To Mike.
I hope you enj
you mak

THE HUNT FOR PUERTO DEL FAGLIOLI

A motorcycle adventure in search of the improbable

By

PADDY TYSON

Shuvvy Press, Hereford
England

THE HUNT FOR PUERTO DEL FAGLIOLI

A motorcycle adventure in search of the improbable

Published by Shuvvy Press,
Tump Cottages, Fownhope, Hereford HR1 4NJ

Copyright © Paddy Tyson 2009
Paddy Tyson has asserted his right to be identified as the author of this Work in accordance with the Copyright, Designs and Patents Act 1988
All rights reserved. No part of this publication may be reproduced, stored in a retrieval system, or transmitted in any form or by any means, electronic, mechanical, photocopying, recording or otherwise, without the prior permission of the copyright owner

A CIP catalogue record for this book is available from the British Library

Portions of this book previously appeared in *Motorcycle Mojo Magazine, Canada.*

Proofing was done by Amanda Little and Siobhan Donnelly but they are in no way responsible for any of the bits that may annoy you.

ISBN
978-0-9564305-0-2

For my mum Pauline, who furnished me with an interest in the world and the inspiration to travel around it, (even if she wishes I'd use a different mode of transport) and for Siobhan, who waited.

CONTENTS

CHAPTER	PAGE

"Come follow me brother
For we come unto this world to travel.
I will take you to the promised land,
Where the days are hot and the beer is cold.
Pray with me so that we might do this again"

-anonymous traveller, one with a great attitude and a slightly beaten up GS 650

PROLOGUE

I'm very lucky. Generally blessed in fact. I don't mean that in any material sense, indeed I'm a bit of a 'mend and make do' person if truth be told. No, I am lucky because I have a loving partner and family, great friends and no real job. I count myself lucky that as I enter middle age I am not divorced, or terribly bitter, though perhaps the fact that I never married has some bearing on this. I count myself incredibly lucky that because of all the above, I am able to load my panniers when finances allow and ride off into the sunset. I rarely do, because I hate riding with the sun in my eyes and because I find that setting off in the morning makes the day that bit more productive before enjoying an evening beer, always so much more refreshing enjoyed beneath a parasol and with a fresh new vista. Then I can enjoy the sunset, avoid the glare and wonder what incredible new experiences the following day might bring.

That's life on the road, enjoying the beauty of the world and the intrigue of its people.

I'm lucky too when I consider this project, to use industry jargon, which started by accident when I was writing home about my journey through the Americas.

My target audience was originally family and friends, which I felt gave me permission to relax and let my writing style really reflect what I was experiencing, both emotionally and physically, without the need to polish the text for a wider readership.

However, I began receiving messages of support from individuals I'd never met and it transpired that my emails, in this interconnected cyber world in which we live, had gone viral. Some people had begun forwarding my tirades to what were, in essence, the general public which left me either embarrassed or apprehensive. I'm still not sure which.

I tried to ignore the fact and carried on writing what I observed, in spite of the diversifying readership, but on my repatriation to the UK, still without a proper job to hide behind and with continuing encouragement, I decided to link my writings together.

The following pages contain a compilation of those emails sent home between May 2008 and March 2009, with overtly personal references removed in the interests of common decency, but with the mood of the moment left intact.

Some say that spending long periods of time alone on the road, especially inside a motorcycle helmet, can have detrimental psychological effects, but I know that I can be a moody bugger whether I'm on the road or not, so I don't believe that is a valid excuse. Instead, I'd like to imagine that travel itself and any incidents incurred, help create the very mood through which those incidents are experienced.

I had set out with a plan, (which I've since discovered was my first mistake) to ride across and around the North and South American continents, for as long as I had the time, money and energy, which seemed simple enough.

There were a few geographical points that I really wanted to reach, for example Prudhoe Bay at the top of Alaska and Tierra del Fuego at the bottom of Argentina, the desire and reason for which I can trace directly to the BBC.

Back in the 1970's, Blue Peter, the children's TV programme, contained regular reports of the exploits of three Mini cars as they were driven around the world. Struggling through all manner of terrain and climate, they attempted to raise funds for charity. So transfixed was I by their exploits, that I have no idea what they were raising money for, but I knew then, as I sat watching, that one day I too would use a terribly inept vehicle to attempt to conquer the world.

Contained herein then, is the story of how I got where I got, saw what I saw, learnt what I learnt and felt what I felt and none of it is meant to be overtly upsetting or offensive. If it is upsetting and you are offended, well tomorrow is another day and I really don't think the sky will fall down. Try and concentrate on the bits you like instead.

PART I

Getting Started

1 HEY, CALM DOWN!

Bugger. I'm sitting writing this on the bus to Gatwick Airport to begin my motorcycling trip of a lifetime and it's just occurred to me that my helmet, gloves, scarf and only pullover, are carefully stacked in a neat pile on the kitchen table. Adventure, inconvenience and serendipity, that's what these trips are meant to be about. It's just that I thought I would have at least left the UK before I started experiencing them.

I've never fully grasped the origins of my organizational ineptitude, because I am after all blond haired, blue eyed and do have some Germanic blood, but I do find this incompetence ensures that my travels always contain an element of surprise, which I've come to enjoy. For now I'll just blame the sheer volume of indecisions I've been faced with in the recent past, like, for example, what bike to get for the trip. Needless to say I couldn't use one that I already owned. Like shoes ladies, I need one for every occasion.

The 'adventure motorcycling' market has become a lucrative one, bursting with choice and possibility offered by bike manufacturers eager to cash in on the pursuit made fashionable by Ewan McGregor and Charlie Boorman. There are now hundreds of models grappling for the attentions of any wannabe overlander. Every manufacturer has got in on the act and because almost all of the bikes sold will never travel any further than the local cafe, it is imperative that they look the part. One element of looking the part is that they should be big. Really big. And heavy. Huge in fact, which is all well and good on the perfect tarmac of Western Europe, but not so handy on a gravel mountain road in Guatemala when confidence overtakes ability with the inevitable consequences, and your film crew isn't there to help you pick it up.

But freedom of choice is a helluva burden as they say and marketing's seductive. Lots of these bikes have names that conjure images of adventure and of exploration, pushing boundaries of independent travel and clearly all designed to play to the egos of middle-aged men in good jobs who are suffering from psychological crises. I, of course am not one of the above. I have been suffering the same crisis for twenty years and have never yet managed to get a good job.

There are bikes called 'Transalp' capturing an all-encompassing image of European mountain travel, the less definitive 'Gran Passo' and the more specific 'Stelvio'. Bit of an upland theme, but close to home and easy to relate to, so at least you can still imagine being able to stop for a latte if you are overcome by the sound of cow bells. Then there's 'Africa Twin', 'Dakar' and 'Tenere' for those who'd like their sand to be more foreign than Weston Super Mare, and fancy a bit of a challenge. There are lots of bikes with 'Adventure' somewhere in the title and even the 'Navigator' if you feel you need to chart your own course. (Duh!) Then there's the more imaginative, nay pretentious

Ulysses, though the manufacturer in this instance leaves themselves open for criticism like "and it'll take you ten years to get home too, if you buy one"

I of course, am swayed by none of it. What's in a name?

I chose an Aprilia Pegaso 650. Born of the gods Poseidon and Medusa, Pegasus was the winged horse, the flying mythos. Agile. A steed chosen by the Greek gods for reliability, for stamina and for trustworthiness. Zeus used him to carry thunderbolts and lightning, and you've got to admit, any horse that doesn't mind that should be OK in a bit of heavy traffic. For me the choice was more serious though. After researching the hundreds of possibilities, analysing the necessary criteria, searching all the small ads and spending much more time staring at Ebay than is healthy, I made a snap decision in five minutes because it was cheap, was super low mileage and I had no more time left to prevaricate. And it wasn't red. These things are important.

To all those saying things as uncomplimentary as "an Italian bike?" I would love to say PAH! Instead I shall reply thus...

You may have a point, but I shall call any foibles simply 'character', a ploy the British bike industry adopted successfully for half a century. Indeed many people still revel in a spot of routine roadside maintenance, so there must be something in it. In a Zen like way it's probably all about bonding with the machine. Man and bike, building a relationship with each other through the intimacy of grease and a bolt fitting snugly in a socket. Or something. A relationship that can endure going o'er mountains and 'cross deserts, through tropical jungle and arctic tundra. Perhaps not. That's probably all a load of romantic twaddle, but just in case it's not, I have decided to call her Peggy. She has to have a name. There will be many days ahead when there will be no one else to talk to. I think Peggy is upright, steadfast and just British enough for a spot of adventure, don't you know! Verbosity aside, I suppose you want to know what's wrong with her?

Well there are just a couple of minor ailments to worry me, apart from not even being convinced that as I write, she is on the boat to Canada, and not instead heading for Australia. The surly stevedores at Southampton docks were among some of the most intransigent incompetents I am yet to meet, and trust me, the amount of professional incompetence I have experienced in the last two months of preparation would shock you. These guys denied knowledge of shipping, refused to look for the faxes they'd received, wouldn't call anyone at their head office, and only took the keys from me when I forced them to. They didn't label the bike up, didn't care where I left it and didn't tag the keys, so I took charge. A job for Nerdy Man.

I rode the bike across to the cage for shipping, where I had taken my other machine a few years earlier for the trip to New Zealand, and there met the only worker who was civil enough to have a chat. A pleasant enough, middle aged chap, he inquired as to the NI stickers on the back of the bike and the 'personalised' number plate.

"Northern Ireland" says I, proud as punch.

"Oh" he says, "We had a bloke here a few weeks ago that had Cornish flags on his machine. What with Cornwall and Scotland trying to break away from the UK, God knows what'll happen if Northern Ireland wants to separate, there'll be nothing left!"

God bless the British media and how well it keeps its citizens informed. I felt like saying, "Word on the street is that it might all turn a bit nasty, maybe even guns and bombs!" But I didn't, thinking I could save all my experimental sarcasm for the North Americans, which might be much more fun.

And so to the mechanical problems. The bike has

developed this intermittent but still rather disconcerting habit, of relieving itself periodically all over my left boot. I have tried reason, discussion about both the price of oil and the ethics of its extraction, in an attempt to curb this wanton display of wasteful extravagance, but to no avail. I have decided therefore to ignore the problem and carry on regardless, leaving much of the journey open to fate and to the possibility that a few enforced days rest in some backwater will be just the tonic I need and an excellent cultural experience. I'm sure it's only minor incontinence, and anyway I prefer to look upon the oil as a protective covering that the bike is sure to need while at sea to protect it from the nasty sea salt.... or something. And I suppose it is fortuitous that my left boot has now a fully waterproof oily coating, though I'm hoping for a beautiful dry summer in which to play out all those Hollywood road trip dreams. Thelma and Louise didn’t have rain, neither did Peter Fonda and Dennis Hopper, so I’m pretty confident.

Then there's the temperature gauge. Not that Italian bikes are renowned for electrical gremlins, but it appears to indicate boiling point if I hold my thumb on the starter button for any length of time. Then, regardless of how hot the engine actually gets, the gauge reads 60ºC. It continues to do this even when the temperature sender unit in the radiator has been disconnected, so it must be true.

The only other little inconvenience, and the reason why I know that the prolonged depression of the starter button has an impact on the temp gauge, is that she refuses to start in the morning. This began three days before departure, so I suppose it’s just nerves. Hers not mine. Don't laugh, if this bonding exercise twixt man and machine is to work, then Peggy needs a personality. British name she may have, I just have to hope her personality isn’t a hot-blooded, cantankerous Latino one. I've had relationships with women like that before and I hope never to repeat the experience.

And talking of cantankerous. Of all the useless idiots I encountered trying to get the bike prepared, the bloke at the Aprilia dealer has got to take the biscuit. And with that one small statement I feel I may have decided the fate of that sponsorship deal. Hey ho! Having explained my 'shipping the bike out of the country' urgency, he promised that the spare parts I needed would be available in 7 days. Three times I asked and got the same reassurance, so imagine my surprise when a week later I get a call from the dealer wondering whether or not I still wanted the bits.

"Ah, so they are in already?" I enquire. No, but they are just checking I still want them.

"You have ordered them?" Of course they have. A week later I call to see if they've arrived.

"They should be in any day."

Three days later, when I ring again "Yes, the throttle cable is here, but the other stuff isn't." I attempt to discover why, given that if it was all coming from Italy, it couldn't go in the same box. The other stuff, I am assured, has left the factory. Like Elvis.

At 21 days from original order and starting to panic somewhat, I go to the shop and attempt to collect the cable that has arrived.

We discuss the delay and the unreturned calls, the promises of delivery time and the tracking of the shipment. He explains how it isn't possible to track the parcels, but can see no inconsistency with his previous claim that they had definitely been dispatched, and promptly blamed the courier. I am forced to inquire as to the strength of the seven day delivery guarantee and am informed that their policy is delivery within 12 weeks and nobody would have ever promised anything shorter. I remain calm, which is no mean feat, explain that I will take the part that is available, but must cancel the rest of the order. I don't wish to inconvenience him, given that I am merely a paying customer and apologise that the parts still to arrive will have to go into stock at his expense.

He, being the proprietor of the establishment, a shrewd businessman and a mature adult, says that I can't have it and if I don't want to wait for the complete order, then I can fuck off. An interesting approach to business, but this I duly do, having discovered that BMW parts are identical and available next day.

I have, in the last two months, had the postal service lose valuable documents, and insurance companies fail to produce them. All the other documents that have arrived have had at least one flaw, and I have had, without exception, every internet or telephone order for parts or services become corrupted. This doesn't just mean wrong, late or damaged stuff, this also means occasionally, twice as much as ordered. I can see more Ebay transactions on the horizon...

The incompetence is so quaint it confirms that Britain leads Europe in things other than just obesity and teenage pregnancy.

Many people would consider it lunacy to attempt to organise and prepare for a trip like this in seven weeks, especially when, at the outset, I hadn't even chosen a bike, but when you've got friends like mine, who are desperate to get rid of me, anything's possible. So with Tom and Mark committing endless hours to the job, Peggy was ready to go.

My Pegaso, my conveyor of thunder and lightning, now has panniers that fit, crashbars that protect the engine and hold jerry cans for extra water and fuel and suspension that at last suspends. She even has a natty little grill over the headlight to protect the glass from flying stones and because it looks ever so purposeful. Not exactly Raiders of the Lost Ark, think more Raiders of the Local Park, but image is all darling! Were it not for these and other friends, the whole show wouldn't be on the road at all and if the side of the road is where I'm left, then of course I'll have someone to blame.

But while I'm bitching about professionals I'll mention how journalists with a desire to create copy regardless of unsubstantiated information, might have their part to play. The journey may henceforth be known as .... drum roll....

The Hunt for Puerto del Faglioli. Catchy don't you think?

The story goes something like this. A local paper in my native Ireland decided to do a story on my departure, a sort of "Local boy goes global" piece. I explained my plans and desires, my past travel experiences, my reasons for going, my influences and I thanked my producer and director, the catering staff and make-up and even added some local interest links to keep it all relevant. Blah de blah de blah. What ended up in print was even more fictitious. At least I hadn't made up the destination and I had bothered to look at a map. According to the article, after I crossed North America and headed south across the equator, I was going to the very southern tip of Mexico, Puerto Del Faglioli!

I reached for the atlas. This seemed like too good an opportunity to miss. Was there really a place called Puerto del Faglioli? Was it in Mexico, or more probably Italy? Was it at the tip of anything, and had recent tectonic plate activity really moved Mexico into the Southern Hemisphere? It certainly sounded like the sort of place I should try to find, for no other reason than to write to the paper and tell them what it was like.

I hatched a plan. Somewhere in the Americas I would find such a place, rather like Gulliver had, but I wouldn't use the hallucinogenics. A village on a hillside, where the annual communal activity would be the tumbling of dominoes that grew in size to include books and beer barrels, sacks of flour and old mattresses, until finally having wound around the village and reached the square outside the church, the spectacle would culminate in the finale, the creation of a masterpiece; a 30 feet high pint of dark beer with a thick creamy head. The villagers and all the farmers who had arrived for the show would cheer and raise their glasses, because I would have witnessed the annual festival to honour their patron Saint (my dear journalist). Or something like that, if some advertising agency doesn't steal my idea first.

Yes. A mission improbable? The more I think about it the more I feel obliged to accept the challenge.

For now, from London's Gatwick Airport, it's good night. I've got a plane to catch.

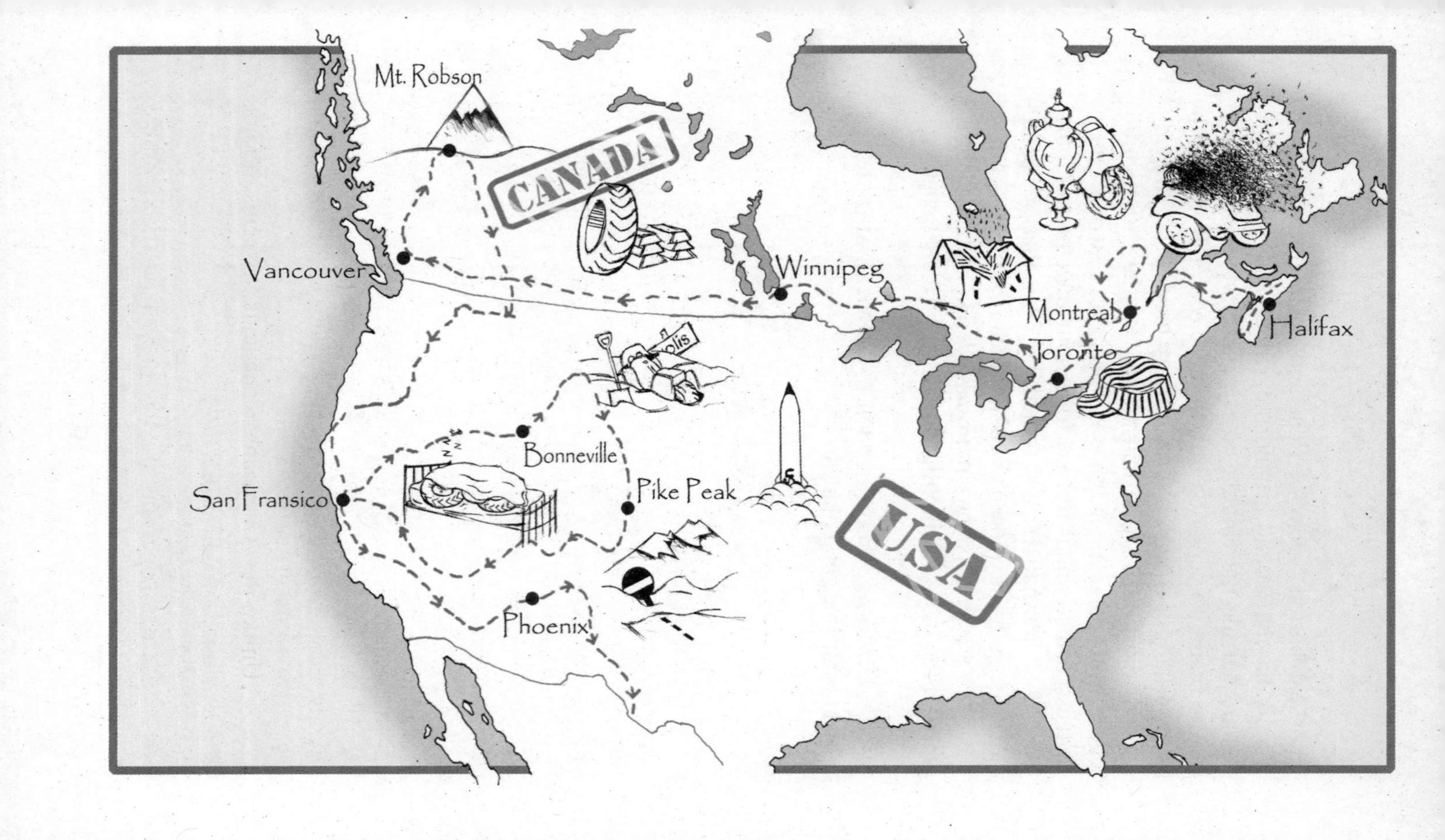
Mt. Robson
CANADA
Vancouver
Winnipeg
Montreal
Toronto
Halifax
Bonneville
Pike Peak
San Fransico
Phoenix
USA

PART II

North America is how big?

2 OH CANADA!

Standing in the arrivals hall of Canada's Halifax airport I read the large sign that says all firearms must be declared at customs. I thought my being in an arrivals hall presupposed certain things, like having been on an aeroplane, but travel is said to broaden the mind and no doubt this was it. My new cultural experiences were beginning.

"Walk this way please sir." "Sorry?"

And it was all going so well too. I had shared a little chuckle at passport control when the security lady said I looked very well for a 99 year old. She was holding the declaration form, that I had filled out in the plane, and was examining my date of birth.

Unlike the Americans, Canadians, it seems, do not put the month and day the wrong way round. They put the year in the wrong place.

"It is a condition of entry to Canada sir, that there

are no falsehoods on this declaration".

But that all passed with a cheery smile and I thought what a lovely place it must be to have friendly officials.

Now I was being accompanied down a corridor by two security guards who obviously suspected me of some heinous crime and although I'm all for safety, I feel security assessments are definitely changing. In Gatwick I noted, as I was removing my shoes, that you can bypass security if you have a small child and a buggy which is priceless! While I was in security though, I had an interesting moment with a young woman. A real "I'll show you mine if you show me yours" moment. Having had my bag scanned and been pleasantly frisked, I turned to Jane Doe as we all struggled to reclaim our particular little plastic trays from the conveyor belt.

"I think you'll find that's mine" I said, as I forcefully took the laptop from her hands.

"Indeed it is not" she replied, in a tone I hadn't expected from a thief.

We both looked at each other in disbelief, daggers drawn in defence of microchips.

"I beg your pardon?" I said loudly and clearly, attempting my best glower of indignance, until another, identical ASUS laptop came down the conveyer belt...

Ah.

"Oh, terribly sorry. Umm, which one is yours then?"

And so, in socked feet and trying to hold my belt-less trousers up, Jane Doe and I move to some seats and fire up our laptops to see which is which. I showed her mine…

I had a fantastic seat on the plane (a fly by wire Airbus, with lots of loose bits that fell off from overhead periodically) right by the central exit, next to Neil, a retired teacher from New Brunswick and my first free offer of a bed on the trip. (In a purely platonic, heterosexual way you understand). We chatted for hours and he was a font of useful Canadian knowledge, none of which I managed to make a note of. He even lent me his pen to fill out the aforementioned immigration declaration, which meant it all added to the burden of guilt I felt as I couldn't stop farting. He couldn't have been more congenial, so why my bowels had to penalise him and all my fellow passengers, I cannot fathom, but as a consequence I am full of remorse.

It was only when I was on the plane however, having gone through so much security: "any fluids, creams, gels over 100mls?" that I realised I had half a litre of water in the pocket of my backpack. Turns out I really am a natural courier. "Couple of kilos of coke? No problem!"

Or did I honestly endanger the lives of all my fellow passengers (asphyxiation aside), by smuggling in the water? Does that make me an international terrorist? I've read in the papers that it really is a slippery slope. Now I can see why the firearms sign is up on the wall in the airport. Perhaps it is for all those passengers who just forgot they were packing heat.

Anyway, back to Canadian customs and immigration and I first meet Gary (wearing his "proud to serve Canada" badge) and we are getting very personal.

"Do you have an ATM card sir? Just how much money can you withdraw?"

What for, is there a charge for entry? Institutional bribery perhaps?

"Just answer the questions please sir. Do you have any other savings?"

Didn't your mother tell you it was rude to ask a person about money?

"How did you get your money?"

I told him of my house sale and journey plans, to

ever widening eyes, his steely countenance ebbing away.

"What, you sold furniture and all? Cool! Where are you staying?"

Everywhere!

"I'll give you 90 days, but don't work."

Work? Moi? We haven't met before.

"Enjoy Canada and have a safe trip, but watch out for the Americans." I wonder if that is sage advice or national prejudice? Let's wait and see.

I thought that was that and Canada was just beyond the sliding doors, until Ian Fitzpatrick and colleague (still proud to serve Canada) guided me into the red corridor. I was one of the chosen few.

"This way Sir. Just wait here. ... Behind the line"

Half an hour passes and it becomes patently clear that officer Fitzpatrick is having a few problems and needs his superior. Working in immigration at a passenger terminal he doesn't deal with the importation of motorcycles all that often.... especially ones that are still at sea. I felt he needed to find out for himself that the people down at the docks would probably deal with that. It's a learning experience. Let's call it on the job training.

With that I was free and officially in Nova Scotia. My oh my, this place has a lot of trees! They have had forest fires burning for a week and they are in need of rain, but I reckon the fires could rage for another few weeks and no one would notice the difference. Right up to the roadside and as far as the eye can see there are trees. The globally screwed up weather patterns are very much in evidence here though. The 2007/8 winter they've just had was one of the longest in recent years, with the most snow and now only a few months later there is drought. Now that I am here in my brand new waterproof riding jacket, I can guarantee that there'll be no rain either. It's an old motorcycling truth. He who carries good wet weather gear is followed by the sun. He who just nips down to the shops gets soaked.

My old friend Mark is now living near the city and I plan to stay a few days with him, but I've booked a hotel in town for the first night, because Peggy is due to arrive in Port in the morning and I'll have to liberate her from the customs officers in the morning, or at least begin the process. It's a terrifically fancy hotel though, so I've now got enough soap and other toiletries to do me for the first fortnight on the road. As an overland traveller I felt I couldn't justify the bathrobe, but just for a moment there...

So anyway, here I sit in Maxwell's, a traditional English Pub in the heart of Halifax. Madness are playing "House of Fun" on the jukebox, I've just eaten and there are sixty, yes 60 different beers actually available on tap. Although ten are from Ireland and I'm Irish, I've only heard of five of them! With that kind of beer selection, happy friendly staff with great product knowledge, good, hot, tasty food served all day, and without a single fight occurring or a bloke trying to sell me anything dodgy, I think they are way off the mark with their descriptive claims. A traditional English pub? I think they could face a misrepresentation suit.

But that's theming for you. Take an idea, embrace the nostalgia, ignore the reality, package the image and sell the dream. I remember when they started opening Irish bars in Dublin so that the English tourists could find the "Real Thing".

The famous Nova Scotian sea mist has rolled in to town, seemingly cutting the tops off all buildings over five storeys high, and acting like an acoustic blanket, adding a stillness and quiet to the town yet leaving the ground completely dry. Spooky!

3 PLEASE CAN I HAVE MY BIKE?

"Friday and it's Day Four in the big brother household".

This big brother is the Canadian Border Security Agency, CBSA, and they are the ones who have my bike. I'm on first name terms with most of the staff in the office in Halifax, though they did get a superior to kick me out of the office yesterday.

"Please go home Sir, you can no longer stay here".

"But the closest thing that I have to a home is parked on the quayside and you won't let me near it."

This exchange came after I had been told that although it had already been four days, the process would take much longer because I needed to apply for Canadian number plates. I, yet again had to explain that I was just passing through Canada and their argument that all vehicles in Canada had Canadian plates was somewhat flawed given that there were three cars in the street outside that had United States plates.

Oh dear, it seems I'll never learn the consequences of challenging authority with the blindingly obvious. Sometimes there is just no room for rationale. Introduce that when you talk to a uniform and I find I'm either ejected or end up staying much longer than planned.

It's a shame really, I had grown to like that office and its quirky posters, my favourite being:

Gary William Stone, WANTED in Alberta for "offences against wildlife", and a picture of mister Stone looking like he may well prefer more than just a bit of huntin' shootin' and fishin!

"CBSA: Canada's moral guardians." (Just not very good at the paperwork)

I'd got into a bit of a routine. Arrive at the office at 9am, make a few inquiries, settle down with a book and my walkman and give it a few hours before heading out to the Cabin Cafe across the street for a cuppa and a read of the papers. The Cabin is, as you'd expect in north eastern Canada's lumberjack land, all split log walls and rough hewn solid wood serving counter tops. The chairs that aren't wood are leather sofa things and there are old photos and paintings on the wall, various seafaring artefacts and the odd stuffed thing. All very atmospheric, till you realise that it is one corner of the ground floor of a 10 storey concrete monstrosity.

Then I'd pop back to customs for an hour or two, maybe get a spot of late lunch, do a little shopping and return until they closed for the day. Mark would then pick me up and take me back to his house for the night before it all began again. After the first couple of days he had taken pity on me and insisted I stay with him, his wife Sheri and three great kids.

Being thrown out of a government building did mean that I could head off and fill my time being a tourist, so I visited the Museum of the Atlantic. With the sea so integral to the history and existence of Halifax, I hoped it would be an illuminating experience and wasn't disappointed.

Among other things, there was an excellent display about the Halifax explosion in 1916, when a French armament ship was struck by a Norwegian boat in the harbour and the whole plot went boom. The explosion was heard 483kms away and the anchor of another boat that had been in the harbour was found 3.5kms inland. Many thousands died because the city was essentially flattened. The whole display was brought to life for me (excuse the pun) because I tagged on the back of a class of school kids and got all those extra nuggets of gory info that are thrown in to keep the kids engaged and stop them rubbing snot on each other.

Over 3,200 bodies were officially recorded, but many more were never found. 1,600 buildings vanished, 12,000 more were damaged and 25,000 survivors were left with no shelter as the December snows arrived. As incredible a tragedy as it was, the story of the huge mobilisations of aid that followed were every bit as dramatic. A message sent down the line by telegrapher Vincent Coleman before he died, to stop an incoming train and raise the alarm, meant that the relief effort could begin immediately. By 9pm that night a relief train full of supplies left Boston USA and headed north, complete with a 500 bed field hospital, medical supplies, 25 doctors and 68 nurses. Money and supplies poured in from around the world in the coming weeks and the locals and military took the law into their own hands when it came to dealing with looters. The effort was all the more incredible when you consider there was no functioning phone network, let alone email, TV, radio or aeroplanes, and really puts to shame how long it takes the world to react to disasters today, now that there are hundreds of tiers of management and an infinite number of forms in place for just such an event.

The museum also had a good "Titanic" exhibition, because it was here in Halifax that the MAYDAY was received, the search and rescue boats set out from and where all the recovered bodies were landed. Class distinctions had to be upheld though, even in death, so First class passengers came ashore in coffins, second and third class came in bags, though many thirds were "buried at sea" according to the records. Handier I'm sure. It turns out that the unsinkable design of the Titanic may well have had one slight flaw in that the high sulphur content of the steel meant that it was particularly brittle if it got cold and was then struck by a large object. Oh dear.

There's an exhibition in Belfast too, where the Titanic was built, and where you can get t-shirts that say something like "It was OK when it left here". Maybe the design brief was for a Mediterranean cruise ship.

Halifax isn't a huge city, so I was a little perturbed to be recognised by some of the museum staff. "Hi there! So you had a real good night at O'Carrolls on Tuesday eh?" A little embarrassing to be recognized in such circumstances in a foreign city perhaps, but in my defence there were mitigating circumstances: I bumped into a man who was from my home county of Fermanagh, though he'd moved to Canada in '79. That was chance enough. What about that he went to my school and we had the same delightful teachers, or that a friend of his married my sister's best friend? And of course he bought all the beer, so you see, it wasn't my fault, and I am here to experience the local hospitality.

It was during breakfast today (I was having a leisurely start with a paper), that the phone rang to announce that my bike was finally available. None of the threatened Canadian issue number plates or taxes to pay. Just 'yep, go and get it after you've been into the office for a rubber stamp eh.' Hurrah!

The twelve minute, sublimely calming ferry ride to cross the harbour and transfer to a bus for the five mile journey to the Autoport was $2. Two dollars, no wonder it was full. Admittedly it was full of a healthy cross section of the population, but that just made the journey, interesting! Still, what a perfect example of integrated public transport systems working.

I did the last few bits of paper work, was taken to

the quayside by a chap called Bob in his pickup, heart in my mouth with apprehension and there she was. Unscathed and intact! She had arrived, complete with a flat battery and no kick-start.

I only managed four laps of the compound before exhaustion set in and I had to admit defeat and go to find help. Never wishing to miss an opportunity for gossip, the guy on the quayside started talking about foreign bikes. It turns out they've been super busy this year. Three bikes had arrived this month, and there were a couple last month too. There was lots of snow before that, so I had to agree, five this year was pretty busy alright! When you think that this is the main arrivals port for goods and services on the east of Canada, and that Vancouver on the West, the other port, seems like a world away, some things are starting to fall into perspective. Vancouver may be further away from me now than Ireland is, but there really aren't a lot of people on the northern side of the 45th Parallel. Seems like it's going to be just me, some bears and a whole lot of trees. Oh, and Peggy for when I need someone to talk to.

Finally jump started from a battery charger, we were off to cheat death in Halifax and practice riding on the wrong side of the road, as another bizarre sea fog rolled in to town. These fogs can happen in a matter of minutes, clear, blue and hot, to cold and foggy in an instant. But I had my helmet and gloves! My adorable partner Siobhan drove all the way down to Gatwick through the night to deliver them. She's such a star and it enabled us to spend one more cherished night together in that most romantic of British establishments, the Travelodge. I don't know when we'll be able to do that again.

And so Peggy and I hit the road tomorrow and the journey begins in earnest. Or maybe the next day if it looks like rain....

4 IS THIS A CULT I SEE BEFORE ME?

Day one on the road proper and it feels good to ride. The sun is out, the temperature climbing and the unspoilt Nova Scotian scenery is soothing. Broadleaf and evergreen stand shoulder to shoulder in a complete carpet of the landscape, the only relief being the black water pools and lakes with their boulder and rock shores coated in yellow lichens. I know I'm seeing it in the best light, not a breeze to ripple the perfect waters, but it is what I'm seeing, so for now it's what I'll recall. This is what memories are made of.

I head north west out of Halifax towards Truro (don't you love the creativity of the early British settlers?), encounter my first sight of agricultural land development, and witness the evidence of the powerful Fundy tides. Salt water rising and falling over fifty feet every twelve hours has a pretty dramatic effect on the shoreline, and I hope to explore the Bay later. But for now, to be many miles inland and see the huge expanse of estuarine mud either side of the rivers I'm crossing, is hard to associate with a landscape that isn't coastal.

It's not just clashing ecosystems that seem alien. All those social and cultural cues and pointers are missing. I'm in an English speaking land, born of European settlers and somehow it's all very "abroad". I can't take shop fronts for granted, don't recognise brand names and logos and as a consequence where services are provided. I don't know where to top up my phone with credit, the phone I had to buy because it was cheaper than getting a sim card for my own! It's true, none of these are insurmountable obstacles, it's just realising that it is a nether world, half of which is instantly recognisable and the other alien. There's a popular road sign in Halifax that is just a white question mark on a brown background. What is that? Underneath it may be something like "centre lane only". So what, is it directions for the perpetually indecisive? I followed them yesterday, just to see where they led, but never found out, because I didn't know when I'd arrived. Perhaps it's a philosophical arts project. Maybe I should buy a copy of the Highway Code.

As I head through rolling fields where once there was forest and aim north towards New Glasgow and then the causeway to the island of Cape Breton, the old dumped car or pickup truck seems to have fashionably outstripped the garden gnome as exterior domestic adornment of choice. It seems that Nova Scotia has adopted more than just music and arts from Celtic Britain, there's also the Irish west coast's addiction to saving that old car, initially just to be cannibalised for spares to keep the new one going, before finally ending up as a chicken house.

The Canso Causeway was completed in 1955, when, prior to all that namby pamby concern about ecosystems and sea water flow patterns, the plucky Canadians thought bollox to building a bridge that they'd have to repair every spring, why not just blast the top off a hill and sling the whole lot in the sea? Then they could drive across from Cape Breton Island to the neighbouring Nova Scotia mainland and get the trains over to supply the industrial mining north.

Of course various other things took a stroll over the causeway too. The bobcat was one, driving the native Lynx up into the hills and generally causing havoc amongst the remaining tasty resident wildlife. The tidal patterns in the whole St Lawrence Gulf area were altered, migrating Atlantic fish stocks took years to work out the new detour system and the eastern side of the causeway no longer froze in winter, which had the handy benefit of enabling the building of that other environmental friend, the oil refinery.

I stay at a campground in the Mi'kmaq Indian named town of Whycocomanagh and begin what will no doubt be a long and enduring friendship with the mosquito population. I'd passed on an earlier site that was completely vacant save for the employee with a strange faraway look in his eye and nervous tick. He said I could head in to town if I fancied a beer, it was only 35mins away and he'd 'be here for me' when I got back. The high asking price and dreadful facilities didn't really add to the overall appeal of a possibly gruesome death, so I'd declined.

Whycocomanagh is really just a collection of buildings and a campground at a cross roads, but I went to explore. The Farmers Daughter seemed to be the place to go. Purveyors of ice cream and fudge they seemed to do a roaring trade with my fellow campers in their big RVs. 'Buy a pound of fudge and get half a pound free' seemed like an offer I could easily refuse, so I opted for a two scoop ice cream cone and took my place in the queue behind some gigantic teenagers. I wasn't really paying attention because I was paralysed by indecision given the array of possible flavours, so when it was my turn and I watched my cone being prepared I had to stop her after the first scoop in the interests of common decency. It was so big I didn't know how I'd cope, but she was taken unawares herself and didn't really know what to charge me for a half order!

As butterscotch and caramel engulfed my hand and ran down to drip from my elbow, I gazed in amazement through the window of the bookshop. A bookshop! There are about eight buildings in the whole town and one of them is a bookshop, but then I suppose the population needs something to do all winter and the evangelical brethren that seem to populate this area, may not utilise lingerie with quite the same gusto as I noted when travelling in Scandinavia.

As I enter the town of Cheticamp it is clear that I have entered a French speaking Acadian enclave. Towering over this windswept coastal community is the massive 1893 Catholic church of St Pierre. Its size seems strangely out of place after becoming accustomed to seeing the small sheds used by the Episcopalian English speaking communities. The other give away that this may be an Acadian area is all the French language road signs and the hundreds of Acadian flags that aren't just flying, but are even painted on the sides of many of the buildings. Fiercely proud of their heritage, having settled the area long before the British, its preservation adds to the terrific musical melting pot that is this region's renown. Eastern Maritime Canada produces a prodigious amount of artistic talent, and is vastly over represented within Canadian culture as a whole. Of course it might just be something in the air, as I even found myself scribe a few jolly melodies inside my helmet as I rode along.

The community spirit here, though redolent of so many communities that struggle within hostile climates and write catchy little ditties about life in the rain, must also be responsible for the growth of the cooperative movement. Cheticamp was at the forefront of communal life a hundred years ago, with a fisher folk collective, artisan collective and others. The fishing collective has gone to the wall only recently, no doubt in part due to all the confused fish that take the scenic route to the Atlantic now that there's no direct route. Even as I rode through the town, there was still a cooperative shop, a Credit

Union and an Arts collective, who I suspect can class as one of their members, the nutter who makes all the weird scarecrows around town. Of course it may be the French connection too, every child born with a union card!

I was here to watch whales.

As a statement of fact, I grant you, it doesn't sound dramatic, but the whole process really was. From getting kitted out in thermal buoyancy suits and clambering down off the pier into an inflatable dingy with outrageously powerful outboard motors, to seeing my first real live monster of the deep, it was fascinating. There was no real health and safety pep talk, just a brief explanation of the fact that the water was bloody cold and that if I didn't hold on I'd probably fall in. Enough said. It was only after this and we were speeding out over the waves feeling like Greenpeace activists, that I realised I had been allowed to take some responsibility for my own actions. How refreshing. I expect if I ever tell anyone, Tony my captain will get the sack, so best not eh?

There is nothing more suitable for demonstrating the advantages of digital cameras, than whale watching. I sat all evening deleting the hundreds of pictures of black ocean, taken just after someone went "Oh, Look!" and I spun round a moment too late. But I did see some and now all the emotion that goes with whale watching actually makes sense. They were Minke whales, and as such weigh only about 10,000 pounds (divide by 2.2 if you left school after 1985), so are considered tiddlers, but to someone whose illustrious fishing career involved catching a single perch, they were huge. They are also known for engaging in a spot of people watching themselves, so they criss crossed under the boat and swam alongside now and again. It was one of those moments when you are sure there should be an emotive soundtrack overdubbed on the whole experience. Complete strangers all grinning inanely at one another.

Captain Tony had hoped we could see a Right whale, so called because they were perfect to hunt. They floated when they were killed and could therefore be towed back to port, and they provided excellent oils and blubber. They are, not surprisingly getting scarce, but at nearly twenty times heavier than Minkes and twice as long, they must be a thing to behold. Another thing to behold would be one of their balls. At 1100 lbs each, or twice the weight of my fully laden bike, they are comfortably the world's biggest nuts.

This far north on Cape Breton there is only one road and I followed it: the famously scenic Cabot Trail, named after John Cabot the famous fifteenth century explorer who neither discovered the area nor was actually called John Cabot, but what are a few facts when writing history? One of Canada's most scenic roads, it winds its way around the north of the island, through the Highlands National Park. A black strip of tarmac perfection, it twists and turns offering stunning vistas of sea and mountain, moose and eagle. It didn't actually offer me any eagle sightings, but it certainly showed me moose.

What a huge, ungainly and terribly stupid animal the moose is. I suppose I should grant them a little slack when it comes to their grasp of the green cross code, after all, the moose population of Newfoundland for example, is widely regarded to be based on just 4 individuals, one boy and three girls, that were introduced in the early 1920's. Conservative estimates are that almost one million have been hunted to date. You've got to admit, they may not offer the greatest challenge to hunters given the size of the gene pool from which they descended.

My first moosely experience left skid marks in more than one place. With a perfectly straight road cutting through endless forest ahead, I, for some unfathomable reason, chose to look down at my map. When I looked up again this massive dark silhouette seemed to block out the day. It just stood there, broadside to me and for an instant I considered trying to go underneath it.

Disaster averted, the rest of the day gave me the opportunity to have close calls with a whole host of extended family members, but I suppose that's riding in the country for you and I just have to adapt. I've made the decision that while I'm in Canada I'll never be tempted to ride at night. While I'm on gene pools, rumour has it, that were it not for the Vietnam War and AWOL American soldiers, these northern communities may be renowned for their manual dexterity, if you know what I mean.

Heading south down the east coast towards North Shore (you figure it out) I spied signs for a campground ahead, with restaurant and bar. Very handy, as feeling that I deserved a beer and didn't fancy cooking, it offered great promise. Twenty kms later I found that it was closed. Actually closed, unlike so many of the businesses that I had lately been encountering that just looked like they had been closed for twenty years but weren't. This place was firmly shut, a season or four ago.

As with all brief disappointments, it led to a great experience, or at least one that now, with a few days hindsight, was a novel experience. I pulled in to another establishment advertising camping and food etc. Paul from Massachusetts met me at the door to the big converted barn, in an apprehensive manner.

"Hi there, I see from the sign that you offer camping space"

"Umm, yeah, we can do"

"And you have a restaurant with drinks license, and WiFi?"

"Yes, but we're very busy now, so it won't be possible to serve you until after 7.30".

I looked around at the empty room, but for a table with two people sitting talking and consider my rumbling tum.

"If you really want a beer I can get that for you now"

"That'd be great thanks"

"I'll just put it on your cheque. Please, just stand there and drink it, don't go outside". I went to sit down.

"Sorry the restaurant isn't open yet"

"So I can't sit down?"

Instead, I stood by the front door and pondered his bookcase, always a window on the mind. He seemed interested in philosophy and sociology and I thought it was a shame he hadn't read any books on hospitality. This was all starting to seem just a little weird. He gave me directions to the camping area and seemed generally taken aback when I mentioned access to sanitary facilities, but said he'd find a key for me so that I could come up to the house later and use the shower room in the basement.

So why did I stay? I've really no idea. I followed the track into the woods and found a clearing that I could share with the clouds of mosquitoes and giant black fly/ant things. I wandered up to the barn closer to my allotted dining time and settled down to check my email near the fire, with a second beer. There was lots of activity as the tables were arranged to suit a party of eight that were milling around in the cavernous room. I waited my turn, my presence having been acknowledged by Paul, and with permission at least granted to sit. With the group ready to dine and still no sign of a menu forthcoming, I was a little taken aback with the announcement

"We are delighted to be joined tonight by our special guest all the way from Ireland who is travelling through the area. Paddy, please come and join us"

What the? Special guest? Is this a closed sect, a cult? Travelling through? Is it such an odd experience for a campground and hotel to host a visitor? As if led by a rope I take my place at the table and am made to feel instantly awkward.

"I'm giving up my lobster tonight so that Paddy can have some" announced Paul, "but it's alright, Barbara has managed to prepare me something else."

Well that's big of you Paul, but as a special guest, and someone who loathes seafood, maybe it would be an idea to ask what I'd like? What about a menu?

Hungry, and burdened with pathetic British reserve, I grimace and attempt to break in to the creature that is sitting on my plate looking at me. This appears to be something that cannot be achieved with any sort of decorum. The accompanying potato salad may or may not be the harbinger of gastric doom, but I need sustenance of some kind. The conversation begins and I am at once central to it and yet still an amazed observer.

Paul and Barbara are middle class academics who are getting away from it all, by moving by degrees from the US to here to start a new life in hospitality. This is the third year and things may not be going quite as planned, since they have arranged for some business and marketing gurus to fly in from the States to attend a three day conference to discuss the way forward. This conference is what I have gatecrashed.

None of them take this networking opportunity to discuss possible needs and desires with an actual customer. They are all mad. Their heads are so far up their own corporate restructuring managerial arses I want to scream. Who are the bigger idiots? Paul and Barbara for paying these twits or them for not noticing any of the glaringly obvious things around them? What about cutting the grass, or providing wash basins for campers? What about greeting customers as though they aren't some nutters who have just walked into your house and asked to have sex with your daughter?

As if to demonstrate just how in touch these gurus were with the service that was meant to be on offer, they talked at length and with great surprise about the fact that the main road was only two lanes wide. Clearly exploring the wilds and beauty of nature and discovering the rural Nova Scotian experience was not something they were attuned to, but felt able to advise on. I tell you, these financial and marketing whiz kids are going to get a reality wakeup call sometime. Reality is bound to bite them on the arse soon, in the way that the mozzies did to me during one al fresco call of nature by the tent later in the evening.

Just to perfectly round off my culinary nightmare before retiring to the tent, Paul asked for $22 for the lobster I hadn't chosen and had barely eaten.

I felt obliged to sit up until 1am with the three interesting characters who walked out of the forest to join me at the tent. Sitting smoking joints and regaling me with tales of derring-do on the high seas, I couldn't help myself but look around for the hidden cameras that were filming for some new reality TV show, or perhaps gathering material for the next "Police, Camera, Action" where a gang of salty sea dogs tear a hapless tourist limb from limb in the forest and then feed the remains to the bears. Am I being melodramatic? The whole night made me feel like some peripheral being looking in on a form of alternate reality from behind a glass panel, but helpless to get anyone to snap out of their caricatured roles, so I was grateful when the thunderous rain had me up at 5.30am and away to enjoy the low cloud and short vista sightseeing.

It seems as though packing waterproof gear isn't a failsafe way to ensure fine weather after all, but this time I don't care, because I saw a black bear!! At least I think it was a bear, but it wasn't very big. I'll tell you later if I'm right when I see another one, but maybe it's like the Pyramids in Egypt. You see them in books for so long, that the real thing is somehow a little disappointing.

I splashed on, rising and falling through the cloud layer and wound my way around the 100kms long inland sea that is Bras d'Or lake. Although saline, the salt content is low due to the number of rivers that flow into it and its minimal connection with the sea, so it supports a fantastic array of wildlife, next to none of which I saw, but stopping for a late lunch on Ile de Madame another of the Acadian French communities, I met a man that made me realise how lucky I was. Sitting having a cup of tea and the daily special, that was so good I've forgotten it already, a short haired, thick set but fit looking man in his early fifties came in, ordered coffee and then approached me without making eye contact. He sat at the table just behind my right shoulder.

"Northern Irish plates?" he said in an English accent, by way of introduction and in reference to Peggy.

"So you did a few tours then?" which I thought was being just presumptuous enough. It cleared the air, because he was indeed ex British military, but listen to this for a story:

In the last two years he and his wife sold up in the UK and started a new life in Nova Scotia, but then had to go back briefly because his daughter's husband left her 8 months into pregnancy. Then his mum died. In the next few months both of his wife's parents died and then when they came back to settle down and start again, his wife was diagnosed with cancer and died! He was making do, and certainly had a great spirit, but shit, the worst that has happened to me lately is discovering that my insect repellent doesn't repel and my new waterproof jacket isn't!

As I get on to the '104 Trans Canada Highway' at what is effectively it's most easterly point of the mainland, I wonder if it's wise to try and romanticise the road. To start an ethereal relationship with a scar in the landscape and create a focal point for a book, hoping to meet it again off and on during my travels west, before realising that it is utter nonsense and the sort of thing TV documentaries do with has-been celebrities, to fill air time on a Sunday evening. Since no one has offered me an advance, I can pretend I am a traveller with integrity and shun such fatuous gimmicks. Unless there's anyone reading this with an idea for a road trip TV show and needs a narrator...

After the very real possibility of a gruesome death in the woods a few nights ago, and while I am doing battle with my paranoia, I opt for a few nights in official campgrounds and engage in conversations with fellow campers, so many of whom seem to be Albertans from out west. I find all these little conversations are essential to understand where I am. Even if the talk starts with something as benign as the weather and a few pleasantries, what is important to people always bubbles to the surface. I've been hearing repeatedly how all the young people have gone to Alberta for work and I'm meeting retirees who have come here, shocked to discover that their properties are now worth a small fortune and that the east coast will let them live very comfortably if they relocate. I can see so many similarities with the North South divide in the UK or even closer to home, the way that generations of Irish had to leave home for work overseas. This though, is meant to be the New World, the land of milk and honey, so why the regional disparity? Well it turns out that there's oil in them there plains and as many people that tell me it's Canada's saviour, as tell me that it is an environmental and social disaster. I hadn't planned on visiting northern Alberta, where the huge oil sand fields are located, but perhaps I really should, just to see for myself.

I took the free ferry from Pictou, where a representative of the town council presented me with a pin badge of the town crest in honour of my passing (!). I docked an hour and a half later, on the shores of the smallest of Canada's provinces, Prince Edward Island.

5 SPUDS AND THE GOOD EARTH

I'm currently sitting in Moncton, New Brunswick, the only officially bi-lingual province in Canada and I'm having a major sugar low. My hands are shaking so badly people must be convinced I have Parkinsons. I expect it's my recent diet. Food is available cheaply everywhere. Eating isn't quite the national sport it is in the US, but I am having real problems regulating my diet. Chips and burgers, pizzas with chips and chips with chips. Oh for mash and vegetables. Even just mash!

I spent four days on Prince Edward Island. The main export of which is potatoes, but I didn't find mash being served anywhere and surely it's an easier way to prepare spuds. In fact, the only product that comes out of PEI is the potato. And maybe songs about potatoes.

102.9 Spud radio is "all the music you'll ever need" Having spent a few days listening though, I beg to differ. Stompin' Tom may be a big hit here, but I'm not sure he'll export that well outside Maritime Canada.

I need to tell you a few things about PEI, some of interest perhaps, and some not. First it has no rocks. The whole province is an island made of red sand. One big sand spit in the Gulf of St Lawrence that is particularly good for growing spuds and making sculptures. The annual sand sculpting competition is a big event, and the red sand lends itself to some truly amazing creations. One particularly fine way of combining the island's two main activities was on display outside the visitors centre: a huge sculpture of a big potato man sitting on top of the globe, bags of spuds at the ready for export.

Summer here is beautiful, winter less so. People tried to convince me the waters were really good for a swim, but couldn't deny that only 3 months ago the island was surrounded by ice. My school geography days said something about large bodies of water being slow to heat up and slow to cool down, so I declined, not least because of a childhood scarred by having to go into the North Atlantic when at the seaside, because "it's fun". No doubt the "fun" part was watching small children turn various shades of blue.

The population of Canada's smallest Province, more than doubles in the summer. The capital Charlottetown (named after George III's missus) is the most European looking town I've seen to date. It has red brick terraces beautifully mixed in with more vernacular 'new world' wooden houses on tree lined streets and to top it all, sight seeing tours are provided in old Routemaster double decker buses straight from London and, it would seem, still prepared to take you to Kensington, Charing Cross or Camden. Many believe the spot was chosen as the Provincial capital because of it's bay, and indeed that bay was occupied while I was there, by a cruise ship that was about ten storeys taller than any other building in the town. However, my guidebook says it was chosen in 1765 because this was the poor side of the island and the "fair play" British colonizers thought it was only "cricket" to bestow a few privileges on the needy.

It was a centre for Loyalism after the American war of Independence, when all those who longed for subjugation by a divinely chosen individual on the other side of the Atlantic, fled here from the newly free colonies down south. It must have really pissed them off then, when less than a century later, Charlottetown was where the first conference to discuss Canadian confederation should occur and the first steps were taken towards some kind of autonomy from Britain. In one of those funny twists of political history, PEI of course, having got it all started, didn't end up joining the new Confederation until six years after everyone else.

PEI was the home of Lucy M Montgomery who wrote Ann of Green Gables so I went to have a look at the house that is "Green Gables". (White Gables, green roof actually). This is probably the biggest single tourist activity on the island and it has oddly spawned another huge tourism industry around Cavendish on the north shore. Not a literary industry as you might expect, but an industry of utter tat. Ripley's Believe it or Not, fun fairs of every description and a Life size Space shuttle. How very random. Is it possible to overdose on spuds?

PEI has a mixture of cultures, but clearly doesn't have the diversity of Nova Scotia with its Gaelic, French and English road signs. It doesn't have any of the ruggedness of the other province either- well not having any rocks does make mountains and cliffs a bit tricky- but this is no flat English East Anglia either. Rolling hills, potato fields and a mixture of trees make it really beautiful. When the sun comes out.

Even Belfast with its white picket fences, mature trees, well kept grasslands and roadsides full of flowering Lupins, somehow exudes peace and tranquility and could not be further from its namesake back home.

Marathon days in the saddle are always fun, but the other day I really travelled. From Bedford to Margate, up the Tyne valley, through Norway past Kensington and West Devon before nipping through Alaska (pah, what bears?) and stopping in Glasgow for a bite to eat. Can you imagine the surprise of the Scottish pioneers setting off to start a new life and finding a place called Glasgow? And what's more, it was right on the banks of the Clyde. What are the chances of that eh?

But as small as these settlements are, and as diverse as their founders may have been, what I find culturally heartening is that there are theatres and bookshops everywhere. Since I've arrived in Canada I've seen that in the tiniest settlement there'll be a bookshop. Was it Noel Coward who said, upon being introduced to a Canadian, "Oh, so you are a North American who can read?" It'll be interesting to see if the trend keeps up when I move west towards the conurbations of Ontario and Quebec, or if it's just because of rural escapism when there's nothing else to do.

Apart from the aforementioned potato radio station, the print media seems a little parochial too. Not in a bad way though. I love the visual creativity of this tag line: The Guardian "covers PEI like the dew". Isn't that great?

A few other things I've noticed: In the north cape of the island the garden ornament of choice is a boat, anywhere from 20 to 40 feet. It seems everyone has one, in various states of decay. And everywhere, apart from the big towns, no one has any driveways. I didn't realise what was so strange for ages, but the houses just sit, completely surrounded by grass. The sandy soil doesn't get boggy, so you just drive in off the road, across your 5 acre lawn and park up, quite often beside your last 4 cars which are dumped somewhere around the property.

I experienced some of my most expensive and cheapest legal camping on PEI and the start of some of my worst weather. I used Beethoven on the walkman to drown out the sound of the rain on the tent when I was trying to get to sleep and am now used to putting away a wet tent in the morning. Oh, and I'm not being a wuss about the mozzies either. I read in the Guardian that it's the worst year they've had for mosquitoes and they are going to try spraying Listerine on the breeding grounds. I have no idea why, but no doubt it's because they want them to have fresh breath when they bite.

Oh how fortunes change in a day on the road. I awoke Friday to the sound of rain and a wet sleeping bag, opened the inner tent to get my boots and found that the tongue of one, having fallen forward, had been catching a drip and redirecting the water into the boot. Nice. All the rain and potatoes was becoming just a little too much like Ireland for me, so, wet and unimpressed, I decided to try a new Province, New Brunswick.

First I had to travel over Confederation Bridge, an incredible feat of engineering which links both Provinces across the Northumberland Strait. The bridge is 13.5kms long, two lane, one each way, and was opened in 1997. There is one little 3ft concrete siding, but break that and over the edge you go. At it's highest you plunge 70ft to the ocean, and then 120ft to the ocean floor. A civil engineering masterpiece that is able to withstand the summer temperatures (up to 30) and the winter (-30), and shrugs off sea ice and high winds. So that's Sydney Harbour, London’s Tower Bridge, the one from Sweden to Denmark that I can't pronounce and Confederation Bridge all ridden, so I suppose The Golden Gate and the Bridge of the Americas in Panama are still to do. Oh what it is to be as nerdy as me!

The Confederation is a toll bridge, (because you only have to pay to leave the island…) but the chatty bloke on the booth made it all seem painless, especially since he charged me half the advertised rate, I didn’t mind paying to leave.

Crossing a body of water and entering a new Province did little to stop the rain, which was disappointing, I thought the weather might acknowledge administrative boundaries, but apparently not. It’s a shame, because there is nothing quite like rain to put a dampener on a road trip. All romance vanishes. The swarthy traveller, cruising with his swag bag from adventure to adventure becomes just another frozen idiot huddled over the handlebars and laughed at by the smug occupants of passing heated SUVs.

In short, it pissed down until I reached Moncton, where I had heard there was to be a bike rally, and I really fancied a weekend of motorcycle hedonism. The global traveller, engaging with foreign cultures and enthralled by native customs was having a break. I intended to be an unashamed petrol head for the weekend and check out a beer and the Canadian bike scene. And what a scene it is.

First, there is no such thing as a central rally site so I had to find a campground outside town. It seems the first big difference on this side of the pond, is that a bike rally involves hotels! Maybe the culture vulture in me was still going to learn something! The second thing is that bikers are clearly not the second class citizens they are often viewed as in Britain. The reason there was no out of town central rally site, is because the whole town centre was the rally site! The main street was closed, there were stages set up for bands to play. Stalls from all the main manufacturers were interspersed with spares and accessory suppliers, clothing outlets etc. Show winning bikes covered in chrome lined the streets for all to see, and then at the end of one group, somebody had managed to get a filthy Aprilia Pegaso passed security and into the thick of it all. Nothing like grabbing a bit of the limelight!

As I write this I am hoarse from conversation. The romance of travel is alive, even in the rain! After meeting the staff of Motorcycle Mojo magazine, I was catapulted into a whirlwind of concessionary this and complimentary that. I was granted free registration to the event, free food, presented with various goodies and t-shirts perfectly timed to save on laundry. I gave a TV interview and a few paper and magazine interviews and was asked to model a new clothing range that one of the event sponsors had, cos baby, I'm a star! I'm a celebrity! I'm famous, though of course I won't let it affect me and I won't be nasty to common people. My agent can deal with them…

What splendid people. Being uncommonly nice appears to be a Canadian trait, just like apologizing and saying 'eh' at the end of every sentence, and the number of addresses I'm collecting means that my old tent just may get to rot away quietly in my roll sack for a few weeks.

6 FAME AND EVERYTHING AFTER

Today as I write, there are no creative juices I'm afraid. They have been washed clean out of me, leaving only a residue comprising distain for the manufacturers of all motorcycle apparel. When the rain is heavy enough, gloves always leak, granted. That damned new "guaranteed" jacket, made by Rev'itt however, has all the moisture repellent properties of a paper bag, so that is all the product endorsement it deserves. I rode for hours through a torrential downpour but was grateful for the accompanying lightning. If it hadn't been for that I don't think I could have seen where I was going. And so comes to an end an otherwise glorious week spent in New Brunswick. 30ºC, humid and generally very foreign. Now at last it feels like a roadtrip!

If I recall, I was about to embark on a career as a supermodel, and generally play the role of media personality. Well, the kick-backs were good. I scored a whole new wardrobe of m/c fashion, though not, I hasten to add, a waterproof jacket. Everyone thought I was very brave and that Siobhan was remarkable for letting me go. I was invited to a gala breakfast and after an auction of custom painted helmets and other goodies to raise charitable donations, the awards began. Best bike in the show, hardest working volunteer during organisation of the event etc and then it all went quiet as one prize was introduced. It was a huge trophy, in remembrance of a famous New Brunswick biker called Ben Richards. He was renowned for travelling anywhere he could by bike, whenever he could. If there was a short way and a long way, he always chose the latter. He was a real celebrity in the motorcycle scene. His nephew and then grand nieces and nephews mounted the stage in readiness to present the award amid tears and respectful applause. Not knowing this great figure wasn't a problem, I could appreciate his impact on the community merely by association, surrounded by the emotion in the hall. The difficult bit was hearing my name being called so that I could receive the award for furthest travelled attendee and take the mic to say something appropriate!

I'm hoping that the laughs I achieved weren't in bad taste and by the way people shook my hand afterwards, with some even trying to hoist money upon me, I think I didn't disrespect his honour. Over the whole weekend I was inundated with free food and beer and hundreds of addresses and offers of accommodation. The upshot of the whole event is that my route is changing to accommodate (be accommodated by) some really lovely people, like Ian, Angela and Suzanne. I am, in a (few) words, the luckiest man around.

It is therefore just, as a way of ensuring that my feet stay on the ground, that I have had the heavens open on me and that the deluge began as I was sitting in a newspaper office, giving another interview. I had been waiting in traffic at roadworks earlier in the day, when the chap in the car in front (and it was a Toyota), came back for a chat and to ask if the Irish flag on the front of the bike in any way signified my nationality. A meeting like this isn't as strange as it sounds. You have to realise that in Canada roadworks can be many miles long so when you reach the stop/go lollypop lady (invariably a lady), you switch off and think of something to do because it'll be a very long time till you can proceed. And I suppose given that I ended up drinking tea and setting the world to rights with an MP in her house in Nova Scotia a few days earlier just because I met her husband at a set of traffic lights, just goes to show how normal these meetings are!

Anyway, this chap was called Mark and he was the editor of the Victorian Star (a bit like your local advertiser on Slimfast) and he "sure would like to do a story on me if I was going to be around these parts for a time eh". I told him I was happy to loiter and would be much obliged. (Though for the first time in my life I was moved on for loitering yesterday- another story, but I felt like a real traveller!) I did a 250 kms detour so that I could meet Mark back at the office late afternoon. I hadn't really meant it to be that long it's just that once you set off on a route there are often no opportunities to alter your course. This was one of those occasions. Off into the northern Appalachian mountains and, it turns out, there is only the one road. Luckily it wasn't raining when it became apparent that they hadn't finished building 50kms of it.

So there I was, sitting in his office stressing the importance of my miniscule budget, the incredible generosity of Canadians who have put me up to date, and watching the clouds get darker and darker. I listened intently while Mark regaled me with story after story about his motorcycling past, about his dogs, his new truck, the floods they had in May, how he got to go up in a helicopter to take photos and there was never to be any offer of lodgings forthcoming. After I had listened to him for 45 minutes, his Dictaphone recording his every word, he had the gall to complain that the rain had started before he could take some photos, and that he didn't envy me riding off into that storm! I'm intrigued as to what kind of story he'll write, he certainly has an interesting journalistic style.

And here I am, thus ensconced in a particularly scuzzy motel, costing more than my total daily budget. That'll teach me to take the milk of human kindness for granted! So while I'm here, with an internet connection and surrounded by dripping clothes, I'll summarise the last few weeks.

I went back to Nova Scotia and got a couple of days away with (my old friend) Mark using his car to travel around the south of the Province. We spent time exploring the Bay of Fundy and its incredible 58 foot tides. Annapolis Royal, the old Nova Scotian capital which is architecturally beautiful, with its grand four storey veranda'd wooden houses, is the site of the world's only tidal power generator. Of course it was built before there was full understanding of ecological interconnectedness, so it's just a big causeway with a generator fitted into a gap in the middle, but the embracing of renewable energy has to be applauded.

I watched a tidal bore come up a bay, not just a river valley, complete with surfers and paddlers and speed boats and I found the village where I'd like to open a small bookshop, eat lentils, burn incense and regrow my hair, Bear River. It is miles inland, but the river is still very tidal and many of the houses near the bottom of the wooded valley, are built on stilts to deal with the altering water levels.

The south east of Nova Scotia and particularly Shelburne, was decorated like Portadown in Northern Ireland on the 12th of July. It was decked out in the Union flag of British Loyalism only without St Patrick's red cross. Here though, the people celebrate the defeat of Loyalism in the 18th century at the hands of the American colonial upstarts, instead of its victories. The good news is that they use the pre 1801 flag and it is impossible to hang the old flag upside down as so often happens in the UK with the current one, so I was able to keep the angry pedant inside me, safely locked away. The area is proud of its heritage as a haven for escaped slaves who pledged allegiance to the Crown and is known as the end point of the 'underground railway' smuggling route for those slaves who fought the Americans and were promised land and a new start, as reward. The not so oft discussed truth is that very little of the promised land was ever forthcoming and conditions remained little better than they had escaped from. Many ended up leaving and founding Sierra Leone, most of the rest of Nova Scotia's black community ended up in the ghetto of Africville in northern Halifax, until it was bulldozed at the end of the 1960's to make way for a bridge development. The NS government has since apologised for the homelessness and heartache the overtly racist action generated, and even built a memorial. After 40 years it hasn't quite managed to sort out recompense yet, though I'm sure it's working hard on it.

When I visited Pier 21 in Halifax, (the main point of entry for European immigrants and refugees), I found the records of my great uncle Owen Swiney, who arrived on 5th April 1924. My grandad's eldest brother, I know that he subsequently died in a snow storm and was found, with his dead horse, relatively near the house he obviously couldn't reach, but I have decided to track down any relatives I can, and luckily there only appear to be 2 entries in the whole of Canada's phone records with Swiney spelt thus, and not Sweeney. It looks like he procreated (officially at least) before death. Rumour has it that one of the reasons he left was his inability to control himself in Ireland! I'm going to spend some time in the capital Ottawa, to see which province he settled in and whether or not there are records of any offspring before I foist myself upon unsuspecting Albertans who just happen to be listed in the phonebook.

Remember Peggy's poor starting and funny

temperature gauge? Well I finally fixed her! Now that is news. I can't believe I've already put 8,000kms on her, so I'm going to have to ignore any weird noises because my plan wasn't to service her until Toronto. I know that'll be 12k or so between oil changes, but those old Rotax engines, "they're bullet proof you know", everyone down the pub says so!

It took me a day at Mark's house back in Halifax, to pull the bike apart and find one damaged wire in the loom, but oh what a sense of achievement! The oil leak has stopped and I'm in two minds as to whether or not I should check the level, but there aren't any horrible new noises emanating from the belly of the beast, or at least none that I can hear when I have my earplugs in. Of course one outcome of that little oil leak problem is that my left sock is the only dry item of clothing I have today, it being the one that lives in the oil soaked boot.

But having a purring steed beneath me has enabled me to see more of the world's precious gems. Like the world's largest axe in Nackawic. Umm. Well. Not sure what to say really. Certainly very big, and axe like. About 20metres in total at a guess. The blade is a good deal taller than me, and as for the shaft... "Oh, I'm a lumberjack and I'm OK...." I don't know a lot of lumberjacks so I suppose it isn't my place to comment on whether or not they spend time in the forest comparing shaft and head sizes.

It is clear that New Brunswick seems to work hard and has less time for 'quaint' than the other Maritime Provinces. All those lumberjacks mean saw mills and paper mills abound, but New Brunswick makes up for it with intriguing tourist attractions of its own. Like the famous frogs of Fredericton, the 1897 covered bridge in Hartland which is the worlds longest and one of only 62 remaining in the province, and of course the big axe.

Then if that wasn't enough excitement, I rode in to Florenceville, "French Fries Capital Of the World". No

Freedom Fries here. I did think to myself, either they grow a lot of spuds in Florenceville, but surely not as many as PEI, or they have a dreadful diet.

Well this spurious chippy claim to fame was indeed fulfilled when I turned into Main street and saw the corporate headquarters of McCains. Then the McCain French Fries Research Institute and the McCain Numerical Centre ? (Yup, there's a lotta chips in that bag). And what a processing plant! There are 50ton 'Spud shuttles' (that's what the trucks are called) feeding those baking ovens round the clock. The McCains are a New Brunswick Family and to say they have slightly more political influence than the 'one man one vote' democratic ideal may intend, would be something of an understatement. Allegedly. What I don't know is whether or not they are responsible for the sacrilege that is the instant mashed potato in a packet. I know it was a Canadian that invented that little culinary disaster, but I don't know which one. Yet.

I spent last night with Bob who has taken advantage of the national economic disparity, left Alberta, retired early and now has a beautiful house with 10acres, a pool, double garage and a lifestyle he loves. In fact he said, quite casually, the bloke he bought the house off had moved it 500meters up the hill because he wanted a better view of the valley! These old wooden houses are fantastic and I now realise what it means in the adverts when it says "as is, where is". I subsequently saw one that had been picked up so that they could install a basement!

Bob is a member of the Iron Butt Association, and for those who don't know, Iron Butt members are, or rather have, exactly that, an Iron Butt. Do you fancy competing in a rally that involves riding 11,000kms in 11 days chasing waymarkers? Or a handy 2000kms in 24hrs if you only have the weekend to spare? He found someone on the internet who would make him a custom seat (to ease the sores?) and told his wife he was just popping out to get it, from Southern California!

When I quizzed him on Alaska (somewhere he goes most years) and the furry people eater situation, he mentioned a motel where he sometimes stays, rather than camping. He just casually said that the motel cook had stepped outside for a smoke and they found most of the rest of his body next morning. You see, smoking kills! He said the diners were a might pissed off too that evening. On the plus side, Angela and Ian who I stayed with for a few days in Moncton, told me of a friend of theirs who camps most of the time he travels that way and has always come back, and I met a couple from British Columbia on a pair of KLR 650s who have experienced bears quite a bit on their travels with no major ill effects of the laceration kind. Apparently I shall become so used to seeing black bears that I won't let it interrupt a conversation. Well, we'll see about that. I have infront of me something that I picked up in tourist information for this area and it says "don't attempt to outrun a bear, you have no chance" (Better to outrun whoever you are with!). It also says, "Photographers! Use a telephoto lens" which is succinct.

Ah, tomorrow, another day another Province. It's schoolboy French from here on:

"Une grande tasse du té au lait et un croissant buerre, pour moi, silver plates" in the morning. Au revoir!

7 LE PETIT FRANCE

"It might just be that Canada's gonna bite your ass!"

Perhaps not the most eloquent of quotes, but certainly apt, and it would appear, becoming more relevant by the day. It was the parting line from Ian as I was leaving Moncton, when both of us were sitting watching the weather channel in disbelief as hail the size of golf balls caused white-outs in Ontario, tornados touched down in Saskatchewan and Quebec got 50mm of rain in less than two hours. However the very literal nature of his prophecy keeps repeating itself as I do battle with the mozzies.

Until a day or two ago I thought it was just me that the mosquitoes found tasty, but what with the Listerine spraying on PEI and now OFF! insect repellent, sponsoring some of the weather channel programmes I feel exonerated. More to the point I have embraced the fact that I shall look a little blotchy until I reach.... well until I reach the UK I suppose!

And so I enter Quebec, bastion of French culture in North America, or as many would have you believe, nothing more than a bunch of belligerent Canadians with a different language and a penchant for shrugging their shoulders. But no, it really is a bit of France, especially

Quebec City. It looks like a southern French city architecturally, the kids all race around on scooters wearing shorts and flip-flops, the petrol station attendants smoke beside the pumps and there is a truly laissez- faire attitude to road traffic laws. The weekend sees the roads full of cyclists, there are patisseries and boulangeries everywhere, the pastries are fresh, the waiters roll their eyes when I ask for tea, and I even saw a Citroen 2CV!

The only really truly amazing difference though, is that all the facilities, all the shops, the bars and cafes, they all open! It's incredible. In the morning they open for business and in the evening they close (except the bars). There is no second guess as there is in France, no desperately trying to remember, 'ok, so it's Wednesday. That means the post office opens at 10, shuts at 10.30 til 2pm, except every third week, when they open at 8 and close at 9.55, unless there's a holiday or a strike, when they open in the evening, or they are immediately opposite a library, in which case they only open on Saturday, Monday and Christmas Day'. No, for the truly culturally French experience I'm afraid Quebec falls far short of the infuriating norm, but that's no bad thing.

On leaving New Brunswick I had planned to cross the St Lawrence river by ferry where it narrows at Riviere du Loup, which means a crossing of 1 hour and 15 minutes by way of demonstrating that it's some river. According to the map and my last encounter with a journalist, the roads on the other side of the river are incredibly twisty, "truly awesome, nothing else like them, eh". The thing is, when you can barely find the road because of the rain and the visibility is down to a few hundred feet, there seems little point to me in taking the mountainous route. Instead, keeping off the highways, I headed down towards Quebec City on the south side and the villages all began changing. The houses were all closer together and right on the road instead of having driveways, and for the first time on this trip the use of stone in construction. Maybe it's being alone in the helmet, but I notice these things...

I stopped in Saint Louis du Ha Ha, for a photo and a laugh, but the laugh was on me. The black flies were so thick they got in what's left of my hair, so the next time I took off my helmet it was full of blood. I just hope they were monogamous.

I passed in and out of rain storms but the head wind never eased and so I pulled into a McDonalds for a cup of tea and to check my emails. There, it's in print for all to read, I went to McDonalds. As you all know I believe it is better to give than to receive at such an establishment, and I usually can park close enough outside to check my email from the seat of the bike, but in the rain I capitulated.

After happening upon a really quaint motorbike museum that didn't have any Harleys in it, I met a German family at a roadside picnic area. Both parents were riding BMWs of course, dad with a huge sidecar to seat both the kids, although they usually fought over who got to sit on the back of the bike instead! They were considering taking off their waterproofs but I advised against it, given they were heading from where I had just come, and in return they gave me the address of a cheap B&B in the very heart of the old city of Quebec. This turned out to be a real gem, I can only hope my advice was as good and that it rained on them. Though that may not sound quite right.

Quebec City was celebrating its 400th anniversary and Sarkozy had just been over from France to join the celebrations and cause a minor constitutional furore by referring to Quebec as a country. And so, I suspect, begins another referendum campaign for independence from Canada.

The celebrations meant the city was packed, there

were stages set up all over the place and free concerts going on continually. There were street performers and parades and I couldn't have been better placed to take some of it in, than smack bang inside the old city walls.

Of course there's just one thing. Bikes are banned from the old city and there is no m/c parking to be had anywhere. I couldn't understand why so many people were looking at me and why the traffic wardens seemed to want to chase me. It's a legacy of all those open exhaust "oh look at me" bikes, that a blanket ban on motorcycles is in force. The reverberations off the high stone buildings and narrow streets must have been unbearable. So, ah, thanks for that!

Instead, Trevor who ran the B&B (a teacher over from Alberta- see a theme yet?) got me into the carpark of a hotel nearby, though I had to pay $8 for the privilege and the Vietnamese proprietor viewed the whole event as some clandestine operation. Free to wander (the rain had stopped, fancy that) I revelled in the atmosphere of the place and all its European architectural familiarity. Dare I say it I even became a little homesick. And the image was real. Everyone I spoke to in the city had either lived in France or in Italy. It was really strange, this was no pastiche, no Disney land, and I fell for it.

I saw the evening out in a fantastically atmospheric Jazz Bar. With Dave Brubeck playing on the record player on the bar, (remember those?) and a barman who treated the job like a trade not an extra wage, I was really enjoying myself. Then a jazz quartet came in at about midnight and began setting up. I gave them 3 tracks I think, and they were so amazingly discordant I had to leave. What's really incredible was they were using sheet music. I just wish they had all agreed on the same sheets before arriving! All very avant garde I'm sure, but incredibly hard to listen to.

The following morning I took full advantage of the late checkout time and Trevor's decency (getting him to do a laundry wash for me), to continue exploring the lower old city, before heading north again on the other side of the St Lawrence river this time to explore those “incredible” roads. I circumnavigated the Ile d'Orleans in the middle of the St Lawrence river, a beautiful island, all chocolate box style houses and postage stamp strawberry farms and then watched a tourist reverse his hire car into a huge ditch, to the accompaniment of a lot of gallic shoulder shrugging and raised eyebrows.

It was on this little island that I also got my Quebec souvenir. Every province has a strap line for its number plates, and a separate registration authority. Nova Scotia- “Canada’s Ocean Playground” is imaginative, but Quebec’s “Je me souviens” is apt, for me at any rate. Other Canadians may not be entirely sure why Quebecois say “I remember”, or indeed what it is they do remember, but for me it was the trip and what then could be better than finding a souvenir number plate on the side of the road, that I tucked under my duffel bag. Part of me even thought I may end up coming across one of those decorated pubs somewhere in the middle of nowhere that I could contribute to if I had become sick of carrying it.

I pressed on north and camped up almost where the ferry would have docked. The weather had cleared so the morning promised an assault on the twisties, it was just that first I had to find them. A few abortive attempts, looking at the map, led to gravel forestry tracks with warnings that I had to register with the authorities before continuing into the forested isolation. My idea of 'scratching' involves neither copious amounts of gravel rash, nor lacerations by bears, so I kept turning back.

I did take a lot of photos though and the one main route that was tarred, was entertaining, insofar as there were some corners. Nice gentle rolling bends to swing through, gently humming to oneself, as opposed to an Alpine physical workout. But life seemed particularly good all in all. It ended up being a 600km day almost by accident and I finished up at one of those semi permanent campgrounds where you have a little tended plot of a few square feet and a wee shed to keep your golf cart in. Not bicycle as you might expect.

There was a bar on site and a live performer with effects box. Bless him, but no matter what he tried to play, the over 60s audience line danced. True, they had, as best I could see, 3 different routines, but that was it. The nightmare began later. Every one of those aforementioned golf carts was placed in the hands of some very pissed pensioners, calling to each other, swigging from bottles and trying to light fags! Some mad grand prix ensued and was definitely a responsible social model to be aped by all the youth present!

"Really, the old of today... I just don't know"

4 am was when the heavens opened with enough force to bend the tent. It never actually leaked, but my main concern by 6am was whether or not it could float. The particularly jaunty angle it was at when I finally ventured out at 7 was due to the excessive weight of one of the tent pegs. Sounds bizarre perhaps, but I lost a peg a while ago so the big "Peggy" now acts as the main guy rope stay. Problem was she had sunk into the mud and was pulling the tent with her.

As I crossed the bridge onto Montreal Island and into the city itself, the rain temporarily eased and I remembered my first adult experience (your mind not mine) in the city in 1987. As an angst ridden teenager with a well decorated denim jacket I had enjoyed the company of the local constabulary on occasion, usually for offences such as walking with intent to get somewhere. So perhaps it shouldn't have been a surprise when, having ridden less than a kilometre on the island, my mirrors should be filled with that familiar light show of authority.

"Where is your Quebec license plate monsieur?"

I don't require one, I am not Canadian.

"But ave you a permit to drive?"

"Oui, ici", as I hand him a sodden lump of papier maché that had been in my inside pocket.

"Ah ha" said the colleague who was inspecting the bike and who had just recovered my booty. "Ere is de plate. You mus display monsieur".

"Well, you see the thing is... it's not really mine"

"Ow is dis possible? But if you fine it, you must return, oui?"

The souvenir play on words seemed a little inappropriate after the 2nd time I tried to explain it, but the conversation moved on when they wanted to know if I knew anyone in Montreal.

"Yes, I 'av a coozin (must stop that) in Pointe Clair" I said, not yet sure whether she still lived there, or indeed where "there" was. My god! All of a sudden the police were as nice as pie, offering directions, welcome to Montreal etc, before finally parting with " Av a nice stay", or perhaps day.

Turns out it's like saying my family all live in Knightsbridge. Blessed with the good fortune of a class system and a prejudicial police force, I was soon on my way as the skies unleashed another torrent and when I booked in to a motel (well I didn't actually know where my cousin was) to dry off, there was one thing that I had never expected.

True, it wasn't the most salubrious place, and they asked if I wanted the room for the whole night, but watching the weather channel (which I've fallen in love with) and seeing the screen go red to accentuate a particularly severe weather warning, I had a bit of a shock.

Picture the scene. Slightly dank motel room, with imaginative stains in the most unexpected places, décor of the crossover late 70's early 80's style, if there is such a thing, interspersed with fading and peeling Formica, my tent draped on the furniture with all my other clothes. My notverywaterproof jacket is dripping in the shower cubicle and there's a red screen on the telly saying "Beware heavy rain and flash flooding". Now that is the way to deliver a warning and mean it. When all of a sudden the roof fell in and there was the rain again, right there, in my room! You couldn't make it up. Well Ruth Rendell could perhaps, but it's not anything I'd have thought of.

It took just a moment of stunned disbelief before the uncontrollable laughter set in and it hadn't fully subsided when I did a Hugh Grant in the reception.

"I'm terribly sorry to disturb your thrilling and intellectually challenging afternoon televisual experience, but it would appear that I am having some difficulty avoiding the rain today, now that it is also falling on my bed. So I was rather hoping that you could relocate me to a room with slightly more indoor qualities."

The establishment was very accommodating and after the move I went out for a meal with my now located family, arriving back as the police raided the premises for that truly authentic north American, big city experience! How cool is that? Like every cop series I watched as a kid. In the morning the police returned and in true TV style they asked if "Drummond" had stayed the night, before showing a picture and saying he used various aliases. They even wore jeans with their uniform shirts and body armour. It was all so very rufty tufty, mean streets, until the meanest nastiest looking one asked if he could possibly use the washroom. Well, this is Canada!

Just up the road I treated Peggy to an oil change at a huge BMW dealership. I asked first if I could use a drip tray and give them my used oil if I bought oil and filter off them, but Caroline, on the service desk, said she'd get the whole lot done for $50. Now when was the last time a main dealer would even sell you oil and filter for the equivalent of 25 quid, let alone save you getting oily hands and provide a complimentary hot chocolate? I like Canada!

I moved out of my motel after just one night, but enjoyed watching a wee scam unfold at (the included) breakfast before I left. This old chap with big grey beard, sports jacket and tie and raincoat, came in with a paper and got himself a table. He was not a resident, and appeared to be homeless, but helped himself to coffee and some toast and jam and then spread out the paper and proceeded to read every article with his huge magnifying glass. As well as being quite blind he must have been deaf, (or French!) because I couldn't engage him in conversation at all. The establishment must have tolerated him, because the maitre d' had a novel attitude for one involved in the hospitality business. This big mama wasn't takin' no shit off nobody and the way she kicked the bin lid across the floor when it wouldn't sit on the bin correctly, and was ready to fly confrontationally at me when I asked where the hot water was, it was clear why many of the long-term residents exuded church mice timidity. In fact the look of sheer terror and distrust that filled their eyes, told a pretty complete story about how part of the forgotten underclass exist in motels in the big city. It was the only information I could glean from them because I couldn't engage anybody in conversation, French, English or Spanish.

Maybe I did look like a mugger, but the Dutch couple I managed to talk to mustn't have thought so, so I'll put part of it down to fear and part of it down to a more extreme version of the standoffishness that I have experienced throughout Quebec province.

This reserved, uncommunicative attitude was a strange thing to deal with after the incredible friendliness that I encountered in the more easterly Provinces. For the first few days in Quebec I thought it was me as traveller, beginning to put up barriers which others merely reflect, as I was doing my utmost to speak as much dreadful French as I could muster, so presumed it was my attitude. However I began to notice at the campgrounds and at the petrol stations or rest stops, that no one would engage with each other. If three bikes were pulled in at a rest area and three or four more pulled in they would park separately and completely ignore those who were already there as they walked passed. This little insight really helped my psyche. It wasn't me. I wasn't becoming morose. Hurrah!! I could continue my cheery "bonjours" and "bonsoirs" safe in the knowledge that my recipients were possibly just stunned into silence.

Oh I must tell you a thing I saw at one service area. A carload of girls who pulled in were getting changed from long-sleeved to short-sleeved tops and each added skin coloured heavily tattooed tights to their arms. Have you ever seen such a thing? Preparing to go out clubbing no doubt and desperate to create an image, but who manufactures such a thing and where on earth can you buy it? (Can't you tell that I'm tempted?)

8 THE OLYMPIAN FIASCO

Time spent in Montreal has been an interesting mix of being family member and tourist. My cousin no longer lives in Pointe Claire, so instead I slept soundly near downtown in my uncle's basement, only waking every hour when the basement 's sump pump automatically rattled loudly into action for two minutes. I had last been here about 12 years earlier, but unfortunately in the meantime my uncle had lost a large part of his mind, though he regularly told me he was hoping to find it any day soon. He still has incredible wit but then can't remember who anyone is the next minute, which makes conversations hilarious. My aunt Adele, now 80, is just incredible, but undergoing chemo and radiotherapy with incredibly humbling grace. Because uncle Charlie can no longer drive it was an honour to start each day by driving her across town to hospital for treatment.

What a terrifying experience and I'm rather flippantly not referring to the radiotherapy! Riding on the wrong side of the road is one thing, but driving and even sitting on the wrong side of a car, is very different. Spatially cramped with a feeling of the door being against my left shoulder, I inevitably struck the door with my hand every time I needed to change gear, which was a truly pointless exercise since the jeep was automatic. This only added to the out of body feeling and complete lack of control that I was experiencing. It was like playing a game in a fairground. Spatially unaware, I couldn't quite position myself on the super wide roads as I pressed the stop and go pedals. And there was this feeling of instability as though I had an appendage hanging off my right side, not unlike a sidecar outfit, capable at any minute of tipping up when I was on the outside of a turn. I don't think I can recall a less involving motive experience. Even in a jet airliner you can convince yourself you are involved, because if it wasn't for you and the 400 others all willing the thing to stay in the air, the pilots wouldn't have a chance.

I'm really glad I could be of some help though, and becoming immersed in family was great given that the rest of mine was so far away. Aunt Adele and I added to the morning routine by trying out a different one of Montreal's thousands of coffee houses each day and passing judgement on the quality of the pastries. That French café culture is alive and well and we fully embraced that joie de vivré, just sitting on the street, chatting, people watching and breathing in the fumes from the city's traffic. She loved the bike and at 80, hopes to go bungee jumping soon, having already tried ice skating and skiing!

I did my best with my diplomatic skills to smooth a rift, born through a mother's love of her daughter, but ultimately caused by the "wrong choice of man", which meant hours of juicy gossip for me and nights in the pub with my cousin. Families- doncha jus luv em?!

As a tourist there are certain 'must dos' in every city and one of those in Montreal is the Olympic Stadium, or Big O as it's known because of its shape. Perhaps more appropriately, locals call it the Big Owe, given that it was scheduled to cost $134 million and be completed for the 1976 Olympics, but actually ended up costing almost $1.4 billion and was finally finished in 1987, so, umm, bit of an over run then. Still, it was only setting the tone for all Olympics to follow. As always, not wishing to be outdone by anything French, contractors for the 2012 London Olympics in the UK, are over running and over budget already, three years ahead of schedule! But that's not the whole stadium story and the costs need to be put in perspective. So here goes, the story is something like this:

French architect Roger Taillibert designed the stadium and its focal point, the 575ft leaning concrete tower structure, which would hold the huge cables to support and retract the roof. It opened, (the stadium, not the roof) unfinished, in June 1976 and like all pale Olympian elephants, is renowned for holding two main events; the opening and closing ceremonies. Actually it apparently seated 72,000 for the football final that year between East Germany and Poland, which is a hell of a crowd, when you consider it has seating for 58,000!

In May 1976, in a valiant attempt to ensure it opened on time, and in the spirit of healthy athleticism, the Quebec government introduced a tobacco tax to bring in more cash, but alas it wasn't enough, and blighted by that other famous French recreational activity, the strike, the Olympic opening ceremony was held in an open air stadium not dissimilar to hundreds of other open air stadia.

As work continued into the 1980s, paid for by Quebec's smokers, there was a fire of all things in the concrete tower, suggesting not everyone embraced the tax! Later it was decided that concrete was probably too heavy for the proposed angle of lean and steel should be used in its construction. Unfortunately that only happened after a big bit fell off the end of the still unfinished tower in 1986 during a baseball game. Luckily everyone was standing together in one corner of the field, as they seem to do for baseball, so no-one was injured.

In '87 the orange roof was finally fitted and the stadium was declared finished. Then they realised that the roof couldn't open very well and couldn't be used at all if it was windy, which meant it famously became the only covered sports stadium where rain could stop play. When it was closed the roof leaked anyway, and in that first winter it fell in with the weight of collected water that hadn't dispersed as planned.

By '91 the place was remodelled and twelve thousand seats were removed, no doubt in case any more bits fell off the tower, but by September it was at the other end of the arena that a 56ton slab of concrete fell when a supporting beam broke. But that's not all, it goes on! The roof continued to leak so was kept closed after '92, until '98 when it was taken off and chucked in the bin, creating an open air stadium of all things.

I suppose everyone must have forgotten that it can get a bit chilly in a Canadian winter, because when the snows came a new static roof was fitted that they got down B&Q for a bargain $26million and then watched as it too collapsed the following January. Then, just as the government was on target to finally pay off the builders and bankers by October 2006 with the last of the tobacco tax, some wit in the legislative assembly banned smoking indoors and the resultant decrease in cigarette sales meant further delay and more interest on the loan.

As stunning as the stadium looks, especially from behind, with the tower rearing up like a giant cobra, a monumental tribute to a huge financial disaster, that is not why I was so intrigued and fascinated to see it. No, for me and now for you too, it will for ever be remembered as the place where, in August '76, just 3 days after the closing ceremony, a small blond 7 year old Irish boy and his big sister competed against each other in the long jump pit and then managed to run a complete lap of the track while their mother sat in the Royal Box and watched, no doubt cheering them on, until security guards arrived and threw us all out.

My time in Montreal coincided with the "Just for Laughs" comedy festival, so I went to see a few shows which were great, but I soon found that Montreal (the city that never sleeps) was similar to Quebec in that there were street performers, live shows on outdoor stages and general entertainment everywhere.

Coming out of one show, cousin Pearl and I stumbled upon a real pied piper street act. There was music and fireworks and costume and imitation bull fighting all done very theatrically with chopped up and rudimentarily reshaped bicycles and things. Loads of lighting either human powered or in battery packs. The circus remained in one place long enough to build a huge crowd before getting mobile and drawing everyone along until finally outside a huge art gallery the musicians (all wirelessly attached to the p.a.) climbed the steps of an old church and we, the spellbound audience witnessed two knights on horseback chase a huge bull down the street before the bull retaliated and so on.

These 'creatures' must have been 25 feet tall and the head and legs of the beasts moved by the most intricate mechanical contraption, but the best bit was that inbuilt lighting really seemed to bring the structures to life. The reality of that life was the 5 blokes pushing each contraption around, but there's no need to shatter the illusion. It was all really awesome (my new young person word) all free in the best tradition of street theatre and involved the closing of loads of downtown streets. The police didn't seem to care, and as they stood around in their jeans and baseball caps, I discovered that they were on strike- upholding cultural values, and hence the relaxed attitude and clothing.

The Sureté de Quebec provincial police force is an interesting one. They seem to enjoy using tazers as much as the Mounties do and with the same fatal results.

"Well it's his own fault he was sitting watching

telly with a heart complaint when we burst into the wrong apartment and zapped him, your Honour".

More interestingly though, during a George Bush visit last September, the crowd of demonstrators arrested three people in their midst with face masks and rocks in heir hands (well this is Canada!) They then realised that their prisoners were all wearing police issue boots. Oops! But then agent provocateur is a French term. The prime minister Steven Harpur said "Hey, it was just some rocks", which leads me to believe that perhaps the political, social, psychological, judicial and constitutional impact of what they were doing was somewhat lost on him! And it made him sound Australian.

My time in the basement passed quickly, doing touristy things, some gardening and a bit of DIY about the house. I also spent some time trying to fend off the advances of the pornographic poet in a neighbouring apartment. Don't you just adore big cities and their colourful populace? I finally wrote and posted some postcards too. When I was in the post office the clerk wouldn't take my quarters because they were American, which is fair enough, but I must have received them in change somewhere in Canada.

"Happens all the time now that they are worth the same, but I can't take 'em dude"

"Nevermind, I can't expect you to, you're right. Sorry."

Then I got my change from him. "Oh, this appears to be US too"

"Unlucky dude", was his response, accompanied by a Quebecois shrug. The shrug has infected the English speaking zone!

But alack, or alas, I felt it time to leave French Quebec, lest I develop a palate appreciative of fine wine and food, some fashion sense or even become a good lover, and so, in a not very direct way I headed for Ottawa, the Capital of Canada, to follow the lead I had garnered on my great uncle Owen. The weather was great, (just thought I'd better say that) so I made my way in a northerly loop that let me play on the perfectly graded gravel roads through rolling hills of grassland and forest, peppered with tiny lakes below the mountains and famously upmarket ski resorts around Mont Tremblanc.

Parking illegally has become second nature now, and while I parked on the pavement outside tourist information next the Parliament buildings in downtown Ottawa, I was approached by a very happy chap.

"Hi, you're not from around here are you?"

No, you're right, I'm not. He took off his shades.

"Ooo, you are a blondie!! All over eh?"

"I am yes."

"Are you staying long? Cos I could show you a really great time eh!"

"Fraid not."Prolonged silence.

"You're not gay are you?"

"Nope."

"Ah, that's a real shame. Have a nice day!"

I then proceeded to get on a city tour bus, which, halfway through the tour, drove down a slipway and into the river. Aquabus. Awesome!

And here's the "bet you didn't know that about Ottawa" section: Velcro was invented in the central government research building, though I can't imagine what they were doing in the lunch-break to think of that. Perhaps someone was having difficulty with that other Canadian invention, the zip, but then you know what they say about academics. Ottawa became the capital of Canada in 1857 because Toronto, Montreal, Quebec City and Kingston all wanted to be, and Queen Vic said "sod this for a game of darts" or something similar though possibly much more Victorian and to stop the bickering, chose a completely different village. Its main criteria was that it was far enough away from the border to be safe from the USA, who had a habit of invading. Imagine that! Still, given that Canada is the only country to ever manage to burn down the White House, they may have had due cause.

Ottawa has a 200mile canal stretching to Kingston on the shores of Lake Ontario, that was built by Irish navvies under British direction for military purposes. It was all to do with defence and the response to American invasion. Well, we all know what a lightning quick method of transportation the canal, and all it's locks, can be. That would surely have got the reinforcements there in no time. Today the Rideau Canal is the world's longest ice skating rink for a goodly percentage of the year, the winter being something of an oversight on the part of the defence design team. In 2007 it was declared a UNESCO World Heritage site, recognised as a 'work of human creative genius', so the blindingly obvious still escapes some.

Near the mouth of the canal, above the 7 locks to the Ottowa River and beside the Parliament buildings, there stands a statue to Samuel de Champlain, seventeenth century French explorer, militarist, cartographer and recognised founder of New France. He is proudly holding aloft his navigational sextant. Unfortunately it is upside down. Apparently the sculptor didn't know what a sextant was, but if you don't look too closely it's still a fine effigy, though not as powerfully emotive as the memorial to the fallen of the Great War. The stunning 23 figure piece of commemorative work was done by 6 siblings from Farnborough and put on show in London before being shipped to Canada and set in Confederation Square beneath an imposing archway. This monument to the War To End All Wars, totalling seventy feet in height, was finally finished in March 1939, just in time for the next one. Ceremonial military now guard the National Monument in response to an incident that took place a couple of years ago, when some youths were caught relieving themselves on the bronze figures in the middle of the night. It's guarded from 9 to 5.

I saw the gate lodge of the Prime Ministerial Residence, but there was no easy access to the house of power. The lodge is now owned and staffed by Mounties since the last Premier, Jean Cretien, had his house broken in to, the burglar having got past the security, police and alarm system. Mrs Cretien, the premier's wife, hit the intruder on the head with a statue, which is all very Carry On Prime Minister don't you think? The house was first used as official Ministerial Residence by Lester Pearson in 1963, which may appear as a pointless factoid to you, but Lester B Pearson was the PM who created the Maple Leaf flag, and due to pressure from his lefty coalition government partners, introduced Canada's famous universal health care system, pension plan and declined Washington's invitation to send Canadian troops to Vietnam to partake in the war against communism. As wars on abstract nouns go, it seemed marginally less ridiculous than the current one, but Pearson chose instead to maintain and develop his remembrance as the father of modern peacekeeping strategies, after diffusing the Suez Crisis and instigating the UN Emergency Force of peacekeepers. So at least we can say he had some great ideas, even if their execution has been a little demure. The blue berets are fetching though.

Anyway, I proceeded to move the bike to the National Archive and park illegally on the huge footpath at the front, under the sign saying no parking. I went in and registered to join the central archive library as a researcher with Bridgwater College, Somerset. (I had to think of something and it was where I last held down a job). I scanned microfilm after film, getting dizzy and adopting weird black and white vision. When I found the right film, it was upside down and back to front, as it was bound to be. The brusque librarian (no hair to release and let cascade, or glasses to remove....), got it turned for me as the minutes ticked by. I'd been in 4 hours already and the place was soon to close. With real panic starting to set in, and with sweaty palms I scanned more and more. Switzer isn't all that Irish a surname, but that's only because hundreds of them seem to have moved from Cork, Kerry and Limerick to Canada.

With two calls of final closing, and with about 6 minutes to go, I found him! He was nestled not very alphabetically after the Switzers, between Pakic Swidzinski, a farmer from Poland who was going to his brother, and Charles S. Swinnock, a protestant Anglo Saxon from England, who came for a health visit from Auckland New Zealand and brought £2,500 with him (his declaration, not mine) as spending money!

Owen Oge Swiney was one of 204 third class passengers on the good ship Marburn, which arrived from Belfast on 23rd April 1924. His port immigration entry reads thus:

Purpose of visit: to learn Canadian farming. £15 in possession. Paid own passage. Was initially going to 1031 Prospect Avenue, Calgary via Canadian Pacific Railways.

Father: Colonel William Daniel Swiney, of Moyagh, Co Donegal, Ireland, registered next of kin.

I'd be lying if I didn't say it produced quite a lump in my throat, but like millions of other individuals noted as nothing more than a couple of lines in the register, he was part of the foundation of modern Canada with hopes for a new life. And in his case, hopes of less rain. That was the only Swiney I could find who had come through the Eastern entry to this great continent, so it's lucky it was him. Now I've got somewhere to go and see in Calgary,

Alberta, as long as Prospect Avenue hasn't been buried beneath a Walmart.

I arrived back at the bike to find a note from someone at the Ministry of Justice, saying what a cool bike I had, that he'd seen me in a huge thunderstorm in Montreal two weeks earlier and suggesting that I come out and ride with his BMW buddies! So that's why Canada's judiciary is held in such high esteem as fair and even minded, they ride bikes! Literally two miles outside the Province of Quebec and people notice me again! I exist! The downside of leaving Quebec and entering Ontario however, is that the signposts revert to default Canadian. Absent or pointless.

I pulled on to a filling station forecourt and endeavoured to get the attendant's attention as he was going inside.

"Excuse me, can you tell me where I can find the four- one- seven highway to Toronto?"

"You need the four seventeen" and he went inside. I called after him.

"Excuse me, can you tell me where the four seventeen is?"

"Yeah, go down Robson" and he was gone. I dismounted, followed and accosted him next to the miles of peanut butter flavoured confectionery.

"I can see you are busy, but could you tell me where Robson is?"

"Yeah sure. Right on the 3rd lights then left at Dairy Queen. Then you need the 416"

"I do? When? To get to the 417?"

"No, Toronto." WHAT? Well which is it 16 or 17?" But he was gone into the office.

I found it, the 417, all 8 lanes of it and not a single sign post, except one on the actual entry ramp, that said 'Toronto' and was the size of a speed limit sign, which with my eyes, gave me about 30 metres to cross two busy lanes of 'Robson' to get it and time to upset only about ten drivers. Profanities aside, it was a piece of cake. And then the skies opened, probably as a result of the profanities, making the journey to Toronto one of those punctuated with bouts of hysterical laughter. How much wetter can I get? The skies got so dark they had some light blue clouds in them, if you know what I mean. At one point the cloud formations seemed to be exactly that of the roof of a dogs mouth. All black and grey and ridged like a crinkle cut crisp.

The roads seemed better than many in Quebec, even though most of them were under a few inches of water and someone had been let loose with the 'overbanding' machine, liberally applying super shiny stripes of pure tar all over the surface. I gave in to hunger with just two hours to go and realised that 'ah shure wernt in Queebeck now, eh!'

The family diner at the crossroads in Havelock, uncannily called The Havelock Crossroads Diner, sure had a lot of them good ole gals and boys in it. Everyone had facial hair and a baseball cap with the name of their favourite tractor emblazoned proudly across the front. They all stared open mouthed and mid munch at this funny feller in their midst, their facial flavour savers doing their job and retaining stray food for a later snack. There were posters up advertising country and western events, so I guess they enjoy both kinds of music round here. I got a burger, one ah mamas best, rang Siobhan's brother in Toronto and said

"I'm coming tonight. I may be very late, but I think I'd like to keep moving!"

9 NICE HAT, EH!

I arrived with Siobhan's brother Paul and family in Toronto and they promptly moved house. I thought a polite, “you smell rather and we don’t like you”, would have done the job, but they rather excessively moved house. They say it was coincidence but… My cunning plan was to help with the move, and therefore embarrass them into letting me stay, which worked. As it happens I was then brought down by something medical which manifested itself in a strange way. Stiff, sore neck and back, incredibly sensitive hair folicles (yes, I still have a few), stomach cramps and a randomly exploding sphincter. Bed seemed like a good cure, after I had tried to ignore it for a couple of days but some elements of the illness were easier to ignore than others when I was caught out in public. “Get out of the way!”

I was in one public convenience in Toronto's underground mall, (they have 23kms of underground shopping for when the winter comes), when I had my second 'approach' of the week. Breathing a huge sigh of relief after another close call with uncontrollable bowel movements, and feeling none too happy generally, I emerged from the cubicle to a young man who asked if I fancied a good time. A good time? What a cheesy line. Not being my usual pleasant self, I said “Yes. Why not. Have you got the keys to a Ferrari and a cork?” Honestly, it must be my hat that attracts the attention, though on second thoughts the cork reference may not have helped my heterosexual case.

I tried to be as much of a tourist in Toronto as I could, determined to see past it's rather unfairly given "boring" moniker and went to look at the CN tower among other things. At its 553metres, it is very tall and the viewing platform is made of glass. Very thick glass, which you walk on, but which, the visitor is informed, can withstand the weight of 14 hippos, Hippos being the common construction industry standard in these parts. The native moose measurement I can understand, but hippos? I don't think they'd be able to get into the lift. How stupid, like someone saying something is the size of Wales, when nobody actually knows what size Wales is. And before someone more nerdy than me writes back, there are bound to still be disputed territories around Hereford and Shrewsbury regardless of that ditch Offa built.

Sorry, I must stick to the plot. Toronto.

There is so much construction in the downtown Toronto area it is said that Canada has 2 seasons, Winter and Construction. They have gone apartment mad and supply is soon going to be outstripping demand, like has happened everywhere else, so "Buy now, to be sure of negative equity in a couple of years".

I took a day trip from the city and crossed the mighty Welland canal which links Lakes Erie and Ontario and lowers ships 327ft in the process, then headed down to Niagara to see the Falls, because that's one of the things you do, and because I wondered if it had changed much since 1979 when I was last there. It has. The whole area is one big casino now, but I think perhaps they've done as best they can around the Falls themselves, considering the incredible numbers of people being catered for, an estimated 20 million in 2008. I found the area slightly further down river more relaxing, especially Niagara on the Lake, but be warned- don't buy anything, you can't afford it. Between the two Niagaras I felt the need for sweet tea, because it was really all I had consumed for a few days, but then I treated myself to a muffin. One of Otis Spunkmeyer's Best Muffins to be precise, now with secret added ingredient- I kid you not! I tried not to think what the ingredient might be and concentrated instead on the banana and nuts flavouring (euphemisms not withstanding), and how strange it was to be the thinnest person in the whole café. I was only utilising one chair and felt somehow aggrieved.

Toronto has so much more than the CN Tower though. It has a legacy of great wealth created during the era of prohibition when all those God fearing Americans respected the ban on alcohol and just got in a boat to cross the lake instead. For a while the unfortunately named Gooderham and Worts Distillery was the biggest in the British Empire, when the British had an empire. The islands just off the skyscraper-lined waterfront, were covered in casinos, hotels and even a baseball pitch to pander to the hoards. The pitch is famous as the first place that Babe Ruth struck a home run, out of the stadium and into the water, if you know who that was. Anyway it's all gone now and instead is the site of parkland, a small amusement park and some very exclusive yacht clubs. There are a few hundred private properties in the east which survive on a lease if the residents agree to live in them at least 300 days a year, after a 25 year court battle was won against the government who had wanted the whole archipelago cleared of dwellings.

It also has Casa Loma, the fairytale castle-house used in loads of movies that you thought were made in Hollywood, and originally built by multi millionaire Sir Henry Pellatt, who controlled the electricity company. You see? Power utilities in private hands are a license to print money and he had so much he told his architect that he could build his own house with any materials that were left over. Guess who was in charge of ordering the building supplies? There's a very fine house nearby that was built at the same time. Pellatt didn't get to live in his castle long though. The great depression meant people couldn't pay exorbitant fees for electricity and the government decided to nationalize his power generation company and tax him on his new mansion, all of which was a bit of a blow after his aeroplane company was taken by the State as part of the war effort. He ended up living with his driver, which is really quite a social tumble. While I'm on electricity, it seems that the electric light was invented in Toronto, it's just that hard up student, Henry Woodward sold the patent rights to a bloke called Edison, who thought there just might be something in it.

The city is now the most ethnically diverse in the world according to the UN, but who knows how these things are measured. The amount of money spent on drink in the 8 blocks that make up the entertainment district is reliably measured however, at $4m every weekend, so I think it is fair to say that Toronto isn't Montreal's prudish municipal sister as she may once have been. Or else it's those immigrants. How dare they go out and have a good time.

One of those immigrants, Joe an old school barber from Campodimele in Italy, gave me a haircut. Now I've never been shaved by a barber with a cut throat razor before, and in the interests of giving it a go, I thought I'd give it a go. After the haircut though, he flashed the mirror behind me where I caught a glimpse of the dribble of blood on my neck and made a hasty exit rather than risk a full Sweeney Todd experience.

After a little nudge from Siobhan I headed to the doctor on day 6 of my mystery illness. After all, as she pointed out, it's all social research so I called the walk in clinic and duly walked in as they opened their doors for business. I then sat, for 1hour and 52 minutes, with various ill people, where I attempted to catch other diseases while listening to the Philippino receptionist call all her friends for a chat, before being finally shown in to the doctor's room. He wasn't there, so I sat some more before he finally appeared and stood with his back to me, mumbling to the floor. It was refreshing to see that he came from the same western "let's ignore the patient" medical school of thought. I really wasn't culturally that far from home after all.

"What's wrong then?"

Well, I have a very stiff sore neck and back and sensitive nerve endings, kinda like meningitis, and severe stomach cramps and explosive diarrhoea.

"Is there any blood in the stools?"

STOOLS? That's not the concrete noun I'd use.

"How long have you had the sore stomach?" he says, still keeping his eyes firmly down on his note pad. "What about the nervous system", I proffer.

"Have you a temperature?" I don't know, but I've been sitting under an air-conditioner for nearly 2 hours waiting for you!

"And is there any blood in the stools?" He repeats, still looking at the bits of paper, exploring his bloody bowel fixation and not listening to a word I say.

"Well I suggest pepto-bismol and you should be fine", he didn't touch me- not that I was there for male contact, I can get that myself using my hat- but the consultation took less than 2 minutes. I can see why you have to pay the $50 up front, or I'd have walked straight out of there.

I went and found a small micro brewery in the historic quarter by way of recompense and for medicinal purposes, where they were advertising free tours and tasting. "I'dlike to try your wheat beer please".

"Sorry, it's not on as a taster, how about the coffee

porter, since you are Irish".

No, I don't really like porter, but I'll try the organic Pils then. "Sorry, just run out".

I stood there and looked at him. He went to the fridge and took out a full bottle of the wheat beer and handed it to me.

"Nice hat". Oh, Jesus.

The recuperation from my mystery illness was aided somewhat by the swimming pool and hospitality at Paul and Brigitte's and by playing with the three lovely kids, but it was all too soon that I had to leave. (Which isn't meant to sound a little suspect…)

With new brake pads which I had to buy from BMW at three times the normal price, (well someone had to pay for the granite staircase in the three storey showroom and because Aprilia, would you believe, don't keep them as a stock item), and with my new Corbin super comfy seat fitted, I was ready to do some miles, and get filmed doing them. On the way out of Toronto in the heavy highway traffic I had three different cars pull along side and take pictures with mobile phones, and one couple who filmed me.

And so it was, after more than two months away from home, I rolled into Enniskillen, the namesake of the town where I was born in Ireland, which is situated on a big hill called Big Hill. Now let me tell you a thing or two about Enniskillen Ontario. It isn't the largest hub of economic activity, what with its one store, one phone box and two stop signs, but things weren't always thus. At its height this town of 230 souls had 4 churches, so the northern Irish settlers clearly didn't leave all their old ideas at home when they pioneered a new beginning. Reading the names on the various gravestones brought a lump to my throat: Fergusons, Farrells, Swans, Gallaghers and Mclaughlins aplenty, all names so common at home.

It was one of those McLaughlins that really put Enniskillen on the map though, by founding a small blacksmiths shop making sleds in the winter and farming equipment in the summer, before diversifying into buggies. True, you may never have heard of the McLaughlin Carriage Company, but in 1876 they outgrew their premises in Enniskillen and moved to Oshawa, Ontario, concentrating a few years later on making new fangled automobiles. They ended up doing a bit of corporate re-branding, changed their name to General Motors and made quite a go of it by all accounts.

McLaughlin's eldest son Jack was more interested in explosive chemistry than cars and liked nothing better than messing about in the lab trying to make something that tasted better than the water out of the Great Lakes. He came up with Canada's first dry gingery ale and it must have taken hundreds of marketing seminars to think of an appropriate name for the product. I expect it was the tea lady who said "What, are you still discussing that Canada Dry Ginger Ale stuff?"

While I was outside the shop enjoying one of the justly famous Kawartha Icecreams, I got chatting to Dave Loughlin, the policeman in these parts. Having seen the Irish flag on the bike, he wanted to tell me that his town was named after a place in Ireland, so was delighted when I told him that was where I had come from. He lived in one of the oldest houses in the town and he and his wife turned out to be a real font of local knowledge.

I didn't go to visit all the neighbouring villages whose names are from the same vicinity back home, and couldn't bring myself to go to Little Britain to find out if there really was only one gay in the village, even though I expect I'd have had little difficulty finding him if I wore my hat.

This was really just as well, because I am less than half way across Canada and when I do get to the west coast I hope to head north, further than the whole distance across the continent, so that I can get into Alaska and properly ride 'Into the Wild'. The first snows are expected at the start of September up there, so I'm a little behind my meteorological schedule already.

10 INTO THE WILD WEST

In Barrie, Ontario I stopped with some friends I had met in New Brunswick, Glenn and Gwen, the couple who had pulled so many strings for me at the bike rally, and during my stay with them they pulled even more strings. They organised the Yamaha play day and are wholly to blame for all my current aches and smiles.

I arrived after dark in Barrie, Ontario, where I planned to meet Glenn and Gwen, some friends I'd made in New Brunswick and found the 'open all hours' Tim Hortons, national symbol of Canada and a great place for a sticky bun and coffee. It shone like a beacon in the night and I thought the crowd of bikers outside might help me find their address. They were auto workers, waiting to start the night shift and to a man, they were stoned out of their heads. I'm sure it's not the most exciting job in the world, but I wonder who it is that keeps an eye on productivity and quality control and stops everyone giggling.

I stayed with Glenn, his wife Gwen, daughter Emily (who had promised to teach me Irish dancing) and their hugely huggable Retrievadoddle dog called Diesel and it was they who introduced me to a remarkable lady and one of Canada's best kept motorcycling secrets, Michele Duff, grand prix bike racer in the 1960's.

Michele had a full Yamaha sponsored factory ride

for three years among other things and was the 9th person to ever lap the Isle of Man TT course at 100mph. She is now racing classic bikes and had just returned from Spa Francorchamps in Belgium where an accident had cracked her skull. Although still badly bruised from the incident, she was an excellent host and I had a great time. She knew all the great riders from the 1960s and 70s because she spent so much of her racing life in the UK and Europe, so the anecdotes and stories of derring-do kept me enthralled, especially those involving Alan Sheppard and the people from the MZ factory in East Germany. She still rides a bike at 69 years old and likes finding young guns on the latest superbikes so that she can give them the fright of their lives. Of course you may not have heard of her, a woman with a factory sponsored ride in the 1960's? Well she was Mike Duff until 1984 and it appears that the historical motoring press may have selective amnesia about her achievements.

I had a fantastic time at the Robert's house; fed, beered, entertained beyond belief and given a ride on a Harley. Apart from a Buell, that was my first Harley experience, all 1600cc of it. I can see the attraction now, given the straight roads here. It was great, lolloping along at next to no revs, huge comfy seat and stereo, but heaven knows how it would be with a few corners and some potholes because that is what I am now in search of, and the rougher the better. I'm fully trained you see!

Over the weekend I was treated, by Yamaha Canada, to a day at their off road school It all began with a quad bike, which was hilarious until I broke it going over some logs and another one was issued. Then I played in a four wheeled miniature jeep thing which seemed to be capable of climbing near vertical ascents. It only got better when I was presented with a trail bike, a guide and a piece of woodland (the size of Wales) in which to try and get lost or stuck, and at the end of the day I was shown to the motocross track.

I'd let slip over lunch that I'd really fancy having a go at getting some 'big air' like you see on the telly when kids with broken noses and no teeth fly through the air with such grace, performing tricks during the twenty minutes that they are airborne. I had never been on a proper motocross bike before, light, agile and eager to fly, and now I am realising that I have never before had so many previously undiscovered parts of my body ache so badly. But I couldn't be happier

And I really got some 'big air' as they say in the trade. In fact I got it loads of times, higher and higher, and every time the landing hurt more and more. The thing is, by this time the Yamaha guys were just laughing at my antics, so no one would tell me how to land without spraining my wrists and repeatedly slamming my face into the handlebars! Ho hum, what joy, but now I see why the kids on the telly have no teeth. I just don't think I can afford the reconstructive surgery it may cost me if I decide to keep practicing.

Afterwards the Yamaha chaps offered me anything that I might need, a new jacket or helmet, and me after buying a dodgy rubber oversuit because my Revitt jacket is such a pile of pants! Have I mentioned that before? They said I should see how my kit holds up in Alaska and if I want anything to just give them a call and it'll be at the Yamaha dealer in Vancouver on my return. What kind, generous people and they thought I was writing a book.... You never know, I may do, but in the meantime I feel obliged to say that this edition of The Hunt for Puerto del Faglioli is brought to you in association with Yamaha. You see, I can sell out. It's easy.

Now I just need to find an amenable tyre manufacturer....

So here I am, 600kms a day for the past three, I'm

still not out of Ontario and every bit of my body still hurts like hell! But there are also bits of me hurting that I didn't know could. My eyes hurt from the incredible vistas they have been subjected to in the last few days and from crying with delight after observing the awesome sight of black bear cubs sitting watching the traffic near the town of Marathon, and from seeing eagles soar, as they are wont to do, riding the thermals against a perfect sky.

I stopped in Marathon shortly after and mentioned my bear sighting to some blokes over tea in a cafe. When I said where I'd seen them, one man said "Did they have white chests with sergeants type stripes on them?" "Yes! Really distinctive brown stripes!" "Yeah," he said, "they live near by with their mum and dig in the trash at the Mining company, where I work". Then the idiot tourist, still enthralled with his sighting and brimming with excitement said "Oh, you know them! Have they got names?" This led to a bit of a pause, a silent moment in the cafe, until he said, "Nope- they don't have names. They're fuckin bears."

Even my olfactory glands hurt from the stench of roadkill. Only the big trucks have the bulk to run at night and risk the moose collisions, but the resultant mess on the road even after the carcass has been moved, looks like a diesel spill until you realise it's red. I nearly lost the whole plot on one such gloopy mess this morning. But the flat raccoons and skunks and squirrels and deer all add to the roadside aroma that hits me intermittently and fills my helmet with a stench that the bouts of intense summer heat only accentuates.

This road over the top of the Great Lakes was only paved in 1961, so finally providing a reliable link to the prairie lands to the west and demonstrating how important the inland waterways were to the commerce of the continent until relatively recently.

Sault Saint Marie is the closest I have been to the USA so far apart from Niagara. I turned right at the lights to go north around Lake Superior and in my mirrors could see the border with the Stars and Stripes flying proudly overhead. I was almost close enough to smell the donuts and hear the gunfire! It was a decision that was easy to make. I know I am coming back across the States later and will see more than enough of it. By contrast, the route less travelled, remaining in Canada and going north is the one that appeals. I'd had real trouble staying awake getting thus far, though what I remember of the scenery was nice. It's just that the continuously straight roads pass through a continuously constant vista of trees of a continuous variety set beneath a continuously blue sky, which, in time can lead to a state of continuous relaxation. A good nights sleep in Sault St Marie though, and I was ready for anything, except the distance I had to ride before I found anywhere to get breakfast. Getting an early start is great, but I'd misjudged the isolation I was heading into. It was 200 kms before I came to anywhere.

What am I saying? You see, there is the urban dweller in me. The twenty first century namby pamby cosseted westerner. There were of course lots of places en route. It's just that no one lived in them, had built anything in them, or had given any of them a name. To make up, and to keep my mind off my growling stomach, the road darted in and out from the shores of the Lake. Occasional mists rolled in, imitating the sea, and these bodies of water are so huge they may as well be seas. They can affect the weather the same way and are directly responsible for the heavy snowfalls around here and in the north east of the USA. Lake Superior is actually bigger than the old Czechoslovakia (and you just thought I couldn't spell it) and therefore way off the Welsh scale.

Together all of the Great Lakes hold 20% of the world's and 95% of the USA's fresh water, but 33m people live around the edge and use them as a toilet. Did you know Halifax in Nova Scotia is the first Canadian city to begin treating its sewage before discharging it into a watercourse? In that case the Atlantic. But all the other cities, Kingston for example dumps 30 billion litres of untreated sewage into the St Lawrence river, and Victoria on the west coast 33 billion into the Pacific. I can't remember over what time span that is, weekly or monthly, but that hardly matters. Add to that the agricultural fertilizer runoff and the chemical industry wastes that were buried on the Great Lakes shoreline for years and you've gotta ask, "Swim anyone?"

The road heads inland after Wawa, which is really just a t-junction and petrol station with a café, but it maintains some of its coastal interest. Rocky escarpments, variations in gradient and flora, even a few corners all helped to keep me awake, but also for much of the day I was accompanied by a little grey Toyota whose occupants occasionally overtook me holding up signs that said things like "We Ireland".

Half way to Thunder Bay is the settlement of White River. You might have garnered at least one thing about the physical attributes of the town of White River from its name but you'd be wrong, because there is no river. But there is a huge wooden thermometer supporting a claim to being the coldest place in Canada with a temp of minus 58 Celsius. I have to tell you that there are other, colder places in Canada who don't have wooden thermometers and as such can probably measure the temperature more accurately.

The town is a stop on the Canadian Pacific Railroad that Uncle Owen would have passed through on his way to Calgary, but he wouldn't have been lucky enough to lay his eyes on the 25' statue of Winnie the Pooh that graces the field beside tourist information. Primarily because the Ontario Tourist Board wasn't really thinking about how to market a town named after something it didn't possess, and as such didn't have an office, but also because AA Milne hadn't published Winnie the Pooh in 1924, so White River couldn't claim to be the town Winnie was from. But it really is.

In 1914 Capt. Harry Coleburn was happily on his way to war in Europe when he passed through the town and bought an orphaned bear cub from a trapper on the station, who was probably selling it alongside cups of tea and coffee and prepackaged chicken salad sandwiches for hungry travellers. Harry thought it would be jolly fine to have a bear as a mascot for his men to boost morale on the front line. He brought it to England where someone might have pointed out the implications of trench warfare and the bear ended up in a zoo where AA Milne's son Christopher saw it and fell in love. The name? Well, according to the very well appointed museum in White River, Harry had come from Winnipeg, so called it Winnie and as I read the papers over tea, I got some idea why he might have decided to go to the front line in France. If Winnipeg was anything like it is now, he wanted to take his chances in those trenches.

I read that Vincent Li has just beheaded someone in a Greyhound bus in the town. Apparently he was having some marital issues and, the paper says, is noted as being someone who always stopped to say hello to others who lived in his apartment block, which you'll agree, is mighty strange behaviour. Apparently he calmly leaned over to the complete stranger in the seat in front of him and after slitting the man's throat, began the arduous task of decapitating him, before walking down the bus with the severed head. At least Harry would have known which direction the Kaiser's shells were coming from.

As I continued towards Thunder Bay (town on an inlet, lots of storms, you get the idea) I was either disturbed or relieved to see a lot of billboards relating to domestic violence. Disturbed that there should be a high enough instance of it to be addressed so publicly, but also relieved that the problem was being tackled so openly. Better I feel, to discuss the problems in a marriage and confront the issues, than cut the head off a stranger. I presume it has something to do with the isolation of living in a place like this, but I'm passing through and not really exploring, so I'll never know. I just thought I'd mention the posters because there isn't a whole lot else to see at the side of the road and I may have already referred to the trees?

I camped just east of Thunder Bay with its towering grain silos and docks and had time to ponder the memorial to Terry Fox, the athlete and inspiration who died in 1981 aged 22, not long after reaching this same spot during his Marathon of Hope. Terry lost a leg to cancer when he was 18 and in a bid to raise money for research, began a run across Canada from Newfoundland to Victoria, running a marathon a day on his one good leg. After 143 days and 3,339 miles, the cancer that had resurfaced in his lungs forced him to stop, but before his death and with the help of many who were inspired by him, he realised his dream of raising 1 dollar from every Canadian. $24million. The Terry Fox Run is now an annual event raising funds for cancer research that anyone can take part in, but you don't have to run coast to coast, round your own neighbourhood is ok.

I tried everywhere in Thunder Bay for a tyre, but to no avail, though I had some fun at a Harley dealer, accidentally stealing the show from the new models that were being paraded during an open day, by riding in through a demonstration on my way to the front door. Accidentally!

Then riding due west towards Manitoba I seemed to enter little Finland. Finnish place names and family names abounded and I got into a very long conversation with the very friendly and slightly demented Leonard Soivenen who had spent much of his life at sea before settling in Canada to work in forestry with his countrymen. His ocean weathered features looked out from behind his white beard and from under his cap, and he wore his heavy donkey jacket even though it must have been nearly 30ºC. Leonard gave me lots of advice on how to find a job in the sawmills of British Columbia when I got there. He then talked about the pulp mills when he felt I didn't seem all that interested, before moving on to veneering factories. He didn't really comprehend that if I wasn't at sea, I might like to do something other than work with lumber. We went through the whole conversation four times before another car pulled in and his attention was diverted long enough for me to jump on the bike and get away.

I then rode through an area of northern Ontario that was recovering from a forest fire. I rode through it for 45kms and as far as I could see in every direction the damage was the same, so that was probably the size of Wales. And that reminds me of a news report I heard recently about a fire in northern British Columbia. When it was noticed, it had already burnt 84,000 hectares and was threatening two communities. Luckily all 19 (!) people were safely evacuated. But stuff is so big here. The sky is big, the wildlife is huge, the roads are big and the views are just immense, when you can see over the trees.

Peggy's back tyre is bald, but it has to last me to Winnipeg, the next probable source of rubber. My bum is grand though with my new seat and my medication, so bring on the prairies- I've got a good book to read, the roads through the grain fields won't bore me.

Go West young man, Go West!

11 TRACTORS AND HEALTHCARE

And so from Ontario "yours to discover", as it says on the number plates, through Manitoba "friendly Manitoba" (not terribly imaginative), I am now in Saskatchewan "land of the living skies", which can be roughly interpreted as "Uh oh, twister!"

I have been riding the prairies for the past few days and when people say they are dull, or the skies are so big, or there are a lot of combine harvesters, that is exactly what they mean. Poor Saskatchewan has the smallest of all entries in the guidebooks, barely a few pages, but strangely, I haven't fallen asleep once, nor have I read my book. The miles are just flowing past with me in a state of perpetual awe.

People live here! Not many it's true. There is a Province wide population density of 1.6 per square km, but since two thirds of the populace live in the cities of Regina and Saskatoon, that means that generally there is less than one lonely person per square kilometre, except in the north, where there is less than 0.1 of a lonely person. I met some of those lonely people and you know, when they've been coaxed out of hiding they can be quite nice to talk to. First though, you've got to find them, and with 50kms between dots on the map, dots that often represent little more than a grain silo and a diesel tank, it can all be a little scary at times. The dots may occasionally represent a store, but one that is more likely to sell agricultural machinery than bread.

But I did find Phil, who was, quite frankly as mad as a box of frogs and just a little bit paranoid. He was standing in a field, miles from anywhere, but next to a junction which he said led to some government institution and was busy writing the most incoherent placard I think I have ever seen, listing a host of incorrectly spelt accusations against the government. We chatted for maybe twenty minutes and although he seemed well read, his conspiratorial global power theories were just a little bit 'out there', even for me. He is currently out on bail for arson, but is adamant that burning fields of grain is just nature's way of ensuring regeneration, and is sure that his wife will come back home to him any day soon. It must be the open spaces.

It is now 38C and meeting vehicles is an occasion for a cheery wave. I slowed to chat with Korsten who is cycling from Switzerland to Vancouver and who talked with me for ten kilometres as he maintained 25kmph into a headwind in the heat and wasn't out of breath. I'm sure that can't be natural. Cyclists are weird.

Part of this grassland area looks a bit like the moors of Northumberland, without the precipitation, the bog or the sheep, only much bigger. Did I mention scale? Big is the scale. Infinity big, as a four year old once told me when describing the prairie sky. I drove past a breakers yard, spread over about 20 acres, and half of their stock was combine harvesters and tractors. Practical I know, but just a bit odd. I am staying south as I cross the prairies, within 100kms of the border with the US because everyone who mentioned it said that the landscape was much prettier and the gradients were so varied. It's true, they might have been taking the piss, but somehow I think they were serious. Everything is relative. But do you know the best thing about Saskatchewan? I could drive around here all day because they have sign posts! Every junction says the number of the road, the destination of the road and the distance to that destination. It's Nirvana. Oh my god! I've got it! In a sudden flash of clarity I now know what Ontario means. The tag line on the number plates, "It's mine to discover", because there aren't any bloody road signs to help!

Saskatchewan seems nice. A little rough and ready perhaps, but nice. I rolled into Carlyle looking for a cuppa and a bite to eat. The smell from the bakery was exquisite and as I approached I had a wee chat with a bloke originally from Denmark. He recommended the cinnamon buns. I don't like cinnamon buns, so I asked for a jammy tart thing, one of the hundreds that I could see just out of the oven. The girl put 6 in a 'styrene tray and shrink wrapped them, before handing them to me.

"No, I'd really like just the one please, to eat now".

"We don't sell 'em like that. We wrap 'em and we sell 'em in a tray"

I tried voicing many possible solutions but it seemed there was no way around this logistical nightmare, so I had to leave empty handed and with healthier blood sugar levels. And so, pastryless and eager to find a web connection to post the last email before it was dreadfully out of date, I went to tourist information, who shared the building with the museum that engaged in "the restoration of rusty relics". Step forward and take a bow Michele Moore who, above and beyond the call of duty, let me access the office wireless and then made me a big pot of tea. What a wonderful day!

So I like the prairie for two good reasons. It is the home of the socialist movement in Canada, which is mighty odd given its intensely rural nature, and it is so hot and dry there are no mozzies.

The New Democratic Party, or NDP originated

here, the political party of universal healthcare fame and the communal spirit seems to have spawned from the incredibly tough life the farmers face. Many of them are from eastern European stock, settled under the Canadian Pacific Railway scheme. Poles, Russians and Ukrainians, who originally brought their faith and their cooperative working habits with them. The Mennonites came, as did Temperance Colonies and other sects, settling the land even before Saskatchewan became a Province in 1906.

My initial impression of the previous prairie Province, 'Friendly Manitoba', was anything but friendly. My first campground was run by a German couple, Hans and Ulrike and they made me ruminate on why it is that people who clearly don't like people, get involved in the hospitality business. Like all those matriarchal landladies in B&B's in British seaside towns where you were told when to come and go, what time you would have breakfast and were generally made to feel as unwelcome as possible. Tellingly this couple had a sign up saying no refunds on account of the bugs. I had to keep my helmet on and visor down while I set up the tent. The Winnipeg Free Press that I read in the morning headlined page 3 with "Majority of southern Manitoba mosquitoes now test positive for West Nile Fever". Great, that was about the only thing I didn't get a jab for, with me not planning on going to Egypt an'all.

I was eager to source a rear tyre and Winnipeg was my last realistic possibility. Canvas just doesn't seem to have the same wear or grip characteristics as rubber, so anything that would go on and was round and black, would have to do. The now common request was met with the now common reply of "What's that for, eh? Aprilia? Never heard of it." But in the Harley dealer in Winnipeg the guy got on the phone and rang every shop in the city till he found one the right size for me. It was a BMW and Yamaha dealer. Delighted with my good fortune I thought

I would name drop Yamaha names from head office and get a reduction in price. Nepotism or sponsorship, who cares what the label is, nothing ventured....

I took my wheel off outside on the footpath and while they were fitting the tyre I bought an oil filter and did my best networking, to see if I could ease the financial blow. Nothing doing as they say. $335.00 dollars for a tyre on a loose wheel, and an oil filter "to go". Nearly 170 quid!! Never in my life, etc etc... And it didn't really suit the bike as it turned out, but to wear it in, to deal with my seething anger and because there weren't any corners due for the next week or so, I decided to make my own and find out what parts of the undercarriage touched the road first. And who says the roads in the prairies are dull? Use the centre line as a big slalom course, it's not as though there's anyone coming the other way! Of course I can't possibly condone such irresponsible behaviour unless you are in a safe, controlled environment, like a million square miles of flat prairie.

What all the central provinces have in common other than straight roads, is that nearly every wee town has a municipal campground with great facilities, a tended green lawn and a ten dollar honesty box. Just look for a cluster of trees, usually visible from about 20kms.

Reston in southern Manitoba is a perfect example. A tiny, seemingly desolate village, with a Chinese restaurant that has been open for forty years and not decorated since, hosted me for dinner. The restaurant was a communal multi purpose space, diners interspersed with children having school lessons in Mandarin. As soon as lessons had finished, the old men in the corner moved their coffee cups so that the kids could lay out the draught boards and begin the intergenerational gaming challenge. It was one of those evenings when, with my hands and crockery sticking to the plastic tablecloth, I was able to relax and enjoy the dynamics in the room and ponder why is it that we destroy the innocence of children? They don't question age, or race, or culture. Society teaches them to do that to the detriment of us all. Why is it that we have to learn how to hate and when we refuse to, are labelled as simple or naïve? Surely it isn't all about power structures, but anyway that's tonight's philosophy homework.

I was led to the great little campground by a guy in his seventies on a bicycle, after he had finished his game of draughts with the five year old. After putting my money in the honesty box, the only camper in town on a beautiful lawn, I enjoyed a fantastic shower and watched the sun go down.

As I approached the dot on the map that is Val Marie, hoping it might offer some shelter from the encroaching storm that the "land of the living skies" had given me hours to prepare for and panic about, I had stopped feeling guilty about the carnage under tyre. I was literally killing thousands of grasshoppers who were hopping ahead of the storm. They were thick on the road, and those that I didn't directly squash, were stupid enough to jump at the wrong time and get hit by my legs and boots and other bits of the bike. I stopped once with an overheating problem, only to discover that the radiator guard was full of them.

The guilt of my grasshopper carnage only subsided when I went exploring some abandoned farm houses and with every step sent a cloud of them into the air. I could see there were enough to go round. I saw a lot of deer and antelope today too, along with ground squirrels and other unidentified foreign critters. Always the naturalist!

I took a room in the hotel in Val Marie. The only hotel, and I was glad. The storm that I watched develop unleashed itself with spectacular fury, blowing dust and debris up the desolate street (there's just the one street) and the sign at the hotel (there's just the one sign) really did swing, and squeak. My bike and three pickups were parked outside on the dirt road and there was a notice in the bar that said "We don't call 911" with a picture of a gun. The room cost less than camp grounds in Ontario and I was just told to go upstairs from the bar and find one that looked like it was available. I wasn't issued with a key because there weren't any, but that isn't because they were lost, more just that there weren't really any locks. In fact the front door to the whole premises didn't have a handle either, just a whole in the door and some distant memories. However, the way that the lightning searched for something to track to, I'm just a little bit glad that I wasn't in the tent. The landlady, who I don't think received her hospitality training at The Ritz, said she'd be around at about eleven thirty in the morning if I wanted anything.

That night I ate steak so I could fit right in, but felt naked without a baseball cap and thought it best to leave my hat packed away.

The prairie provinces also have oil or gas. Derricks abound in eastern Saskatchewan and the oilsands of Alberta are driving the whole regional economy, as well as creating an environmental disaster. They've also embraced wind power in the prairies and the side benefit is the large number of tourists who come to stand and look at the turbines! You see, there really isn't that much to do in these parts and anything is seen as respite from the seas of gently waving, mesmerizing wheat. There's an idea to sell to the nimbys in Britain who say wind turbines make a bit of a whirring sound or kill the odd bird. Unlike cars.

But after I'd been through the village of Climax ("come again" as the sign says), I got chatting to a Kiwi called Glen who ran an organic flour mill. He said the best earner he had was the gas wells on his property. The State owns what is beneath the soil, but he gets $1800 dollars a well/ year as "disturbance" money. Once drilled, there really is no disturbance, but on his 3000 acres he has 72 wells. What a handy little earner. We stood and talked as literally miles of railway carriages rumbled slowly passed, hauled by four linked engines. Just as it takes the engines hours to get the train up to not very much speed, it must take a lot of forward planning to stop a rig like that. Have I mentioned the scale of things out here?

After leaving Val Marie and discovering that I could have stayed in the Convent down the road (honestly, there is an open convent on the other edge of the one street town) I encountered the next evening's storm and what an experience. The wind never got to twister status, but I ended up hiding behind a concrete barn base anyway. I simply couldn't keep the bike upright and it was hard to see through the dust storm that ran ahead of the rain. I'm not proud of it, but I also killed my first gopher. That's indecision for you, he should never have changed his mind. He who hesitates is lost and all that. Mind you, he was due to die anyway. The posters up in the area said that strychnine stocks had arrived and were available from the local magistrate to begin poisoning the gopher population.

All of which brought me through Alberta, 'the richest province' though the number plates don't say that. With all the oil, the wheat and the lumber up north, Alberta currently offers zero percent sales tax, no capital gains tax, the country's lowest fuel tax, lowest property tax, highest income tax exemptions and lowest single rate. And everyone still keeps coming here! Hard to fathom why! I was still making my way across the south reaches, but headed up to see the town of Medicine Hat. Well you would, wouldn't you? Sunniest place in Canada, home of the world's largest tepee at over 200ft high and possibly oddest town name, after England's Nempnet Thrubwell of course. There are various legends as to where the name comes from, but the one inscribed on City Hall is as plausible as any. The Blackfoot tribe who lived in these parts, were suffering with a bit of a bad winter, possible starvation and extinction so sent out a young adventurer to find a food source and save all the people, so no real pressure then. He took his new wife and dog and set off down the frozen river until he came to a sacred hole in the ice, where the spirits from the river come to breathe. A spirit popped up and said he'd swap a hat of knowledge and hunting prowess for the young man's wife. The man took him at his word, chucked his wife in the freezing water, which leads me to think it may have been an arranged marriage, and waited till the next day when he would find his special hat. Even if you are suffering from hypothermia and hallucinations due to hunger, these visions from the water always seem to come through, and so it was that he found his 'medicine hat' and then a herd of buffalo. Luck or magic? Well the sacred breathing hole still exists during winter, now in the middle of town, but I believe there has to be a great communal imperative before you chuck your wife in. It doesn't work if you are hoping for a new car.

Then, after a 3000km prairie headwind, there, rising directly out of the plains, were the Rockies.

I had chosen my route via the town of Mountain View- well I had a hunch- and the jagged dark blue outline of the range was just an incredible thing to behold, stretching as far north and south as you could see. I rode towards them, mesmerised and it was only after about 20 minutes staring, that I realised most of the clouds above them were in fact the row of taller snow covered peaks behind, not clouds at all.

I stopped at a call box at a filling station in the foothills, to ring mum and say I had reached "Beautiful British Columbia". A bloke loitered for a bit near me and I thought whether you need the phone or not, I'm making this call. When I finished and went to the bike he came over and said

"Are ye rightly? Jayz you've a quare locka miles behind ye hi, if yiv rid all the way on that bike" in a strong Northern Irish accent. Ah sure we blethered away there for ages till his wife hauled him away....

Just a couple of hours later and not even a day from the 38ºC of the plains, I was climbing my first pass. Just 1774m or 5,800 something feet, surrounded by towering mountains and with the rain coming down in sheets, I was aquaplaning my way up at a steady 100kph when the cars coming down the hill started flashing their lights. Peering through the spray, I saw the police car attending a car that had stuck itself in the side of the mountain, at precisely the time I also realised that the rain was now hale and there was close to, if not more than 2 inches of it on the road. Given the gradient, I think I hit it about as fast as I could have. Any speedway fan would have been proud of me as I lurched into a huge slide, the policeman certainly ran behind his car, but like a hero I kept the throttle open, got it all back in line, and rode the next 2kms over the summit and passed another crashed car.

It's the 10th of August and I couldn't be further south in Canada! Am I far too late already? Have I missed my window of opportunity to get north to Alaska? It has already started snowing north of Fairbanks and the bears are hungry. The weird weather has meant a food shortage for the bears and they have now come in to Vancouver. A woman was mauled in her garden in a suburb yesterday!

Where will your intrepid traveller go next? Watch this space for the next exciting episode of "Aprilia? Never heard of it eh. But I like the hat!"

12 A DESERT? DON'T BE DAFT!

Before I continue, just an aside for any couriers reading this. I passed a truck the other day that had emblazoned on its side, the following words- "If this delivery is on time, it must be a Fluke"

John R. Fluke and sons, as it happens, but just another example of two nations divided by a common language. Or what about this billboard at the side of the road- "Randy Kamp MP serving your every need". No punctuation, but with a picture of politician Randy, or should that be Randy politician.

Now let's look at time zones, they were introduced by a Canadian after all, Sanford Fleming and if you had a name like that you too might find yourself sitting around on your own pondering things. I know they make a lot of sense, and for the West bound motorcyclist they provide an extra hours riding every few days, but they are so arbitrary! Man decides, but the geographical line in the sand is so... false. Ok, the concept I get, unlike a certain North American who couldn't understand why the Brits got up in the middle of the night... but I know it gets dark at a certain time in the summer at a certain latitude and I can almost navigate by that. Then, within a mile, all my reckoning is out the window. Now it's not quite as arbitrary when a political boundary is used as the demarcation, after all that's every bit as random, but have any of you seen a map of North and South Dakota? There the time zone goes around villages and crosses the street, cuts diagonally through fields and neighbourhoods, in the same state.

"Should I nip round to Bob next door and borrow some sugar?"

"Good heavens No! You know they'll already be in their beds!"

Canada, luckily, has time zone demarcation that (almost) follows longitudinal Provincial boundaries, except Ontario, which is too big. This makes their crossing geographically logical. But the funny thing is, Canada has four or five time zones. OK, four and a half. Does that make sense? No.

You see Federalism is a wonderful thing. You agree certain laws and standards nationally, and then leave some interpretation of local situations up to the provincial parliaments. After all, the Yukon really couldn't give a monkeys about the transportation of potatoes and PEI doesn't have a huge problem with polar bears. So you nationally agree the time zone lines in your massive country. Then Saskatchewan says, "yeah ok, but we're not having that stupid daylight saving thing in the summer". So half the year the time in Saskatchewan is the same as Manitoba and the other half it's the same as Alberta.

The tourist finds this out when stopping for water, tea and a sticky bun in Assinaboia. Escaping from the 38 degree heat into an air-conned restaurant, in the town whose name in the local Indian language means "where the food cooks on the stones", I thought that the heat was playing games with me.

"Excuse me" I say to the waitress, though everyone stops to listen because it's that kind of place, "Is that the right time, or is your clock slow?" All the customers give me that "Dummy" look, and the waitress tries not to patronise the biker with learning difficulties. "Yes, it's 3 o'clock, like the clock says, with the big hand on...."

Well there aren't any signs up to tell you, and there bloody well should be, this isn't Ontario.

Where there is a great time zone sign, is Australia where you cross from Northern Territories to Queensland at a place called Cammoweal. It says "Welcome to Queensland. Please put your watches on ten years".

What continued to gladden my heart in Saskatchewan though, regardless of not knowing the time, or feeling like I was in an oven, (fan assisted if I opened my visor) were the little signs that said "Point of Interest, 1km". I'd get all excited. Something to look at in this desolate landscape. More often than not it was a plaque that told how there used to be a village, or maybe just a shop, on this very spot. But there wasn't now, either because when the railway came they moved the village 10 miles south to be near it, or because everyone just left. Isn't that great? I love that the government puts up signs to tell you benign stuff like that and gives you count down to the spot. It's a 'Point of Interest' something once happened here, "be ready for the next one, you might get to it by tomorrow, depending on whether or not you miss closing time at the petrol station because you've got the time wrong!"

Anyway, I'm in British Columbia now, 8 hours behind you Europeans and as beautiful as it is, I can safely say it has the worst drivers in all Canada. I have now witnessed, or come on the aftermath of, an accident every day. From just driving straight off the road to spinning on the motorway when failing to control a fishtail because your hands are full of coffee and telephone (I was behind her as it happened).

Maybe it's all the drugs, BC and specifically Nelson, have the reputation for a lot of high quality drugs. Indeed everyone I met in Nelson either ingested or produced. The town is in a beautiful setting between mountains and lake, was never "developed" in the 60's and 70's so is architecturally beautiful and has been discovered only recently by the beautiful people. It's isolation, both geographical and economic, created the drug trade and helped attract the artists and those with liberal attitudes who went to live there, including some Vietnam draft dodgers, like the ones I stayed with. The youth of today prefer alcohol, it being unseemly to do the same drugs as your parents and there was a five day music festival drawing to a close 40 miles down the road at Salmo while I was there, where alcohol was banned. It always has been. Other drugs aren't, because they don't cause fights apparently, but there is a strict no alcohol policy. So strict in fact, that the organisers last year raised $4,000 from the return deposit on empty cans and bottles they found during the clean up. Kids eh?

But here's a thing. How many of you knew that there was a desert in the middle of the Rockies?

I got the shock of my life. It started with a bit of yellow grass here and there, and the low valleys seemed worse. I knew they'd had low rain this year (it all fell on me in the east), but this seemed extreme, until I went down the corkscrew road into Osoyoos and the whole valley was a desert, except where they irrigate like mad from Canada's warmest lake and grow wine and other fruit. The area has the lowest annual rainfall and highest temperatures in the country, and is the most northerly reaches of the USA's Sonora Desert. Not surprisingly they take the utilisation of their water supply very seriously in these parts and advertise the country's longest golfing season! It really is a hot, arid desert, snow capped peaks either side, and on the wet west coast of the continent. On the plus side it did mean a very pleasant night camping safe in the knowledge that the bears find it too warm here. And I found out that the rich Albertans say that BC stands for Bring Cash. Never miss a bit of regional bigotry, that's what I say.

I thought I'd take this opportunity to discuss the religion and prejudice (separately) that I have so far encountered, but I still plan to cross Iowa and Kansas so that should give me some time....

Instead I'll just say that I am writing about non specifics because I am holed up in Vancouver, overlooking the Pacific, undergoing some tests and medical exploration into a left foot which has sort of stopped working. As I approached Vancouver I found it increasingly difficult to change gear and by the time I arrived here I couldn't walk.

It may mean a route change because of the weather up north and time ticking away, but in the meantime, John and Penny, who I met in a restaurant four provinces earlier are putting me up in their apartment. They are being particularly accommodating given that I arrived on them at very short notice and have become incredibly immobile since getting here, but their cat is quite simply an incarnation of Satan. It is possibly the most vicious feline psychopath I've ever met. Some days it won't let me use the corridor to my room and once it wouldn't let me back into the flat at all. I tell you, the thing is a killer and can lash out in the blink of an eye, severing major arteries. The growling and body language is often enough though, it being a master of psychology and clearly able to sense the weaker disabled foe. When the guys are at work I am imprisoned…

John is one of those 'fix anything' people and together we have fashioned a hand shift system so that I can get back on the road. I'm going to try it out tomorrow, just as soon as I have worked out how to get on and off the bike...

Should be grand! The very good news is that the local medical staff have taken pity on me and are charging me little or nothing. Awesome! Eh?

13 SHAME ON YOU

Vancouver is undeniably in a beautiful geographical setting. The ocean to the west, mountains to the north and east and pretty much to the south too, the city is bisected by the mighty Frazer River. Only two current river crossings mean there are the usual traffic bottle necks, but there is a third bridge under construction about 15 miles upstream. I never knew they made suspension bridges by hanging a wee section at a time off the main uprights, slowly stretching out across the water. A great thing to see, but having said that, I can't now think how I ever thought it was done before. Perhaps I never did think about it. Have you? Better even than watching a bridge grow, was watching the sun set. Downtown skyscrapers silhouetted against a multicoloured sky and everything enveloped in this strange soft all pervading light. I know that being all pervading is a defining factor of light, just not usually in this way.

Architecturally Vancouver looks like all of the other cities really. There's a high rise financial downtown and a 3 or 4 storey surrounding city. The rich live around the edges in the mountains and the middle class live in the West.

What I have never seen anywhere in my life before though, is the four or five blocks to the east of the financial centre. With the junction of Hastings and Main at its heart, this area is where the city has consciously concentrated its mentally ill, it's destitute and it's hard drug users. This is not some "Oh it's a bit rough and seedy down there" comment. Today I saw a girl on the footpath holding her obviously cadaverous friend, rigid limbs, blue lips and staring eyes. She was so out of it I'm not sure she realised she was holding a corpse. The footpath was awash with crack smokers, drunks, collapsed smack heads still with needles hanging from arms and legs. Individuals of indeterminate sex or ethnicity so disfigured through violent assault some looked like discarded piles of rags. It was hard to comprehend. I don't mean the odd doorway here and there on the block. I mean thick with people, like central London at 2pm on a Tuesday afternoon. Destitution in central Manila doesn't look like that.

The bag ladies and shopping trolley men mixed with the severely schizophrenic and the sufferers of every 'ism' and diagnostic label imaginable. There was a policy of selling off asylums in the nineties (great real estate) but no "care in the community package" to soften the blow of expulsion from institutional life. It's hard to make informed choices and be a good effective consumer of outsourced private services when the organ that makes those choices is the one that is not functioning terribly well. I was so stunned I didn't take any pictures. The voyeurism didn't seem right.

The policeman I stopped to chat to said the containment in one area was the best thing because it meant that the rest of the city didn't have to be inconvenienced. While we chatted three old men came past, one of them bleeding profusely from a wound below the eye.

The copper called out "Hey, Richard, you didn't look like that five minutes ago, what happened?"

Richard explained that four lads gave him a bit of a beating at the other end of the street, for fun he thought, but wasn't sure.

"Well you watch out, eh?"

He turned to me and said it was great that they knew many of the people on first name terms. "Great" I said, "but what will you do about the assault on Richard?"

"Oh nothing, the lads were probably just looking for a few bucks or maybe having a laugh." I thought that sort of behaviour amounted to aggravated theft, or GBH or something. Clearly it doesn't, but as long as the nice people in the city are OK, sod the poor and the destitute.

The police cars here all have huge bull bars on the front. Maybe it helps them clear intransigent beggars. That might have been where the perpetrators of last year's drive off fuel thefts got the idea to drive over the attendant and drag him for five blocks until very dead. The outcome of that horror, for about 20 dollar's worth of fuel I believe, is that all petrol pumps in BC are pay first. This may work well if you are using a credit card, or know how much you want to put in your tank. It's incredibly infuriating for a biker who needs to fill up and pays cash.

There's a series of events that go something like this: the cashier is approached and cannot comprehend that I don't wish to use a credit card at the pumps. I'm then told to pay up front for what I want. I don't know what I want, so in the end it is agreed that I pay over the odds and then come back in for change. I am not given a receipt; the pump issues the receipt for fuel taken at the end. There are multiple staff working. When I come back in I begin the process of tracking down the staff member who has gone for a break to prove that I paid $20 for the $17.62 of fuel that I took. Infuriating? Just a little.

But the good news is that I am back on the road. There is a mark one version of a handshift system in operation on occasion, (made by cutting off the side of a deck chair and attaching it to the gear lever, then attaching the clutch cable to the end of that) but generally my foot feels like my own again. Hurray! No more do I walk down the street dragging one foot like a palsy victim. I even found that my left hand did that funny wide swing out thing, at the same time. As infuriating as it was, it did mean that the beggars didn't hassle me. They just all withdrew their hands and empty coffee cups and gave me a look of compassion as I hobbled past!

I spent a week with John and Penny in the end, which was very good of them considering we met for 20 minutes in a diner in Nova Scotia, though I couldn't really relax and always felt I was intruding given the way I just arrived out of the blue and colonized their spare room. That's the ever-changing psychology of the traveller for you. Accepting hospitality is great, and always so very welcome, but knowing that the independence of movement exists is invaluable. To have that removed and become wholly reliant on others, really alters the state of mind and in my case always seems to manifest itself in some weird guilt and feeling that I am a burden. This strange subordinating deference probably leads to me actually becoming the very burden I wish never to be, and so the spiral begins.

The local Vancouver medical staff though, were excellent and the whole experience was a million miles away from my Toronto clinic experience. Doctor Lau S Kam couldn't have been more accommodating. The $50 fee was only paid the first time, which even then was odd because he should never have taken me in off the street as a non national. The next consultation was free, as were the remainder of visits. The whole practice took pity on my transitory state, so they negotiated reduced rate x-rays for me and immediately arranged for a clinic to do a range of blood tests for … $15. Awesome, eh?

I realise that means that ordinary Canadians have subsidised my treatment with their taxes and I would therefore like to take this opportunity to thank any of you reading this.

And so I rode out of Vancouver, independent again with my hand gear change mechanism ready for deployment when my recovering foot relapsed and headed north towards Whistler, where the 2010 winter Olympics are going to be held. The "from sea to sky" highway is exactly that. Seeing the mountains rise straight from the ocean helps illustrate the point.

The vistas were stunning, but the bulk of the road is being dualled in readiness for the 2010 games, so the progress was slow. The other thing Vancouver is considering in time for the games is Institutional Asylums, but maybe just for a trial period to see if it works.... I know I'm not cynical, but you'd think they wanted to hide something in Vancouver, for a little while.

From Whistler on, my progress was even slower. The views were truly amazing and I just had to keep stopping and taking photos. After a while I realised that the more I took, the better the views became, and I just had to decide that they were all lodged in my analogue memory and the digital camera memory would have to remain empty. The greenest of glacial lakes, pine and old growth hardwoods, stunning waterfalls, long and short drop, wide and narrow. Valleys and gullies, gorges and peaks. Glacial snouts and all set against a stunning blue sky. The road twisted and turned, rising and falling, sometimes dramatically, and when it rose for me and I met vehicles coming thundering down the other way, especially those pickups that have a 5th wheel so that they can tow huge RV trailers, there was always that familiar "have you left the handbrake on honey?" aroma, and a look of panic in the driver's eyes.

The wonderful Duffy Lake is full of translucent turquoise glacial waters, but one end of it has been dammed by natural timber wastage, where the lake narrows and eventually forms the outflow river. The timber has piled upon itself and seems to almost reach down into the depths of the water, making a secure walkway across the water. It may be the summer, but it's glacial water and as I watched some lads jump in off the logs to impress some young ladies with their manliness, I couldn't help thinking that just at that moment, their manliness wouldn't have looked terribly impressive at all.

Oh, and hear this! I was talking to Pastor Paul (on a BMW R100 GS) and pastors don't lie. He said that the town of Whistler had names for all their regular bears, so I feel exonerated. It wasn't a stupid question to ask back in Ontario! Pastor Paul reminded me of one of the things I did to pass the time when I wasn't walking much in Vancouver. I watched Pastor Rick (famous celebrity American vicar whose book has now sold 25m copies) interview Obama and McCain in front of a live audience in his church. They were questioned separately, but with the same questions. What was striking, was that Obama seemed well read, politically astute, had an understanding of the world and not just America's place in it, but also the real perception that the world has of America. His answers were reasoned and very well delivered especially when it was obvious that they weren't going to be huge crowd pleasers. McCain appeared to be the exact opposite. Nothing was answered directly, unless some populist flippancy would suffice. Every answer included an anecdote. There was no political substance to anything he said. It was then that I realised he might be the next President. Even the pundits afterwards said "Obama needs to tell a few stories, that's what America likes". I know the audience were good church going types, the ones (given their reaction to some of the evening events) that believe evil wears a turban, and everything is black and white, but they are the ones most likely to vote. Reason and rational argument appears to have no place in American politics.

Harrumph! There. Now I'll move on.

By the time I descended into Lillooet, the terrain had become mountainous desert again, being the northern reaches of the desert at Osoyoos. The descent was done in stages and each was accompanied by a marked increase in temperature. It's easy to forget, when surrounded by towering mountains, that you are still above 1500m and need at some point to dive. The day before, I was told Lillooet had seen the temperature rise to 41ºC, so needless to say I was relieved that it had fallen to a paltry 40!

I scoured the map for other towns with a surplus of vowels which seemed to indicate desert and therefore bear-free camping and thought I'd aim for Kamloops in the morning.

Because I camped on the hard parched earth and needed to find a rock to get the tent pegs into the dusty ground, it shouldn't surprise you that I was woken in the night to the sound of rain. It only continued until about 7am to ensure sleep was fitful and that the clothes I had left out to dry after washing, hadn't. The early start was good though, ensuring I was marvelling at the aftermath of the huge 2003 forest fire on the way into Kamloops through the clear morning light.

However fire isn't the only great danger that the forests face. The mountain pine beetle has been munching through lodgepole pine trees in BC at a tremendous rate, or rather its larvae have and is only reducing its spread recently because there isn't much left to destroy. Since the infestation began, 14.5 million hectares have been affected, nearly six times the size of Wales! The further north I went the greener and cooler it all became. Again I tried to limit the photo stops, indeed any stops, because I knew really bad weather was due in from the Pacific and I was desperate to get to see Mt Robson, (Canada's tallest Rocky) and the beautiful Jasper National Park.

One of my precious stops, timed to coincide with finding a phone and it being a sensible time to call the UK, was all going to meticulous logistical plan. Point on the map located, fuel level assessed, ETA decided, thirst and bladder ignored. Roadhouse approached, call box spied, vehicle parked by box. Remove lid jacket gloves and earplugs to dissipate heat (well maybe not earplugs), check time in UK, find calling card in tank bag, gulp down water, turn to call box, and find someone has nicked the phone. In Canada?

Mount Robson is one of those things that gets you. BOOM. I'd seen it on the map, knew I was getting close, but until you go round the corner there's no sign of it. Then bang, in your face this huge wall of rock just blocks everything in front of you. The evening sun lit up the whole thing, save for the top 4-500metres that were in its own cloud. A near perfect triangle, only the pointy bit was missing. It had that really stupid effect of making me go Ohmygod, gotta stop NOW to get a photo. Right here in the middle of the road. No time to lose in case the moment escapes me, or the mountain scampers into the undergrowth like the wildlife....Twit.

I did the 103kms from there to Jasper town just letting silly exclamations out with every view or new wild creature, and was terrifically glad not to be like Ewan and Charlie and miked up for all to hear. The terrific day ended with a slap up meal and a beer courtesy of Mike (Canadian) and Dan (British-Zambian) who had rolled into town in the final legs of their trip. They'd ridden the famous actor's route starting in London and going east through Russia, before flying in to Anchorage and were just blasting across to Halifax to complete their three months. Like Ewan and Charlie they had been met by their parents who were now travelling part of the way with them in the support truck, and they too were thoroughly likeable fellows!

With all accommodation in Jasper incredibly expensive and booked up (inc camping) I found a youth hostel with the biggest mixed dorm I'd ever seen, (my bed was number 50) and lay in bed watching the most amazing lightning show. It was almost continuous for an hour, nearly good enough to read by, before any thunder arrived and it rolled and cracked with a voracity I only ever encountered before in Italy. Then all hell let loose and just a teensy weensy part of me thought "I'm ever so glad I didn't camp."

All the power was lost in the storm, including all the water pumps.... "Would sir like a bucket?" so I set off to ride what is often billed one of the most scenic roads in the world, the Icefields Parkway. It mattered little that I rode it in the rain, what I could see of the Rocky Mountains majesty still stunned. This world famous incredible north-south thoroughfare was built during the depression to provide some work for the regional unemployed, but I reckon there would've still been a few Irish navvies who got in on the job. As low as the clouds were, it was still awesome, and much of it was above the snow line so why complain? At the Columbia Icefields, where you can get a balloon tyred icebus to take you out across the glaciers, the clouds lifted, the sun came out and I just wore a silly grin.

I rode and rode, tar or dirt it didn't matter. Watching long horn Rocky mountain sheep, deer and bears. I stopped, actually stopped to let a fully grown black bear cross the road! Then it was Buffalo. Big woolly buffalo, prehistoric monsters, grazing on the plains all around the road as I approached the fantastically named 'Head Smashed In Buffalo Jump'. I don't suppose you can imagine for a moment what used to go on there.

And so I gingerly rode to the sign that said

"Stawp right there Kid. Get auwf your motorsickle and approach the booth with your passport. NOW Kid!"

Or words to that effect.

Welcome to the YOU ESS of AAY

14 LOW SKY COUNTRY

Border security agency officer Manszweski was going to deal with my application for entry, but first I had to wait in line while he dealt with a Swiss family, giving me time to observe.

Officer Manszweski was about 5'11" and 280 pounds (which just means fat) and I was very much in HIS office now. The older Swiss lady closed the inner door to curtail the cool mountain breeze that was flooding the office and unleashed a furious "You cannot close my door ma'am. That is my door and I say when that door is closed and when it is opened. Open that door now please ma'am." She was a little taken aback, not having too much English, though she certainly understood the tone of delivery! Any question the family had, arising from the filling in of the entry forms was answered by the officer as before, just more loudly, so at least it was obvious that no matter how many centuries or revolutions pass, the founding cultural principles of the British Empire remain: Just shout at the bloody foreigners if they don't get it the first time!

And what a form it is. If any of you have been to the states recently you'll know, but as I fretted beneath the huge poster of a smiling Bush and a sneering Cheney, alongside one picturing the twin towers with "we shall NEVER forget" emblazoned beneath, I really started to wonder about my criminal past. Had I undertaken any crimes of moral turpitude? I wasn't entirely sure, but figured the subjective nature of the question wasn't something I should discuss with officer Manszweski.

"Was I now, or had I ever been a spy, or involved with international espionage?" I'd be a good one if I said yes... Of course the old version of that question was famously "was I a member of the communist party", but no doubt that doesn't matter anymore, unless it is immoral to imagine a health care system free for all, in which case we no doubt come round to moral turpitude again....

You see, it's not an easy form to fill. Then there's "Are you currently involved in terrorism or genocide?" and "is the sole purpose of your visit the overthrow of the United States Government?" Helpfully it reminds me that if I tick yes to any of the above I may be refused entry. As for firearms, why bring any with you when they are available in every corner store? Allegedly. I mustn't let my prejudices run away with me, there'll be time a plenty to see if that one is true.

I got away without fingerprinting, but was told to fill in the form bent over beside a small camera, so maybe my iris has been scanned. In total it only took 50 minutes to gain access to the States and this is the part when I should write, and you should sing;

"Hey 'Chelle, you know it's kinda funny
Texas always seemed so big
But you know you're in the largest
State in the Union,
When you're anchored down in Anchorage,
Alaska"

But alas, I was in Montana, Big sky country! I've no idea how big the skies were, because they were just above my head and contained millions of gallons of water, but the roads were twisty and what I could see was lovely.

Certain things had changed though with the immediacy of that say, “Please don't litter. Think of others and the environment”. Here, that becomes, and I quote “Litter and it’s going to hurt!” Strange thing is, for the first time, I began to see litter at the side of the road. I'm also informed that I need only wear a helmet if I am a passenger under the age of 18. In this weather?

I headed for Glacier National Park and stopped for a cuppa before entering, but oh how a line on a map can change everything. “Tea? Iced tea? lemon or lime?”

“No, just hot black tea”

“There’s pre sweetened black iced tea in the vendor with the sodas”.

And so I had my first hot chocolate in the States and sat in the cafe marvelling at how fabrics suddenly appeared incapable of covering girth. I headed into the Park and took the world famous “Going to the Sun road” which winds between some of the Park’s 50 glaciers. I was up in the clouds after nearly a mile and imagined all the amazing sights, not least the sun I was meant to be going to. Occasionally there would be huge dark shapes through the gloom and I knew there were vistas galore, all hidden from view yet tantalisingly close due to the guard rail free tiny twisting road I was on. There were a few moments of better visual clarity, when the cloud thinned and it just poured with rain instead, but I knew it was beautiful and was the start of five straight days of fantastic twisty, challenging road.

I took a motel on my first night in the states, in Kalispell. I had ridden through “Hungry Horse”(Starving Donkey?) where Ewan and Charlie took a room for the night, and enquired at the only motel, but at $105 plus taxes, I thought not. Montana's streets seemed to be lined with churches and temperance societies, intermingled with Casinos and bars. There seemed little else other than fast food joints. What juxtaposition!

Since I was going to be in Mexico sometime, I grasped the opportunity to try the food somewhere I could speak the language reasonably well. After all, I'd tried just about enough North American cuisine, though when I passed through the town of Wonder, there was the Country Folks Kitchen that advertised it served "Juss plain gud food" or was it "juss gud plain food". I juss wondered and rode on by.

I perused the Mexican menu for a while, finding a terminological glossary at the back particularly useful.

"Eh, you wa sum ting to dring?

Yes, what beers have you got?

"You gaw eye dee?"

I.D.? God bless you, but I'm almost 40!

There was no humour in his eyes.

"You gaw eye dee?" he said again, more seriously this time. I show him my passport before he calls the manager and possibly the police and I ask about the heat of the special red sauce to diffuse the situation.

"De sauss es naw haw señor. Dis ees naw eh haw resstoron"

His words still echoed in my ears fifteen minutes later as I slid under the table gasping "wa'her, wa'her."

If the sun in Mexico doesn't get me, no doubt the food will. It appears 'hot' is a relative term.

In the meantime the weather was still extraordinary for the middle of summer. It was now measured in Fahrenheit, so I'm not sure, but 54ºF didn't feel hot. Here's how bonkers the weather has become. Spokane, not far away in Washington, had its last snow on 6th June (usually end of April), then had zero precipitation for 57 days (it's the wet west coast, near Seattle!) culminating in a highest ever 103ºF three days ago. According to the weather channel, it will be 45F in the morning as I set out to ride there.

Two things are now obvious to me. First, Greek

mythology should be taken much more seriously than it is, because it was said that anywhere that Pegasus touched his hoof on the ground a spring was born and water became plentiful. I should arrange a sponsorship deal with the US farmers union and ride to all the drought ridden places, as I seem to be something of a harbinger of torrential rain. Or secondly, there's incredible climatic weirdness afoot.

Now in a conversation with Bert, (the first Texan I met) back in Canada, he said that there is no funny weather, it's just that we have better news coverage now, telling us about it. I take issue with that, now that I am in the States, and not just because I know he is a twit. The Weather channel that I had really come to enjoy in Canada, is crap here! There are no news stories from around the world. There is only local stuff, interspersed with hurricane reports from Florida. Although 24inches of rain on the east coast of Florida in two days? Tell me that's normal Bert.

Somewhere in his deepest consciousness there must be an acknowledgement of climate change though, because he went on to tell me that he made as small a carbon footprint as he could when taking his boys camping. His pickup was as small as was possible for two boys and their bicycles, and it did nearly 10 miles to the gallon, which wasn't bad. Give him his due, that is an American gallon, so maybe 11 to an imperial gallon. With that understanding the planet has nothing to fear.

Bert and I talked about lots of stuff, like how he balanced his Christian principles with his working for the arms industry. Turns out there is no problem, "cos there's a lotta folks what don't know right from wrong and need to be taught". His main concern and the greatest threat to civilisation, was the use of profanities.

I rode across Idaho's panhandle and loved it. Fantastic roads, beautifully paved and surrounded by lovely mixed leaf forests, all in the pissing rain. Then into

Washington and it cleared up, leaving me riding through dry prairie where tractors and combine harvesters created miniature dust storms, before I entered the Cascades with the best possible weather to see Mount Rainier (and it wasn't!) and Mount St Helens that had erupted so violently in 1980, sending a vertical column of ash 24kms high whilst killing 36 people and leaving 21 unaccounted for. (I reckon they didn't all vanish for the insurance payout so it may be safe to say that they perished too). After 160 miles of constantly twisting roads in the Cascades, I stopped to see the smouldering mountain and the new bulge that is continuing to grow like a festering tumour, signalling the possibility of another explosive catastrophe in the not too distant future.

The whole Cascades area which runs throughout Washington and Oregon is dotted with the snow capped perfect cones of volcanic peaks that rise from the surrounding topography, sometimes dramatically so, being almost a mile taller than the neighbouring landscape. This meant I was faced with the drama of a row of perfect white jagged cones in front of me and simultaneously in the mirrors behind, delineating powerful tectonic activity.

The brilliant roads continued as I headed south, with no traffic to blight the experience and with my foot now generally working as it was originally designed. And there, in the Columbia River valley, that divides Washington from Oregon, I came across the wee town of Stevenson, which was full of bikes, and not a chromed cruiser in sight. I had happened upon a 'training rally', with road books, daily riding lessons in the mountains and guidance on all aspects of riding. At 150 dollars for the 4 days, the camping wasn't cheap, so I tried to blagg my way in, to no avail. AMA insurance rules sir- sorry! Instead, I was advised that if I went west a few hundred yards, there was another entrance that came really close to where all the tents were but which was actually public land....

I had a rare old time, met lots of folks, including some KTM Adventure riders that had managed 12,000 miles a year using their bikes for nothing more than visiting micro breweries! It's a huge growth industry that hasn't happened a minute to soon and is dramatically changing America's beverage palette. Luckily the KTMers had a few samples with them that they were eager for me to taste, but I still got away in the morning before the organisers and security came round, although not before a local chap asked if my license plate was Canadian. Maybe it's not that surprising, I'd been asked twice in the previous days if my accent was Canadian. Given the size of the continent and the likelihood of a foreign bike being here, perhaps that's not an unreasonable assumption. After all, I'm way too pink to be Mexican, so maybe I could be Canadian but Montana, Idaho and Washington BORDER Canada for heaven's sake!

A couple of old boys came out of a bar in Oregon and asked about the bike too.

"Where ya from?" Ireland. "You drove all the way?" Yes. "That's some bike that can cross the water!"

It wasn't his razor sharp wit that surprised me, but his geographical knowledge! The conversation came not that long after one that went something like this: "Where ya headed?" Argentina. "That in Washington?" No the country, down south. "What, you mean south beside Mexico?" Yeah, that's right, just beside Mexico.

The weather remained stunning as I encircled Mt Hood and headed through wonderful smelling pine forests to Crater Lake in southern Oregon, where the remnants of Mount Mazama which erupted 7,700 years ago, are filled with the bluest water imaginable. There are no rivers feeding the lake, which is the deepest in the US and reputedly the cleanest in the world. All the water is from rainfall and the amazing 45 feet of snow the area gets each year. Possibly one of the slowest journeys I've undertaken was the 33 mile ride around the rim, where I couldn't help but keep stopping to gawp at the beauty of the place, even though it never changed! The only blot on an otherwise idyllic Park, is that the Mountain Pine Beetle I mentioned earlier, is causing havoc, killing vast swathes of both Lodge Pole Pine and now, worryingly, Whitebark Pine as well. It seems that the dreaded global warming is allowing the beetles to move further up the mountains where they've found an even yummier species of tree to munch on, but one which is unfortunately key to the survival of lots of other species in the area.

And then it was northern Californ-i-aye, and the mighty Redwood trees. They are immense. I know you know that already. The tallest trees in the world and with the girth of an average American male. 15feet diameter is common, over 370ft high and anything up to 2000 years old, the battle for their preservation still goes on against the loggers. Less than three percent remain standing and still there is a desire to cut them down. But walking through the forest creates a calm that I'm not sure I've felt before, and approaching Peggy I realised she looked like a mini-moto parked on the aptly named Avenue of the Giants. The age and size of these trees is staggering, what they've lived through unfathomable. Some of them had already taken root when some upstart Judean revolutionary overturned the moneychanger's tables and got everyone pissed up at a 'dry' wedding.

Redwood NP is full of some informational gems though. In the middle of a forest full of the tallest trees in the world, there is a sign directing you to 'Big Tree' and another at the foot of the 'Immortal Tree' which explains how, in its youthful 950 years, it has survived floods, loggers attempts to fell it, and at least one lightning strike that knocked the top 45 feet off it. The sign then asks, to avoid damage, that you do not climb it.

While I was in tourist info trying to find out the whereabouts of the shorter but fatter Sequoias, I overheard half a phone call:

"No sir, they are working on certain bypasses, but they are not likely to turn all of the route into 4 lane freeway. I realise that it is difficult for your RV sir, but the County are not likely to cut the trees down just to widen the road. I'm sure you are right and that if there was a freeway it would increase tourism, but I don't know cutting down the trees would help."

I think the trees are safe in Humboldt County for the time being at least. The county has a reputation for being somewhat liberal. It is a county where the smoking and growing of marijuana is legal and the only county in the US where George dubbya Bush's Patriot Act is illegal. Isn't that cool? If the FBI comes into the county to tap someone's phone, the local sheriff can arrest them! The whole place may be a little too "knit your own yoghurt" for my liking, but it was certainly good to discuss Iraq without being called a terrorist. Brendan Patrick Ryan was my host for an evening in Eureka, and you'd never believe he was of Irish descent. Studying social sciences at Humboldt State Uni, he was able to pass on loads of local info.

The Californian coast is a Tsunami watch area, because of the earthquakes, with little signs showing you the evacuation routes, just like the volcano evacuation routes in Washington State. Sweet.

"There appears to be a big wave coming ashore, threatening to destroy everything in its path, now which way did that evacuation sign say we needed to go? No it must be next left, this one says no entry."

Heading south towards San Francisco it's unparalleled as a motorcyclist to see a sign that says "Danger, narrow winding road for 48 miles". Especially when there are also reminder signs for other vehicles that it is illegal to not pull over and let faster vehicles pass, it is almost impossible to contain the grin. "Bring it on!"

Past your famous Californian vineyards and through forests, along valleys and over small passes, I only used the crown of the tyres to change direction. The non-riders amongst you are saying "what?" at this point, and the rest are going "lucky bugger". Yip! I am. I don't know if it can get better than this.

I hope to come back north and sample some of the famous Californian wines, there are vineyards everywhere, but I read that grapes are California's second biggest cash crop. Number one cash crop, according to Californian Judge James P Gray, is that old favourite, marijuana so there must be counties that waste an awful lot of money losing the "War on Drugs" because Humboldt is really very small and the hippies certainly wouldn't clear fell the Redwoods to enable cultivation.

With the sun going down I made it to the Golden Gate Bridge and managed to get a photo as only half of it was lit golden by the setting sun. The rest of it is disappointingly dull primer red, but it was set beneath a horizontally striped sky, with purples, reds and blues, tiered no doubt, by the smog.

As I paid my toll and rode across to enter the city that has been so central to the development of recent popular culture, I felt terribly under-dressed. I hadn't seen a florist open all day and I wore nothing in my hair. I hoped no one would mind.

Pulling off the freeway and knowing I had to turn right at some point, the first street I turned up was a hill straight out of a movie set. Pure Steve McQueen, though I didn't meet any cars flying off each cross street, and I just couldn't bring myself to run a stop sign and get some "big air" of my own. Heaven knows how ungainly the landing would have been with all the luggage, given the problems I had back in Canada on a purpose built dirt bike.

What a groovy city to look at! All tram cars and hills and bendy roads and wooden houses, or art deco concrete ones, built at the strangest angles to fit the hillsides.

So why am I here? It's not terribly Alaskan to get all loved up in San Francisco. What about the promised lumberjack shirts and the grizzlies and mosquitoes the size of small birds? Well they all have to wait for a bit as this is to be Peggy's destination for a wee while. I am flying back to Blighty for some further tests and treatment on my foot as a few of the early exploratory results were a little alarming. Peggy is to stay with Siobhan's cousin Jane and family and as I write this, preparing for my flight, their puppy has just chewed through the power cable to my computer. And only 15 minutes ago he looked so incredibly cute staring out through those beautiful big brown eyes, like butter wouldn't melt…

15 SO I HAD A LITTLE SOJOURN

So I had a little sojourn. A little trip across the Atlantic for some R and R.

These things happen when you plan a trip abroad, just man and machine against the elements, seeking adventure where millions have probably tread before, though, one may be fairly confident to say, precious few may have taken a 650 Aprilia. Through swamp and forest, from downtown to desert, mixing with natives of every colour class and creed, in an ultimately futile search for somewhere called Puerto del Faglioli. Taking everything that life on the road can throw at you; bugs, beasties, personalities of every strain (many of questionable moral turpitude), the bureaucratic ineptitude of officialdom, even North American cuisine, the adventure must continue!

And regardless of the hideous heights of pompous verbosity that all these obstacles may have led me to.... I did get a bit of a sore foot after all.

So I flew home.

However- in my defence of the environmentally indefensible, a flight across the Atlantic is only the same price as seven nights in a mediocre (read sticky surfaces and dubious roofing material) motel. Combine that with getting myself around a strange city from one clinic to the next undergoing assorted tests and doing battle with a travel insurance firm which seemed to have no grasp of geography, and it all makes much more sense. Dammit, this dodgy foot is almost as debilitating as man flu!

My global "specialist" insurance is handled by a single company that acts for 300 other "specialist" insurers. It seems it was certainly worth my time shopping around! Their 24 hour helpline is staffed by Brazilians somewhere in Europe who operate to UK office hours. When it was finally established that there was a time difference roughly equivalent to their full working day, they saw sense and transferred my case to an office they have outside Europe, better suited to North America they thought. Of all the places they could have picked, New Zealand really didn't help.

So I found myself catching a cab to San Francisco International Airport for the flight home. Cabbies to my mind, regardless of their appalling dress sense and social perceptions, should have two specific qualities: the ability to drive and some geographical knowledge of their locale.

"Hi there!" said the chirpy cabbie whilst exhaling the previous drag on his cigarette and reversing blindly out into the main road.

"So, it's the airport eh. Should I go along Panorama and then turn east on to Market?"

Once I'd guided him out of the City that he lived in and in which I had spent 24 hours, we had a chat about all sorts of groovy San Franciscan things.

Originally from Canada, as a 16 year old he had run away from home in the late 1960's when he first went to see "The Grateful Dead" play. He just asked if they needed a roadie, and he never went home. On the road in a Kerouac way, he sought out drink drugs and free love, arriving in SF complete with flowers in his hair in 1970, just missing the summer of love. I hoped, as we took another wrong turning and savagely cut up other road users, that we wouldn't be arriving at the airport having just missed the flight as well. We made it in time, though primarily because Aer Lingus was a couple of hours behind schedule, meaning it would be interesting in Dublin when I attempted to make a connection to London that I had been given 20 minutes to achieve.

When the departure gate was announced and we, the 'self-loading cargo' (industry jargon), were assembling, it was comforting to note the prevalence of complexions that were either ghostly or lobsteresque. Ah, the Irish abroad. And with the complexions came that familiar Celtic cynicism. Note the father and son conversation that took place beside me:

"Now Daddy wud ya luke a' dat plane. It was made in Eye Orland"

"Naw, it wuzzn't."

"Bu' iss gaw a shamrock on it, so it muss be made in Eye Orland"

"Naw. Shure nuttins made in Eyeorlan. Iss problee made in France. Den Aer Lingus wud bouy it, secon han no dout, and give it a coata paint. Den dey floy people about de worl." "Feckin late."

Pass the cynicism on from generation to generation… Ahh shure what's the point of worrying, I may as well just take a wee drink… And so a national psyche is born.

The flight was just like flights normally are. A combination of fear, discomfort, apprehension and complaints about the food, which is no doubt just a coping mechanism, manifesting itself in grumbles about the overcooked, occasionally unrecognisable contents of a small tin box on a plastic tray, eaten by intertwining your arms with those of the passenger beside you and hoping you won't break a tooth on the "fresh last month" bread roll. All this, rather than marvel at the fact that you are in a metal tube at 35,000 ft, travelling at 590mph when you know they've been outsourcing the maintenance contract to the ‘best value’ bidder.

I spent my time playing the general knowledge quiz in my multi media centre and felt terribly smug as I helped my fellow prisoner Brooke Kimble (great name), with his questions, until he noticed that it all had a terribly ‘rest of the world’ feel to it, and how was an American meant to know the answers anyway? Ah, yes, US foreign education.

Brooke said that he had been to the British Isles three times before and was yet to experience the dull grey weather and low cloud that he had heard so much about. It must all be a lie he thought and as we came in to land in Dublin he looked out the window and said, “Oh, look. There are the peaks of some high mountains coming out above the cloud line.” “That’d be the weather you were looking for” says I, “there aren’t any high mountains”.

Dublin was fine apart from my falling out with a security woman who wouldn’t believe that I had been able to fly from the States with 3 pairs of extending curtain pole wall attachments (don’t ask why- she didn’t). She thought if I was late for my connecting flight (as she emptied all my possessions on the table and examined each one), I should have left home earlier. I considered my options. Explain the huge flaw in her own argument, given that we had just discussed my flight from the US and therefore I hadn’t just left home, point out that Aer Fungus was “feckin late” or punch her on the nose.

Given that “rational security” is an oxymoron, I quietly fumed, before looking like an entrant for the Paralympic 1500 metres as I hobbled with my luggage to the departure gate for the next timetabled flight to London.

So now I have been back in the UK for a month, feeling somewhat perforated and sure that I am entitled to a blood donors Gold certificate for the amount that I have contributed to science. Without Siobhan acting on my behalf and doing battle with officialdom I'd still be on the NHS 21week wait for the first exploratory testing. Like they say, get in quick, early diagnosis is all and saves money in the long run. After tests for the most incredible things with improbably long names, and enough x- rays to enable me to glow in the dark, the medical profession had decided (until yesterday) that it was acute reactive arthritis caused by a particular gastric bug, possibly from the e-coli family. (By the time I'd got back from the States it was in my wrists as well and I was wondering what thumb operated scooters were on the market).

Yesterday, when I was at the doctors getting some more blood results, the doctor rushed out and said "Ah, Mr Tyson, please come down to my room, I was just going to call you, you are a most interesting case!" I'm so glad I can still generate excitement among middle-aged women. It turns out my last bloods had flagged up yet another bug, this time beginning with S. (I'm clearly one of New Labour's 'expert informed' patients). On a scale of 0-200 my reading is, guess what, 200! And we all know that points mean prizes. Or in this case, further blood tests.

I knew I should never have entered a hospital in the first place. However I do like to be of service to the greater good, and if I am an interesting medical case that's just lovely.

The terminology that the medical profession has been using throughout this ordeal has occasionally left me speechless though. When the first load of tests in the UK came back normal, a different doctor in the Practise rang me up and said so, but then added: "Your cholesterol however, is very disappointing"

Disappointing? What, should try harder? Too high or too low? He never elaborated, just hung up the phone. All the funnier considering I had asked to get my cholesterol checked before the trip while I was getting lots of other things done and was assured, with one of those condescendingly dismissive laughs, that I was much too young for that and there was no need.

But my flight back to San Fransisco is booked for tomorrow, I can walk, feel fine and I can hear Peggy calling me from here. I've got to get back on the road, who would not want to be touring the USA in the middle of a recession, in the aftermath of big hurricanes and during an election campaign?

What a time to meet people!

16 RUNNING FROM THE SNOW

So! I'm in back country Wyoming. Not so much a place as an experience, with the emphasis being on 'back'. Now you might think that is a little harsh, but don't. I'm in Thermopolis, where they have hot springs and must have once had a Greek linguist. The largest hot springs in the world apparently, but then that might just mean the USA, as these things often do. I’m here “jus ridin’ out the storm” in local parlance, because snow has blocked my onward progress.

This is the kind of place that doesn't do phone reception, and where the supermarket keeps it's coffee mate in the chill cabinet with dairy produce. I always feel such an arse when I let out a little cry of delight on discovering such things. It has a population of 3224, 96% of which is white and owns a plaid shirt, and Thermopolis sits on a plain at 4500ft, surrounded by mountains. You see what happens when you leave me in a motel room with wi-fi? The Paintbrush Motel, which I can only imagine is so called because it badly needs one. I'm about to embark on the culinary sensation that is a Swanson Classic microwave TV dinner, ‘serving the nation since 1954’, which is apt, because that is roughly the same vintage as the microwave it is currently being irradiated in.

My plans are as fluid now as they ever were and with each day they seem to change more, if that is grammatically possible. Leaving Cody this morning, Stacey who cooked me ham'neggs, told me to check in the next town, Greybull, before heading up the pass out of town "on account of the snow an awl". That I duly did and was informed, by the ladies in the "we sell everything you're ever gonna need, cept weird liberal stuff" store, that it was safest to take highway 14, not the 16. She knew the guy who was working the snow ploughs on the 14 and he keeps his ploughs in real good order. With recommendation like that what could I do? The obvious answer would be stay in bed, but here, dear reader, I need to contextualise. In this part of the States it is a very long way from anywhere to anywhere else, or should that be nowhere else. For the last week I have rarely seen temperatures rise above 40ºF (about 5ºC) and I really need to start making headway to lower altitudes. Until now, I haven't been below 5000 feet for a week. That is quite high, granted, but to cross any pass or go upland at all, means regular forays to 9000 feet.

These areas, I have been informed, have been "having a ways of snow in the last week" and I have ridden through the remnants of much of it, feeling quietly confident that everything was still going to plan. But these distances are so vast that every now and again I have to come to my senses. This afternoon was one of those times, though really last night was too. Strange how a satisfactory end to a crisis can alter the reality of its seriousness (I'll tell you later). So this afternoon I was 30 miles out of town, following the advice to take Highway 14 when I was stopped just near Dirty Annie's place, by a couple of pickup trucks.

"Where ya headed?"

"Well, Custer in South Dakota"

"You sure as shit ain't takin no motorsickle there. We came over the pass lessen twenny minutes ago and it's proper white out. You ain't goin to no Custer till April or

May times"

"So just how far up does the snow start proper?" says I, ever watchful for a good photo op.

"Don't fuck with the mountains son, else they'll kill ya".

I was faced with a few possibilities: wait until April as the nice men suggested, head north via Billings, just a 350 mile detour with no guarantees, or head south. I tried south and was turned away from the pass on highway 16 too, with the only vehicles I met on that lonely 50 miles being trucks properly caked in frozen snow. By this stage the bottle of water I was carrying had begun to freeze. So I went further south, with the hope of getting on the 2 lane interstate at Casper and forgetting all about Dakota and Mount Rushmore and Crazy Horse, and I would let the Badlands stay mean and nasty.

And here I am, stuck in Thermopolis, a real big town for these parts, luckily. I am surrounded by higher ground and lots of snow and wind but tomorrow should be fine I'm telling myself. Now all those 4x4 pickup trucks with winches and spot lights and snow tyres and bracketry for snow ploughs, just don't look so brash and wanky. In fact the yellow school buses round here, you know the sort, you've seen them on a thousand TV shows, are really short, sit about 10, the maximum school size, and come equipped with their own snow plough too. I really am starting to comprehend the seriousness of my situation. I haven't seen another motorbike since I left Salt Lake City in Utah, and that was only a few hardcore helmetless riders in the city. There is no 'lid' law in Utah. Mind you there are no beer laws either, save for the fact that there is no beer. But here's a law you'll love: according to Utah State Law, it is an offence for any person who does not have control of their bowels to not wear waterproof swimwear. The sign was followed by some useful pictures of what waterproof swimwear looks like. I can only hope that none of it is supplied by Rev'itt motorcycle clothing. But really, who drafted a law like that? Maybe the same kind of people who think that Alabama should have no dancehall establishment with a trap door that leads to a room used for immoral purposes. Just normal stairs then?

So I perhaps you are asking yourselves how I came to be here. If not, I'll tell you anyway. It all started with a flight from Heathrow. Cue wavey picture and dodgy seventies elevator music.

"Final Call for Virgin Atlantic flight VS19 to San Francisco, boarding now at Gate 32".

In plenty of time I had thought, seamlessly through security and stuck in the maze that is Duty Free, wondering to myself why the stuff for sale is cheaper in Tescos, and if the price wasn't enough to annoy me, I was forced to remember my experience of trying to buy perfume in SF on the way to the UK 6 weeks earlier. Siobhan likes Donna Karan. Now I didn't know that there were different sorts. I smelt them all. Red Delicious, Black Delicious, Be Delicious, and I have to say they all smelt like Golden Delicious to me, so I didn't buy any of them.

So there I was, getting to the departure gate as everyone is boarding, still 30 mins to go before take off.

"Where is your return ticket?" Pardon me?

"This is a single. You cannot get on a plane to the USA without proof of return." My bike is in San Francisco, I can show you my Carnet de Passage to prove it, I am leaving by road. And I'm not Mexican.

"Well I am afraid you cannot board this plane without a return. The US Government says it is a requirement and we are not permitted to let you on the plane without a return ticket."

But you had no problems selling me the ticket three weeks ago!

"It is not our responsibility to check your

nationality sir, you may have been American." Then why did you ask for my passport number and place of birth as well as residence?

"That's because that is a requirement by law for services to the USA." And at no point you saw a discrepancy?

"That is not our job sir. If you wish to get on this flight you will have to purchase a single returning to the UK for £934.40. This is refundable for a £35 admin charge at San Francisco."

I was stuck, hopping mad, but paid and then took my seat on the plane, after reassurances that the refund process would begin the minute I got to SF. I hadn't been sat for two minutes when an air hostess approached me and said "Mr Tyson I believe you have just bought a return at the departure desk"

Don't you bloody start, I'm not in the mood to start digging out receipts.

"No Sir, we'd like to upgrade you to Premium. Would you like to come and choose a seat? Glass of wine? Red or white?"

I had a thoroughly enjoyable flight and am clearly very easily bought, though I don't think I was meant to be part of the "stress free retail therapy experience" they were offering on board. I didn't know how to fully employ all the legroom. I wanted to sleep using the complimentary eye mask, ear plugs and woolly socks, but feared I would miss one of the freebie handouts that arrived every hour. Fruit, icecream, tea and coffee, snacks, wine, beer, cognac after dinner, the list was endless. And the menu: Chicken piccata with fettuccine pasta, vegetable ratatouille and parmesan, spinach and mushroom risotto with pesto and even bangers and mash. Extras included Persian cheese and herb noon slice. I don't know what a noon slice is but it all meant I hardly had time to watch one of the 18 movies on offer or engage my personal games consul. The choice was overwhelming, so instead I read my new book "Deer hunting with Jesus: a guide to redneck America" in readiness for my arrival and so that I wouldn't miss a round of the trolley goodies. It also enabled me to reflect on the fact that if I was a terrorist I would fly Premium, and after being scanned through security, would be presented with glass glasses and bottles and stainless steel knives and forks. But of course the Saudis don't have enough money for Premium.

Touch down was perfect so I didn't spill my champagne and security went as well as can be expected.

Given that we are all viewed as criminals in the eyes of the US authorities, I had to have my thumb and fingerprints taken and my irises scanned. When I was just a road warrior coming overland from Canada these things weren't necessary, which leads me to believe I may have spotted a chink in the armour of 'Fortress America'. And so I headed straight to Virgin customer services as advised to begin the swift and easy refund process, until I discovered the fact that there isn't a Virgin Customer Services in San Fran. The nearest one is in Heathrow. Undaunted, though I confess, a little angry, I spent 1hour 15 minutes refusing to leave a closing check in desk for the return of the flight I had just arrived on. In the end they agreed to start the process of refund which will take up to 3 months and in the meantime I stood in awe at what was effectively an empty airport.

Remember those Thomson holiday ads, "Where is everybody?" except this time it's because no one has gone on holiday. SF International looked like Prestwick. There were clearly more staff than passengers, but who says the US economy is in the doldrums? I'd read on the plane that there was a bus to the city for $3 but no one at information had heard of a bus, (the concept more than the route) so I caught the train. The ticket booth showed me the price to my destination, $5.25, so I put in my money and was offered a $4, $6 or $8 fare! This idiocy continued in the tube when I transferred. The machines take $1.50 in quarters, the man at the desk tells you this and collects the money, though isn't allowed to change your $5 note!

I go to the 7-11 shop three storeys up and buy a chocolate bar to get change and am assured that dollar bills are acceptable, with 2 quarters. They aren't. Though there is a machine next to the kiosk idiot's desk which can change dollar notes into quarters, which I then give to him to put in a sack that have to be taken to the bank and turned into notes! There was a long queue of foreign people finding it difficult to comprehend why the system was as it was. I'm sure some managerial task force has decided this long queue of bewilderment is somehow more efficient as a means of funnelling people through the rapid transportation system.

I missed my bus at the other end.

Peggy was still safe and sound when I arrived back at cousin Jane's house, but had a flat tyre and a flat battery. There are only a few times that you are glad the street you are on is a 1 in 3. After a day with Jane and Ducie's family and the chewy dog that had eaten my computer cable, I got on the road and was treated to a few days in their chalet at Lake Tahoe, the stunning Californian mountain and ski resort.

As beautiful, tranquil and welcome as it was, I feel I cannot emphasise enough the fact that it is a ski resort, and that I was on a motorbike. As I climbed and climbed some more on approach, there was a definite drop in temperature and an alarming number of laybys specifically designed for the fitment of snow chains. I don't generally carry snow chains, so bought some locally grown pistachio nuts instead.

Cold, and having crossed 8,000ft to get there, I

revelled in the luxury of the outdoor hot tub, the fully stocked kitchen, the 1000 channel TV system with not a single educational or informative news programme, and the garage. And it's available to rent so contact me if you want to splurge. It's worth every cent!

I spent a day cycling in the forests and around the beautiful Lake Tahoe, noting nonchalantly how frozen everything was in the morning, and refusing to acknowledge that I would soon be camping.

I met Bruce and Clint, the only year round residents of the street who told me how funny it was that the Nevadans in Reno (other side of the Sierra mountains) lost lots of possessions in the last few months because they weren't used to the earthquakes. Can you believe that Nevadans hang their paintings from only one nail? And they don't have big lips on the front of their crockery shelves to catch everything that tries to leave the cupboards? Oh how we laughed.

Lake Tahoe is so clear that if you lower a white plate on a bit of string into the lake, you can see it until it is 108 feet down. Now that is clear water and I expect you wonder how I know that little gem. Well that was the system they used when the area was being mapped in the middle of the last century. Now there is only 65feet of visibility, but that's progress for you. Presumably that's because a foot just ain't what it used to be, or because old folks tell a lot of lies. No one explained to me how you tie a plate to a bit of string though. I wonder if it involves drilling, to make sure it hangs the right way.

From Lake Tahoe I rode the highest year round navigable pass in the Sierras, though navigable I hasten to add, is a relative term and has a lot to do with spikes and chains. From there I dropped into Nevada and boy what a change. Lets just say you never hear about forest fires sweeping through Nevada. There are one or two trees planted in peoples gardens in Reno, but vegetation is not something that Nevada is generally big on. Instead they do casinos. The biggest ugliest concrete and steel monstrosities you have ever seen and the houses that aren't trailer homes are painted either beige or taupe to blend effortlessly and pointlessly into the barren landscape.

I rode for days, but it seemed like weeks, through the dead Nevadan desert on my horse that does have a name. It felt good to be out of the rain. In the desert you can remember your name 'cause there ain't no one for to give you no pain. Even with the cooling temperatures of late autumn, the sun was intense and moisture something of a premium. The distances are crazy, interspersed with signs that read "Next rest area 115miles. No services". In the town of Fernley I had lunch and was served by big Anne. 26 years she'd been doing the job. I thought it churlish to point out that she still didn't have the hang of it and refused to leave a tip. I don't get the whole tipping culture. If the service is exceptional, sure, why not? Mediocre, well it's your job, so getting the food from the kitchen to my table should really be factored in to the bill. Bad? Then forget it. I need my money too.

I got to Fallon and chose not to take highway 50 to cross the state, known as the "loneliest highway" and instead took 80. Any lonelier and I would have gone mad. The desert bowl of much of central Nevada is so high and dry, that things can be preserved in a very special way here. Things other than cars and pickups from the 1950's that are then exported to Europe for premium fees. Things like the part mummified Cave Spirit Man who was found about 15 miles east of Fallon and is somewhat older than a big finned Cadillac. About 9,400 years older in fact, and probably one of the first ever people to try western style BBQ ribs. I kept my fingers crossed that Peggy wouldn't decide it was a good day to die and that my sun bleached carcass would be the next remains to be discovered.

These immense distances were all just the start of what was to come. I rode like a demon to the town of Elko, somewhat perturbed by the occasional electronic highway signs that warned amber alert of a white Dodge pickup truck with Mississippi plates. I had visions of one of those dreadful road movies starring a psychopath in a pickup truck, the open road and me.

All day I spent in the saddle to get to a dump that really has no reason to exist now, even though it's the biggest place in northern Nevada. It was once a railhead town (though I don't know why) and it has an airport, renowned as being the first destination for a commercial postal flight, 6th of April 1926 if memory serves. The fact that this flight from Pasco Washington State first touched down in Oregon to drop off and collect more mail, seems to have slipped everyone's memory, therefore making it the second commercial postal flight destination, but you've gotta have a hook, especially if you are selling yourself to any tourist lucky enough to be attempting to sleep directly under the flight path of all current flights.

But I am so harsh. Elko is famous for more! It has legal prostitution. Under Nevada law, a county with LESS than 400,000 inhabitants (pretty much all rural counties in Nevada) can have brothels. Less than? Which dirty old legislators with a thing for country girls thought that one up? It is also a town that covers 14sq miles, (though if there is water in the Humboldt River this figure is reduced somewhat) and it is full of casinos and Basque food. Turns out that it wasn't just the Irish and Scots that settled these wilderness areas. Unfortunately this Spanish influence seems to reach into the bars and restaurants too, which are all smoking zones. I'd forgotten how horrible that is.

From there I rode into Utah and to Bonneville Salt Flats. The nearest town is a bit of a trek, so bring a packed lunch if you want to watch the racing. After all this way, to get to the hardest, most perfect surface known to man for racing and speed testing motor vehicles, Peggy and I sank. There had been rain. The last few weeks of racing had been cancelled. Do you notice a precipitation theme entering this whole journey yet? As an aside, has anyone heard the news from Central America? They are suffering terrible flooding and land slides, greater even than the usual seasonal disasters. I'll definitely be fitting some knobbly tyres for that section, but would have loved some here on the salt flats. Of course I would have done terrible damage to the surface if I had got more than twenty feet from the roadside. The salt crust is easily broken, except when it has been baked hard by the unforgiving Utah sun, and there are signs up warning of the fragility of the surface when there has been rain. These signs had meant nothing to the family that were driving around doing their utmost to ensure the body of their saloon organically reverted to its natural state, and who asked me to tow them out when they sank, about half a mile out on the lake bed. The sight of their shocked uncomprehending faces when I told them I wouldn't be able to!

I went to the petrol station at the main highway in Wendover and told the proprietors of their plight. They just rolled their eyes and said they'd send a truck out later. At least the tide wasn't going to come in any time soon.

The salt flats are the old dry bed of the huge Bonneville Lake that once covered much of northern Utah, and which is now represented by the renamed but still shrinking Great Salt Lake. It's size ebbs and flows with droughts and rainfall, but its average depth is only 14 feet. It is one of the worlds terminal lakes, so has no outflow river and is situated on impermeable rock so the water can't drain away either. Hence the evaporation that leads to all the crusty mineral deposits and its salinity, which is ten times greater than sea water.

Utah became the 45th State of the US after it agreed

to abandon polygamy, which was seen as a threat no doubt, to all those other God fearing Americans who preferred infidelity. I decided I didn't really like Utah though it was too cold for me to explore the Uinta Mountains which might have changed my mind and it's not because of the Osmonds or because 62.8% of the state is Mormon. I know, you thought it was 70% but it hasn't been for nearly 10 years, there are so many blow ins watering down the religious conviction. Instead Mormons are exporting their belief and theirs is one of the fast growing faiths on the continent, apparently.

All the blow-ins come for the work. According to the "Jackson Hole Daily" 20/10/08 Mining business is brisk in Utah. There are now 170 quarries, producing 91,000 tonnes of rock and employing 200 (obviously lonely) people. When populations are small, it all matters. Compare that to the 254 people working in quarries in Montana and 224 in Idaho. What a huge industry! The best bit is the last paragraph of the article:

"Most of the rock that comes out of the ground doesn't travel very far though, primarily because it's heavy". Timeless.

For me though, I just found Utah lacking. Colour mostly, and the intense reflection of the sun on the salt meant I spent my time with my eyes almost closed. You are right, it's not a very insightful summary, so be grateful this isn't a travel guidebook and to the whole State, I say sorry, but you just didn't move me. I might reassess the situation when I explore the south later, but even my map doesn't encourage me. It has a list of 'Points of Interest' on the back, beneath which is written: 'Many points listed, especially historical and cultural sites, are not noted on the map.' Genius.

Camping was getting silly by the time I left Utah, waking up in temperatures that rarely got above 28 in old money, (about –3ºC) so by the time I rode towards

Yellowstone and Grand Teton National Parks, I was planning on using more motels and hang the expense. It was a little disconcerting that most people seemed to be travelling the other way, and with cowboys bringing their stock down off the hills and corralling their horses there was this little niggle that I was trying to ignore. If everyone was battening down the hatches, and there was snow by the roadside, should I really be riding up into the mountains?

Looking for somewhere to get a hot drink and warm up, I found one of those grocery/cafes that sell guns and knives, but was turned away because it was Sunday, so I could only buy a gun. They phoned around the town of Logan for me and directed me to a "liberal" place called Ibis in the centre of town that was open for drinks. It seems 'liberal' means vegetarian but they were also liberal with their hot water, feeling bad that they had no tea for me. I like to keep the odd bag about my person, even though I was never a scout, so that was ok. It was in this great little deli that I met Janet and Bob and their friends, who I spent the morning with. Janet, a multiple vintage motocross champion and Bob, who'd been riding for years and was originally from Luton, hadn't been together that long, so it was one of those events very early in a relationship when the new partner gets presented to the old friends and everyone is being scrutinized for compatibility amidst polite and jovial banter. These can always be tense situations, so what better time to be joined by a complete stranger from the other side of the Atlantic? Maybe my random intrusion put everyone at ease. I'd like to think so and may be that's why Bob gave me his address near the Grand Canyon and said I should call in, which I think I will.

I headed north into S.E. Idaho and through Montpellier, made famous on 13th August 1896 when Butch Cassidy and his gang of ne'er-do-wells, robbed the bank of close to $16,000 and then calmly rode away on their horses and into the annals of wild western history. The very plucky Deputy, Fred Cruickshank gave chase on his bicycle, but alas, to no avail. The bank teller, AN Mackintosh, blamed the number 13 for the whole ghastly affair. They apparently raided the bank 13 minutes past the hour on the 13th day of the month, after the 13th deposit of the day, which had been 13 dollars. Incontrovertible evidence. No wonder Americans never build a 13th storey in their buildings, instead preferring a gap. I also rode past Franklin, the oldest town in Idaho, founded on 14th April 1860 by Mormons expanding north as the Good Lord said they should. I'm sure everyone is relieved they didn't get there a day earlier.

Into Wyoming and I spy further proof, if any was needed, that more than just Anglo-Celts settled the Wild West. I ride through Paris, Geneva and Bern, and get a feel for the attitudes the settlers brought with them, passing the villages of Liberty and Freedom (well it's best to be sure). I then reached the sweet town of Afton, which has the largest elk horn archway in the world. Now I was thinking, as you may well be, that to be fair, it is probably the only elk horn archway in the world, but it isn't! There are four of them in the centre of Jackson along with the kitschiest of nasty buildings called the Cowboy Bar which has got a plaque outside honouring the far sighted council who have helped to preserve a building more than 50 years old! All of which reminds me of something I heard on the radio about some US tourists in the library of an Oxford College. When they asked the curator if the 'really cute' building was pre-war, he replied "Madam, it is pre-America".

The Cowboy Bar probably did have world famous steaks behind it's ghastly exterior, but at more than the price of my hotel room, I settled for trying another

Mexican, where, being castigated for dining alone, I was instructed to sit at the bar in front of the telly with all the other sad and lonely diners. I hasten to add however, that by not wearing a baseball cap, I feel that I shone as a beacon of individuality. Back in my room, as I write this, I have just taken a break and tried to find a news channel on the box. WGN9 'coming at me from Chicago' is the best I can do but I really hope that I am not a member of their targeted demographics. Every advert is for a medical condition, but mostly erectile dysfunction. The working man, home after a long and stressful day at the office/factory, trying to stay informed about the world around him while taking a break from worries about mortgage and car repayments, settles down to be confronted with pictures and narration of couples only able to smile at each other after he pops a few pills. All these are accompanied by a ten minute list of side effects and almost all of them seem to cause death in asthma suffers, but remember, seek medical advise if your erection lasts more than five hours and see our ad in Golf magazine for more info.

Then there's bladder control, birth control, allergies, skin conditions and a million other disorders that I'm sure no one knew they previously had. It's good that these advertisers don't attempt to play on any insecurities or frailties of the human condition.

And so I went to Yellowstone, (Yabba Dabba Doo!) after I had bump started the bike. Peggy has decided that she will no longer tolerate these ludicrous morning temperatures. Land of bears and big cats, 300 volcanic geysers and roaming herds of bison, the world's first National Park came into existence in 1872, when President Ulysees S Grant signed the Bill to protect almost three and a half thousand square miles. Wolves were reintroduced in 1995 and because of them the beavers have come back too, because apparently the wolves keep the moose moving so that they don't eat all the fresh willow shoots that the beavers like. Then because the beavers make the dams that create the wetlands that enable the sodium rich weeds to grow, the bird life has improved too, all of which means the visitor numbers are up, bringing in more money which enables more conservation projects and protection work that's needed due to all the extra visitors. Ahh, ecological interconnectedness.

As I approached the entrance I met Andy, a whirlwind from Victoria, Australia. "G'day mate. Streuth, you've come a bloody long way on that bike. You'll have a bonser time in the Park mate, but if you wanna piss in Old Faithful you gotta time it right or you'll lose your bloody dick! And watch for the Rangers, they've got bloody guns like all the other nutters in this country!"

My Yellowstone experience was a little more conservative and to be honest, I have never harboured any desires to urinate into a geyser. Instead I found myself enjoying great moments of solitude and serenity beside Firehole Lake and Great Fountain geyser. It was a fantastic time to visit the Park. Very few of the three million annual visitors were there, it was like being in a land of make believe, a real 'middle earth' experience, with steaming lakes and rivers and jets of boiling water shooting skyward before crashing onto multi coloured tiered mineral formations. The whole thing set against a backdrop of pine and broadleaf forest in autumnal colours and inhabited by seemingly prehistoric bison, who had liberally coated the whole area with excrement and always seemed to have an eye on me as if to say "Yeah, so wot?" There was nobody there but me.

I crossed the Continental Divide in absolute solitude too, the point where all the water to my right would eventually end up in the Atlantic, and all the water to my left, the Pacific. None of it was flowing anywhere when I got there though, being frozen solid.

Of course Old Faithful had visitors, having a car park, hotel and visitor centre that was undergoing a refurb and expansion to cope with the ever increasing numbers in the summer. I can only presume that Australian Andy camped beside the car park. I would like to think he relieved himself nocturnally.

The northern half of the Park had already been closed due to the October snows, which can be deep and arrive at any time at this high altitude, so as the day prepared to end, I asked a fellow tourist to fill my fuel tank from the automated pump using his credit card in exchange for cash and headed for the eastern exit with a little too much gusto. VJ Menagh, one of the gun toting Rangers gave chase in his Suburban and then decided not to officially nick me for recklessly breaking the Park speed limit by four miles an hour. I was given a firm talking to and told that speeding motorists kill lots of the Park's wildlife each year. I think an SUV might do slightly more damage to an elk or bison than a 650 Aprilia, but he was probably still smarting from the death of #264 Obsidian, the ranger's favourite bear, a twelve year old killed by a motorist a few years back. Then I had the experience with the weather that really scared me.

Trying to leave the park, with high passes to cover, many of the roads already closed to traffic and over 110 miles to go to civilisation, the temperature fell, the snows and rain began and there was nobody else on the road. I began the climb to the Sylvan Pass at 8530ft with failing light and rising panic. Strange how the feeling of solitude can be so liberating and enjoyable in one set of circumstances and so terribly frightening only a few hours later. The pass itself, between the Grizzley (9948ft) and Avalanche Peaks (10566ft) was in monochrome when I arrived and the desolate shale sides of the towering peaks either side of the road reminded me of Welsh slag heaps.

The Eleanor and Sylvan lakes were completely frozen but the dash to the exit was now downhill and a huge psychological boost with every kilometre bringing the belief that the temperature was increasing. Regardless of the fact that the bike handled in the snow like it had two flat tyres, it felt similar to descending an Alpine pass towards sea level with each new band of warm air engulfing me. The truth of course, was that the Park entrance lodge was at 6940 ft and it was still snowing when I arrived. An incredibly surprised solitary ranger told me that the nearest town, Cody, was another 60 miles away, but it was a couple of thousand feet lower. The snow and sleet eventually gave way to rain as darkness embraced me and I tried to keep the throttle pinned.

My fear, paranoia and hypothermia combined in the Shoshone gorges to conjure images of fantastical creatures. The rock columns and pinnacles, seen in a thousand westerns, with shapes and faces in them, towered above me, often shielding the final rays of sunlight. Their beauty and majesty would have been stunning at another time, but for now I needed civilisation lest I died, quite frankly.

It was then that my first deer incident caused me to use all the road and more. This was becoming ludicrous, as wildlife took an age to register in a cold brain. I'm not entirely sure how I missed it, but barely 10 miles further my luck ran out when I clipped the third of three deer crossing. I knew it must have been there somewhere, the way the first two crossed something told me there were more, but the third went behind me and caught the pannier. I managed to stay upright and within two miles saw the lights of the most welcoming place I was yet to stay in. Garish neon spelled out 'restaurant and bar' and I couldn't have been happier.

Free tacos because of the Monday Night Football Game were welcome, as were a couple of bottles of

Moose Drool ale, from the Big Sky Brewery in Montana. Funny how warmth and intoxicating liquor can make a frightening experience rapidly pale, and I got to chat to a couple of Swedes who were finding the wild west as scary as I was, and this time I mean socially. They had been spending time on Indian Reservations, studying the poverty and disempowerment wrought by legislation.

I assured myself I'd go back to see the canyon in daylight, but the howling wind and snowstorm that caused a complete whiteout of the hills, put me off, so instead I headed east, to encounter much worse weather as it happens.

17 RACE TO THE CLOUDS

I spent the other night in Shorty's, an all American bar, with all American hats, boots, guns, pickup trucks, misogyny, racism and a drive-by beer window. We were having a rare ole time there, trying not to talk politics or religion, cos them's the rools, but of course failing now and again. It was certainly an insight into small town Western American culture, but I did come away with a glimmer of hope. Between "jokes" like, "what do the KKK and Nike have in common? They both make niggers run fast", and "I won't be sending racist texts no more cos that's criminal, and I ain't black", I was taken aside for a quiet word by Dave (I shouldn't publish his real name for his own safety). Dave said the economy was in a mess and the whole world hates America, so he was going to vote for the black guy. He said that was the only chance the country had, but clearly couldn't say so out loud. My glimmer of hope is that it wasn't the first time I had been confided in, in hushed tones. There are many more who feel the same way and understand that politics means more than saying "Don't ya know it's a WHITE House?"

I did have one moment in that bar of the sort I never had imagined happening. It was a 'pindrop' moment when I knew I had to climb not dig, that I found myself saying, quite honestly (and gratefully), that I was a christened and confirmed Protestant. With that I was bought another beer and we could all go back to hating. There had been a time when some of the patrons might have suspected I was a heathen, or worse, a communist, and I'm not proud of not speaking my mind, but I'm trying to convince myself it was for the greater good of being able to observe the social etiquette. And because generally in a confrontational situation like that I find that I am a coward.

The whole election thing here is such a convoluted, confusing business, it's little wonder that only about 35% of the people vote. Apart from the Presidential ballot, there are also elections for County Supervisor, Sheriff, Congress and Senator and then a huge raft of individual laws or Propositions that are so spun out in the TV propaganda it is almost impossible to work out what to vote yes or no for, unless you read all the new proposals in full.

With a population that is 50% functionally literate, (though I'm not entirely sure what that little stat actually means) it is no wonder that the sound bite is king and there is never any room for discussion, debate or meaningful dialogue. There can be no engagement with politics and that is why we see, as I have witnessed, arguments like the following:

"I can't vote for Obama because he is a Muslim and they attacked our country. If he gets in he'll hand America over to Iraq". I'm sure you can follow that seamless logic, but it makes it easier to see how one of the things the Republicans campaigned successfully with last time was that John Kerry, the Democratic hopeful, "looked quite French". Surely reason enough to decide your economic and foreign policy position!

You might have heard all about Joe the Plumber who is being used this year in the Republican campaign (the true honest working man trying to make good and live the American Dream, but who will be restrained by

Obama's taxation plans). Well Joe isn't actually a plumber, isn't about to buy a company, doesn't earn $250k a year and has state lawsuits against him for non payment of income and property taxes. But what are a few facts that may get in the way of a good slogan?

I've also discovered- I'll talk about that whole motorbike journey in a minute- that Obama isn't the only black candidate running for President. Of the 17 candidates running there are three black, two women (note that they don't have a colour descriptor) and a Mexican who is allowed to stand, but not win, because 'ees foreign. What about that then? Hands up how many of you knew that?

I'll not bore you with their policies, but one of the black candidates, Alan Keyes, is dismayed by how far to the LEFT McCain has gone, and wants to return to a strict pro-life, anti environmental Reaganite free market agenda! The women standing are, not surprisingly, Green and Socialist, (so they've lost their deposits then) and there's one other bloke I must mention. Gene Amondson is standing on one issue. He believes that with the introduction of prohibition there will be no criminals, no illness and no foreign policy worries. I'd like to live in the simplicity that must be his head and ask if the name Capone means anything to him. Finally, all but the two candidates we hear a lot about, want to bring the troops back from the 47 countries they are currently occupying! Now there's a thing.

So anyway, I awoke to a stunningly beautiful day and by 10.30am it had warmed up to almost freezing point. I like to start most mornings with a full cardio-vascular workout. There are two reasons for this: firstly, sitting on the bike for a long time isn't terribly physically taxing and I need to keep in trim and secondly (and more plausibly) because Peggy needs a push start each day. A push start. It sounds so easy but at this altitude and in this temperature a big single cylinder engine is not an easy thing to coax into life. I know there are one or two things that need fixing, but they'll have to wait until such time as my hands don't stick to the metal so I think that'll be California.

Remember the oil leak that developed on the way to Southampton? Well that is, or has become, a protective film that now coats every bit of engine, from the rocker cover to the sump. The slow front puncture is in fact a dodgy valve. Do you recall how old men used to do the spit test and look for bubbles, which as a kid you found revolting? Well I took that one stage further and having found the leak used the steel valve cap from the rear wheel and filled it with grease to make a seal. Just temporary, honest, but it's managed about 2000kms now so I'll see how long it'll last. The clutch is getting heavy, the brake lights are stuck on, one of the spotlight brackets has broken, one front indicator unit is held together with glue and a large amount of Obama's Hope which is en vogue and the front wheel bearings are so noisy and coarse now, I can hear them above the engine when I lean from the vertical.

Oh and the heated grips have become intermittent. They seem to stop working when it gets particularly cold.

So I left Thermopolis and headed south through the really breathtaking Wind River Canyon. I am so glad I didn't try it in the snow earlier. For a start I wouldn't have been able to do the owl impersonation as I tried to take it all in. At one photo stop a man pulled over and offered to take my picture. As he took my camera I noticed that his hands were covered in blood. Just me, a desolate river canyon and a mad killer with a pickup full of implements of destruction! He took two pictures and apologised that the first one missed the top off one the cliffs. What a nice man.

The town of Shoshoni was a perfect example of so many back country American towns I have seen out here in the upland west. The poverty is everywhere, manifesting itself not least in the terrible physical appearance of the houses and businesses. Broken, taped up windows, rubbish and a general air of desolation. Of course the majority of the properties everywhere are "trailers", the mobile home which occasionally moves, but mostly begins disintegrating the moment it is bought and sited in this unforgiving climate of scorching summers and perishing winters. They are as thermally inefficient as many of the motel rooms I have recently found myself frequenting. Single glazing, thin interior style exterior doors, which fit well enough to let just a small hurricane in, and light ply walls. Some nights my rooms feel much like the tent! There are starting to be "insulation aware" adverts on the telly, but prior to this the attitude was one of turn up the heating.

And Fuel prices are tumbling again, as I'm sure they must be in Britain too, given that the oil companies always say that the price at the pumps is not their fault, it's because of the price of crude oil. Oil that they drill for in their own oil fields. Well when I arrived in the US in mid August it was $4.50 a gallon, and now it's $2.50. As I watched one newscaster on a National news bulletin say, "Well that's good, we can all go out for a drive at the weekend, and there's no need to downgrade your car" which is the sort of enlightened responsible journalism that should help save the world.

Leaving Shoshoni I headed for Casper and was on top of a plateau again, now over 6000ft with a bitter prairie wind and just 120 miles of bleak open space till the next bit of welcoming shelter. Powdery snow whipped across the road, but the skies were clear and blue and I chose not to stop for pics lest the same "being blown off the stand" thing happened to the bike again like in northern Nevada. I passed the town of Hiland that proudly proclaimed its population and altitude on a road sign, as so many do. Its population is ten. That was the only settlement I passed. The sign hadn't been tampered with but so often they have. If, upon entering a village, the sign says 67 and the seven has clearly just been added, I never know whether I should mention it at the petrol station. Should I congratulate the community, rejoicing at the news of a newborn, or is there deep sorrow at a passing?

In a restaurant in Casper, one of the waitresses, Annie, asked all the truck drivers who had come from the south whether the main highways were open. All said they were, but I should watch for the wind. Then Annie had a look at my map to see where I could stop if the weather turned, on my next section south.

"Awe hunney, they've just rit a whole buncha names on yer map soaz to fill them spaces. There ain't nuthin there really, but there's still one store in...." and she proceeded to (correctly) identify every possible stopping place in the next 180 miles. It took a minute or so.

The last bit of that journey south toward the Colorado border saw me try all sorts inside my helmet to stay conscious. I have discovered that when I am particularly cold and vocalise dialogue between fictitious characters, as they discuss my surroundings in the minutest detail, I adopt a Lancastrian accent, though sometimes I argue like a Brummie. I am afraid I can shine absolutely no light on why this may be, other than when the brain is suffering a trauma, bad things happen! I tried doing all of my times tables to fight off hypothermia, but didn't quite manage them all. Even my usual recital of pye to 182 decimal places was beyond me, such was the cold, though I confess I might have made that up.

First rule of travelling by road: never go to the first hotel or lodging place you see on the outskirts of town, it'll cost too much. Sod it.

"Hi!" said Diane, as she greeted me in the foyer. Diane was used to life on the road, as she was a long distance coach driver.

"Yes, everyone keeps telling me how much FUN those motorcycles are!" I had no retort, so she giggled as she filled in my registration form because I couldn't write and after thawing out in the shower and getting a revolting Chinese meal next door, I settled down to write and ponder why it is that if the Chinese travel west they bring their culinary expertise with them and if they travel east from China they really don't.

I was in Cheyenne, centre for USAF Missile Command. I felt right at home, on Missile Drive and Patriot Avenue, with phallic symbols of capitalism's insecurity on show at every turn.

With clean long johns and a quickly evaporating layer of morning perspiration after my daily workout, I crossed out of the perfectly rectangular Wyoming and entered the perfectly rectangular State of Colorado, the Centennial State. It joined the Union in 1876, just a hundred years after Independence. See what they did there? Witty eh?

Colorado has 54 mountains which peak at more than 14,000ft, and the State fish is the "Greenback Cutthroat Trout" which sounds financially violent. The Rockies really dominate everything here, with Mount Massive being the... second tallest. They're not quite as literal here as in Canada, or perhaps they got the early measurements wrong.

I was specifically here for one of those 54. Pikes Peak stands at 14,110 feet and holds a special place for me as a car rally fan. In 1915 Spencer Penrose and associates decided to build a road to the summit, roughly following an old trail the US Army signal Corps had used since 1873. It took a year and great expense, but opened in 1916 and to celebrate the opening they organised an automobile race to the summit. By jove, that's the spirit! The race has effectively happened every year since and Pikes Peak Hillclimb was one of those World Series type events that only Americans seemed to be allowed win in their specially prepared hill climb cars. Until 1988, when the Finn Ari Vatanen, famed promoter of milk, demon driver and a bit of a god really, brought a funny little Peugeot rally car from Europe and smashed the record by almost two minutes on his first attempt.

The race always happens in July, what with the suitable weather and the fact that only a portion of the road has yet been tarmaced. So I thought my first attempt at the ascent should be at the end of October, in the snow.

In preparation for the event I had a high cal Burger and some fries and then bought the most expensive, highest octane petrol for Peggy because even that is down to $2.85 and I can be a bit of an environmental hypocrite too if I try. In the further interests of race tuning and preparation, I elected to do it with all my luggage, an almost slick road pattern tyre on the front and just the one operating heated grip. Perfect.

Then I got to the entrance (it's a toll) and they said I couldn't go because I was on a motorbike, lots of it was too slippery and anyway of the 19mile route, only the first 15 miles were open. I stated my long travelled case, smiled sweetly, promised I wouldn't cross 10 mph and really went for it when I'd got of sight of the entry control. They have this slogan “real men don't need barriers” and it means that when it goes wrong, it really, really goes wrong, some of the drop offs being 1000ft. Alas my “RACE TO THE CLOUDS” was more a dreadful ungainly slither through the mud, snow and ice up to the wardens that were parked across the road at just under

13,000 ft. I asked them if they were sure I couldn't get on up to the summit, but they just demanded to know how I had managed to get this far.

I took a few pictures of the panorama- I think I could see New York- and then realised that my little heart was racing, my head was thumping and I really couldn't get my breath. Time to descend, utilising all those skills that the nice Canadian Yamaha off road people had let me develop while wrecking their bikes. All too soon I was down, and not because I missed a corner, and the ladies at the bottom gave me an official Pikes Peak Park Ranger badge and took my picture. How sweet. I think perhaps they were glad to see me, secure in the knowledge they could keep their jobs. It was all good practice for the Andes and I know that the engine management system has no problem altering the mixture for altitude, so that's a bonus.

I explored Rocky Mountain National Park, which containers 12 "fourteeners" and saw a huge herd of elk, but the main routes through the park were closed and the wind was really bitter, so, full of the joys of late Autumn, I retired for food and to contemplate some of the characters I've been meeting.

There are two main themes I keep encountering. The first is that a lot of Americans can't quite fathom what I'm doing. I've encountered a lot of hostility when I say that I'm not very rich, as though I am lying. Most people ask within the first five minutes of conversation how wealthy I am, which is uncomfortable enough, but then to brush off my reply and imply there is something I'm not telling them, just pisses me off. It appears to be so far out of their comfort zone to not be weighed down with material stuff, it is as though it can't be done. Everything seems to be defined by wealth and expenditure. Anyway, what does it matter what I'm telling them, a complete stranger?

The other disconcerting conversational opener is being informed of a person's private life. Being told all about their adoptive upbringing and reasons for name changes, to stories about life, prison sentences and debt to being disowned by offspring, is something I should be honoured to be trusted with, but in a diner, or a car park, at our first meeting? It seems as though the very materialism of this life has been achieved at the complete expense of human contact and any that can be garnered is grabbed and used to offload inner burdens.

Maybe it's not that at all, and I am unfairly assessing these people in the context of my northern European reserve. Are we really so very socially different? Perhaps, regardless of the unrelenting fear mongering in the press, this is actually a nation of trusting, almost child like souls, who can't see how any bad could come from bearing their frailties and concerns to others. Or do I just have 'counsellor' tattooed on my forehead? But to the guy in the elevator in Denver who asked, I'm afraid I don't know just how violent the police in Colorado are if they find you sleeping in your car and I'm sorry to hear that you have only got your hotel room for another two nights, but might I suggest you reconsider your rather strongly worded opinion of the welfare state. Perhaps it'll dawn on you that it's not just lazy commies that occasionally need help.

Gosh.

There was a great road sign on the way to Denver: 'In case of flooding, climb to safety'. No doubt that's the sort of thing that needs saying. It was in a gorge that also had one of those signs that reads: 'Motorcycles use extreme caution'. I'm not sure if there is a comma missing, if it's a statement, a warning, or just advice, but to me it always means fun ahead! While I'm on signs, the cruellest of all must be at the newly created junction 365 on Interstate 80 in the Nevada desert, which is for the ironically named Independence Valley, a penitentiary. Signs 5 miles either side of the junction say “do not pickup hitch hikers”.

I am being so fortunate with the weather now, that it couldn't be better. Visibility is fantastic, all the tourists have gone home, the skiers haven't arrived yet and the snow and bitter temperatures have temporarily moved east to Nebraska and Kansas. Poor old Nebraska. You just never see adverts for “All the best holiday breaks in Nebraska” do you? “Ten fun and exciting things to do in the desolate prairie”. Even a Bruce Springsteen album doesn’t entice me to go there. At least Kansas has a yellow brick road and gives you the excuse to ride along singing “Home, home on the range, where the deer and the antelope roam..”

18 TAKIN' IT EASY

After conquering Pikes Peak (sort of), I headed to Colorado Springs from Denver and was warned not to go out at night because of all the squaddies. Bit of an Aldershot by all accounts, but Joe Biden (Obama's running mate), was there the day before me campaigning for the Democrats, as Colorado is said to be a swing State. How exciting!

It seems to me that Subaru is the automotive carriage of choice for the liberal middle class in these parts. They all seem to have bicycle racks and Obama stickers on them. In the cities and around the very lovely mountain lodges, there appears to be little else, 'sep pickup trucks 'a course. If this is a swing state, there must be a whole other part of it I am yet to encounter.

The next few days were full of awesome mountains and a series of incredible gorges. The mountains were big, the passes high, (lots over 10,000ft) but the weather was improving all the time. The roads were entertaining and I became an unabashed tourist at the Royal Gorge, walking the world's highest suspension bridge which moved alarmingly and was almost 100 years old. The drop was a mere 1372 ft, into the Arkansas River. I took a cablecar back across and wasn't entirely sure that they should have promoted the fact that it had now travelled 229,000 miles since it's construction in 1968, and was the longest single span in the world. But this is the country where if you've got it, you flaunt it, no matter how questionable.

If you were the head of marketing at Pabst Blue Ribbon Beer, brewing proudly in Milwaukee since 1844, would you put on the can that it was "Selected Americas Best in 1893". 1893? Surely it must at least have won a taste test at some local fete since then?

I know, biggest this and fattest that (careful), but that's the kinda place this is. The world's largest ball of barbed wire is in Wyoming. Thought some of you might need that for a pub quiz.

I visited the Manitou cliff dwellings of the Pueblo Indians, carved out of the red Colorado rock a thousand years ago. One of the houses even had some original, rot free woodwork in the flooring and a small balcony which I noted was held together by some original 11th century half inch stainless steel bolts.

I rode so many stunning ravines, all of which seemed to be called "Falling Rock", that I can't remember where they all were, until at last I got to the Black Canyon of the Gunnison River, so called because it is so deep the sun doesn't penetrate parts of it. Some of the sheer cliffs are 2300ft in one straight go. I know that's what sheer means, but I need the emphasis and have a limited vocabulary. The rest of the gorge takes a strange jagged form as interspersed rock layers have eroded faster than others. It is too incredible for words, and being the winter I was effectively there alone, which added to the power of the place. I think it best you Google it for images.

Leaving the rim of the gorge I had a funny old thing happen. I was enjoying the swinging nature of the rapidly descending road, when on one right hand corner and I don't know how it happened, my right foot got pulled off the peg and stuck between the pannier and the road, meaning that my boot was being slowly ground away. I could lean no further for the tightening bend, nor use the rear brake for balance. Oh how I laughed afterwards, when it transpired there was no truck coming the other way and there was just enough road to make the turn without barrelling off the side of the mountain.

The night before I stayed in a real dump, where I accessed the room by walking across the roof of another part of the building. Everything was broken, including the lives of the people in the neighbouring rooms. The paper thin walls let me eavesdrop on conversations, even though I really didn't want to hear jealous boyfriends start rows about text messages before expressing their apologies and undying love when their libido was raised half an hour later. Alcohol fuelled scuffles and arguments about what channel the telly should be on, came from every quarter and filled the night.

More beautiful mountains followed as I headed south west through other Colorado towns and discovered why it was a political swing state, and saw turtles swimming for the first time in an old goldmining town. Well in the pond at any rate. I just adore that ostentatious Victoriana in previously wealthy western gold mining towns. Really nothing more than a dusty street in a valley, high in the mountains, but with the most lavish shop fronts and hotels that have survived because the place was deserted when the gold and silver ran out, but hadn't quite fallen apart before the yuppies rediscovered it. Now Silverton has more coffee bars, head shops, antique dealers and Subarus than a place 100 times its size has a right to, so somehow that same grandiose mentality survives. There are still signs everywhere that say no entry without a shirt and shoes, but all of the State seems to like using those.

Crossing back towards southern Utah and enroute to Monument Valley in Arizona, the scenery returned to that of physical desolation and I had one of those seminal motoring moments. I say Pah! to route 66. I went one better and rode route 666. It was an evil bit of road though and I hadn't packed any garlic, so I didn't go far.

Then the cartographer in me had to go to Four Corners, which is just a brass plaque in the ground where 4 US States meet, and an opportunity for the Navajo to make a few quid. Colorado, Utah, New Mexico and Arizona joined by the lines drawn on a map in an office miles away, across an unknown wasteland. I bought a sticker and had my picture taken by a huge lady from Ohio who told me she was pure Irish, being a Maguire. Umm.

Tuba City and not a musical instrument in sight, but a suspect looking collection of pickup trucks weighed down with firewood were lurking in the shadows of waste ground. All very suspicious, because I haven't seen a tree for a very long time. I cruised up and down for a while attempting to find somewhere to sleep but very aware that this was not somewhere to put up a tent. Every other house was boarded up and there were a lot of government initiative buildings behind barbed wire. The mangy dogs of the last few days were again in evidence but what wasn't, was a cheap motel. Night fell rapidly and with no street lights the desert is a very dark place. Come to think of it, most places are, but I'm building suspense (mostly my own). There was no bidding the manager down in the cheaper of the two motels, so I had an expensive night and in retaliation set up my stove and cooked in the bathroom having been turned away from the drive through burger bar because I wasn’t in my car. Then I found a TV station run by Arizona State University and watched an hour and a half long documentary about LBJs presidency with no ad breaks! Did you know…, oh don’t worry, I’ll keep it all to myself.

It turns out I was right to feel funny about Tuba, it is said to be the nations’ centre for met amphetamine trafficking and use. But they are pretty good at alcoholism too. The whole Four Corners area is to be honest, and the evening's drive from Colorado through the bottom corner of Utah and into AZ was interesting insofar as every single inch of the roadside glistened with the glass of smashed beer bottles. With the sun falling at the right angle to catch all the shards, it was like riding through some kind of glittery Disneyland. And therein lies the case for recycling! Not one of those four states pay return deposits on their glass bottles, like so many others do.

Of course that won't help the fact that this waste is produced by those people who stop off on the way home, buy a case of beer and drink it going up the road. Remember, if it's 70 or 80 miles between settlements, it's something to do. I'm convinced a major contribution to road safety and environmental protection, would be the removal of screw tops. Or not... but you know what I mean!

Much of this land is Navajo territory, though it surrounds a smaller Hopi Reservation. I had a long chat with a woman from the Hopi tribe about this drink problem, among many others. Kathy Sahmie works for KUYI 88.1 Hopi Tribe community radio and helped me a lot with understanding what was going on and what the suspicious pickups were doing. Young men bring the dead wood in from the back country apparently to provide heating materials for those old and infirm who can no longer go foraging. It was her that explained the huge drug problem, the alcoholism and how the Native American tribes are battling with adversity.

The granted land the reservations are located on is of course the poorest, least productive of any in the State and in Arizona's case that is going some. After a couple of days riding huge distances I had formulated the question, "Arizona. What is it for?"

The poverty on the Indian lands was even more pronounced than elsewhere in the midwest. I was riding through towns that seemed simply to be a collection of broken buildings, broken machinery and vehicles spread amongst the dust and tumbleweed. I had believed they were inhabited by broken people with broken spirits, like so much of what I had seen in Aboriginal Australia. Kathy assured me that as destitute as they were, and as rapidly as they were losing some elements of their cultural identity, (she for example could not speak her own language though she could understand it), other elements of their identity were holding the tribe together. Unfortunately as more of the youth go to the cities for work they are bringing back an urban gang mentality and drugs to the reservations. In the cities they are still the lowest of the low but their difficulty in finding work and lodgings remains an unacknowledged issue. I am yet to hear a single Native American reference from either Presidential campaign. Of the various Native tongues that I have been hearing, the common denominator from an otherwise incomprehensible language, is that they all lisp. Can any of you linguists out there confirm this?

Temperatures were rising fast as I rode south and the longjohn conundrum was becoming prevalent. Mornings and evenings are bitterly cold, but the middle of the day is proper toasty. Letting it all hang out at the side of the road while I change, is sure to mean a passing car even if there hasn't been one all morning and you can see for 5 miles each way. Trust me, it happens.

In this parched landscape the road takes you over massive plateaus, so large and flat that you forget you are on one, till nearing the edge you can see further than you can ever imagine. For miles and miles the panorama is of nothing really, save for the classic western flat top mesa and the odd weathered standing column like in Monument Valley (which is amazing). The landscape is so immense it's difficult to capture on film. The distance you can see from the edge of a mesa is comparable only to perhaps standing on a chair in East Anglia. For those of you in the Fens with a head for heights, give it a go and you might get some idea of what I mean.

By the time I reached the Painted Desert National Park the colour of my surroundings had changed. Diminished was the yellow and brown, instead here the reds and whites and stripes of blue and grey are like nothing else and over such a huge area- probably about the size of Wales. Aren't most things? From within these eroding layers of sedimentary rock a petrified forest has emerged. A forest of giant trees that have been fossilized and perfectly maintain the pattern of the wood. Their colours are such that most of them appear red or brown and woody, until you get close and realise they are perfect mineral facsimiles and much heavier. Here too, as with Wyoming and southern Colorado there are incredible Dinosaur remains, which the various states seem keen to promote, so it must be safe to assume that these are not the states that teach creationism.

I'm not entirely sure what I was expecting of Holbrook. Probably some nostalgic idyll, where all the houses have an art nouveau feel in funky pastel colours and all the cars are from the 50s and 60s, or at least have white wall tyres. No I don't know why the two periods should coexist so seamlessly in my mind, but they do, but this is old Route 66 country. It runs right through the heart of the town. This is where the chicest of concrete teepee motels is and that isn't a collection of words you hear everyday.

I found it, an icon of 50's popart, right there on the strip between all the other motels with their whacky sign designs in funky neon.

Alas it was one of the very few that was still in business, most having been boarded up, or vanished altogether, just their 30foot high signs remaining to beckon you into an empty parking lot. The wandering human inhabitants, like a goodly number of the vehicles in town, had seen much better days and many were finding it remarkably difficult to navigate the arrow straight footpath at 5 in the evening. I couldn't afford the asking price for a night in a pointy concrete tent, which is a shame, as the opportunity my never arise again, but after my expensive night in Tuba I had assured myself that only absolute degradation was affordable for the foreseeable future.

I followed the 66 out of town until it was swallowed up by the main Interstate 40, but it occasionally reappeared alongside the highway in a dreadfully forlorn state: broken tar, perhaps single lane where the I40 had eaten directly into it, grass poking through here and there and every so often it would be just a gravel farm track. Desolate buildings, some still advertising services to the passing motorist, were rapidly returning to their constituent organic parts. It was all terribly sad, but I rode the 8 or 9 miles that are still accessible west of Holbrook, until the last mile became a much underused concrete dual carriageway and finally I stopped, dismounted and found myself

"Standing on a corner in Winslow Arizona,
oh it was such a fine sight to see.
There was a girl, my Lord, in a flatbed Ford
who slowed down to take a look at me.
Well, I took it easy, I really took it easy,
I wasn't going to let the sound of my own wheel (bearings) drive me crazy.
I may lose or I may win, but I doubt very much that I'll ever come back here again,
so I just sat and took it all in. Oh yes, I took it easy."

And may I just say huge apologies to all the writers of iconic rock anthems that I have ever abused in the past and will doubtless continue to abuse in the future. You should however be flattered, Mr Eagle you wrote the soundtrack to my angst ridden Irish youth, and provided momentary escapism from the weather.

I ate in an old Winslow diner by the side of the 66. It was all formica counters and gaffer tape holding the vinyl seat covering together. I sat in a booth that Harrison Ford had once sat in (yippee!) and was waited on by a couple of the campest Mexican Americans I have seen. The place was full of real men in cowboy hats and women who were so fat they could only sit in a way that would normally be described as pornographic. There was Z92 FM Country King playing on the radio, 'United We Stand' posters everywhere proclaiming allegiance to the rapidly changing and increasingly misunderstood ideology of the Flag and these two mincing around between the tables. Fantastic! What a land of contradictions!

In daylight it is easy to see that Winslow Arizona has very little going for it, except a corner that people come to stand on, where they can pose for their photograph beside the brass statue of an American dream, a vagrant musician. There is a red flat bed Ford truck parked up and two souvenir shops selling Eagles and Route 66 memorabilia. To all intents and purposes that's it. It is still on the railroad, but Interstate 40 takes most of the traffic around it, and a goodly number of the buildings, both commercial and private, are in poor condition. I stayed in a room in the Winslow Inn Motel which smelt like it had been scrubbed from floor to ceiling with disinfectant. The hostess said her cleaner was meticulous. I presumed it was just after forensics had been.

My plans for the immediate future involve Sedona, the Grand Canyon and Las Vegas of course, so that I never need to work again. But they are just plans, and the plans of man are but thoughts and ideas easily revoked should anything more interesting crop up in the meantime. Speak to you soon.

19 GETTING MY KICKS...

Riding out of Winslow on the original two lane, sectional concrete, one way system that so defines the town and its history upon Route 66, I headed for Sedona. Rumour had it that there was beauty in Sedona, and that there were trees. This I had to see.

Approaching from the main Highway, I took the Schnebly Road, because it looked twisty on the map and had a very funny name. The map didn't say it was gravel, but hey ho, off I went anyway. After about 6 miles I was greeted by an amazing vista of red rock mountains rising from a base of green. Trees! There really are trees in Arizona! As I sat at the top of the overlook, taking it all in, two pink jeeps appeared and pulled in. Full of "Tourists on Safari" as it said on the side. I said hello and was simply stared at, which was a little disappointing. At least if they had been Japanese I'd have been photographed but the descent towards town from the viewpoint helped me fill in the answers to a few questions that were written on the people's faces. For me, "on Safari" as scrawled on the sides of the Jeeps, had seemed a little excessive for a trip up a gravel road, even if most people are used to perfect 4 lane black top. When I started down to the valley it all made sense, as did the way everyone in the jeeps had stared.

The track became a single, narrow, gouge in the

mountainside. It was steep, strewn with boulders and deep sand, had wash outs that were so deep I caught the sump of the bike in them and tight turns with no protection from the edge of deep ravines. The views of the reddest red rocks were stunning, all weathered into stacked tiers with horizontal crevices and topped off with giant boney fingers reaching to the perfectly blue sky and lit by the late morning sun. So at last I was getting some practice in for the more challenging roads I'm sure to meet south of the border.

I had passed a big warning sign saying that passes for the red rocks must be purchased at the bottom of the track, but there had been no mention of that when I pulled in off the highway 12 miles earlier, so I planned an exit strategy. It involved my throttle hand and worked admirably. This is, of course, a complete fabrication should you, or anyone you know, work with the Sedona Parks Authority. I did, of course follow the arrowed route to the payment booth and did not, at any time, choose the more direct one past a barrier and towards the main road into town.

Honest.

Sedona is a very beautiful town. Not with the grand architecture of Cambridge or Bath you understand, but in an American way. It has blue skies, colourful buildings and a backdrop of red rocks and bright green foliage. It is wealthy, white, and has an inordinately large number of people with beaded hair. Sedona has energy..... man!

"The majestic red rock scenery and evergreen vegetation are two reasons for the unique energy of Sedona and its tangible regenerative and inspirational effects. The red-orange colour of the rock is one of the most neuro stimulating of colours. It enhances creative thinking and problem solving. Because Sedona is framed year round by green, visitors are also bathed in a sense of hope and renewal, regardless of the season. The spectacular trails and overlooks provide numerous opportunities for prayer, and contemplation. Sedona is also internationally known for the uplifting power of its Vortex meditation sites. Two aspects of those sites make Sedona truly special. First within a very small geographical radius you can easily access all the different types of vortexes (upflow/ masculine/ electric, inflow/ feminine/ magnetic, or combination/ electromagnetic, etc.) Second, the Vortex sites are interwoven with the real world of a growing city. As a result, seekers have experiences in how to live their spirituality as they go through their daily lives. Rather than having to escape from civilization to find peace, visitors discover that Sedona's splendour gives them insights for how to create an inner harmony they can maintain once at home."

WOW! Tourist brochures.

All that energy must be why Sedona is the only place in the world where the McDonalds does not have golden arches. Apparently the council thought they would "Like, totally clash with the redness of the rocks and create a really bad vibe, man." So the arches are turquoise, which is much more Navajo, though there isn't a lot of room for actual Native Americans round here. Turquoise arches or not, it's still bloody McDonalds though. Don't the ethics of a company like that "create bad vibes and karma and stuff"?

But Sedona is also famous for its residents as well as its arches. Apart from various actors, John McCain, down to earth war hero, man of the people and presidential hopeful, has a ranch here. One of the eight properties he owns. Well, he is Senator of Arizona, though perhaps not for much longer, if the Arizona Daily Sun is anything to go by. There are many articles about his failing in the polls and a very entertaining letters page with some very savvy letters from fundamentalist Christians discussing taxation, economic policy and the Christian Right itself and America's place in the world. They all seem to rationally discuss the new Republicans and especially Sara Palin which is refreshing, except one chap.

Step forward, Donald Young.

"The issue of abortion transcends the taking of life. It has to do with absolute truth. We believe there is absolute truth. Without absolute truth there are no ethics."

Following so far?

"McCain is closer to a believer in absolute truth than is Obama. Obama is a post-modern believer in relative truth; that is, your truth is good for you but not me. He is willing to sit down and talk to those who hate us"

See the seamless link?

"If Obama is elected and continues his path of appeasement, a war will surely follow".

A war eh? Blimey! America wouldn't want to get into one of those! One other article that caught my eye was about white supremacists from Tennessee and Arkansas, caught with a plan to behead blacks across the States and to assassinate Obama, all whilst wearing white top hats. It was thought that although they had managed to stockpile guns and machetes they were probably too disorganised to instigate the whole plan. I suppose that's because there isn't a Moss Bros outlet in the south. There was no mention of sentence, so perhaps they'll be taught to read and write…

Americans have assassinated four of their 43 Presidents already, so assuming Obama makes it to be the 44th there is a good likelihood that someone will have a go, law of averages and all that, which isn't a great advert for electoral college style democracy. That isn't what I find disturbing. What gets me is that in this time of enlightenment at the start of the 21st century, the number of white supremacist organisations in the US has increased from 602 to 926. Can there really be that much hate and stupidity around in these days of that great educational tool, saviour of us all, the internet?

I headed north for the Grand Canyon and passed a wild fire that started with a lightning strike on 7th of August. It had been assumed the monsoon rains of Sept had put it out, but it rekindled itself two weeks ago. The plumes of smoke meant that the sunset was affected in the canyon, but it really didn't matter. The main thing is that the Canyon is a very, very, big hole in the ground, and I feel there are many who can describe it better than I. I sat and looked at it, which seemed the best thing to do. Then I got on my bike, rode 20 miles down the road and looked at it again.

There's no point me giving you all the stats, other than it is a mile deep and unfortunately, on 22nd October 2008, Robert Jenkins 58, from Chicago, was the 5th person to fall over the edge this year. They lose 12 a year on average, though half of them are heart attack or heat stroke victims. The rangers reckon that one person over the edge for each million visitors isn't a bad average.

I went to a lecture in the evening on the Californian Condor, which lives in these parts and is the biggest bird in the continent and is slowly recovering from almost extinct status. It stands four and a half ft tall and when it flies, has a wingspan of nine and a half feet. I have to say that I didn't see any, and although my ornithological expertise doesn't extend much past, "look, a little bright blue job," I do believe I would have noticed a bird that likes to feed on deer.

I met a bloke called Matt, who rode down from Alaska on his 650 BMW and managed almost 50 miles a day in the snow while he was doing it. That was in September, which I believe in youth speak, qualifies him as Hardcore. He shared my campsite for the night, because he is even tighter than me and in the morning I did some work on his bike, which desperately needed servicing. His chain was on its last legs, and his tyres really short on air. Having got out my tools I was fired to do a few of the outstanding jobs on Peggy too, and figured that anybody with such a laissez-faire attitude to maintenance was cool enough to travel with for a few days. If we were going to cruise the old Route 66 and throw away our watches, we both needed a cruising buddy anyway and for me, Matt seemed perfect.

Of course I didn't actually throw away my watch because I find it terrifically handy to tell the time, and it was a present from my sister, but time certainly went somewhere as we cruised the concrete and tar, stopping at the surviving cafes, motels and little stores. He bought me a bottle of Root (66) Beer in the famous Hackberry General store, which although tasting strongly of Germolene, I grew to rather like. I should mention here that there weren't exactly any other buildings in Hackberry, but I couldn't work out if there ever had been and whether the I40 bypass was to blame yet again for destroying a community. The surrounding tumbleweed didn't seem to be hiding any collapsed civilization and it's not as though things have rotted in this climate.

Many of the bigger towns on the 66 had the "two streets, one way system" of Winslow, and it meant we could do a real easy rider cruise side by side past the boarded up buildings, admiring ourselves in the windows of the few that were still in good repair. I knew that there was a barber somewhere on the old road, called Angel, who had been responsible for the whole Historic Route 66 Association and the revival of the nostalgia, and since I needed a haircut, I thought that he should be the man to do it.

Finding a very art deco hairdressers, I went inside to inquire. Eadie Desoto told me that Angel was now 92 and had retired, though he was occasionally to be seen in the town of Seligman where his shop was. As disappointed as I was, both that he was retired and that I was in the wrong town, I really am no connoisseur of barbers and can't tell Vidal Sassoon from Red Ken (even now that he's out of office). So I thought given that Eadie had a pretty cool shop, made as it was from an old Texaco garage, and that it had an old car on the roof, here was as good a place as any.

As luck would have it, I met Angel the next day, riding his bicycle, and he confirmed he had retired, and nowadays only cut the hair of travelling Irishmen. Sadly I had none left, so he posed with me for a photo instead, beside his 1950s Dodge pickup outside his shop. What a lovely man. Seligman is the town that the movie Cars was based on and where we stopped for the night, camping in the village next to the famous "Roadkill Cafe" - you kill it, we grill it! The site was full of Bullhead thorns, so cleaning our tyres kept us busy for a few hours in the morning, but at least I was relieved to learn that the rattlesnakes have all pretty much gone into hibernation now, though the tarantulas are mating and the scorpions still hanging around…

Having a few beers in the Roadkill, I discovered that Holly, 5'8", 210 lbs, dark blonde, who was working behind the bar, had moved out here to the Arizona desert from San Francisco under the witness protection programme.

Oops. Sorry.

From Kingman to Oatman and on to Golden Shores, the 66 is as original as is possible. It is narrow, twisty and off camber as it makes its way across the desert floor and then climbs into the mountains. This was real motorcycling heaven: the ride and the peace and quiet, not so much the nostalgia, but because all the other traffic was on the new freeway. It is true that many people used this route to reach LA and start new lives, especially families like those in Steinbeck's The Grapes of Wrath during the 1930s and all the movie stars came this way with hopes of making it big in Hollywood, but does that make it historic? There aren't many roads in the British Isles that are younger than Route 66 after all, but I suppose emotion isn't a tangible thing. There haven't been that many songs written about the B4 to Enniskillen, but it's been taking people to market since Mr and Mrs Columbus had dreams of their little Chris growing up and broadening his horizons. Billy Bragg may have tried to inject a little mystique into the A13, but what a road to choose!

Camping was getting more difficult for me as soil gave way to rocks and my tent uses tent pegs. Matt found my efforts to weigh down the corners with stones very entertaining. It was at least successful, unlike his attempt to find us a place to camp outside Oatman. Going up a small rutted track he settled on a spot. Bare in mind this was Halloween and the village of Oatman is an old haunted mining town that is populated by donkeys. Really. He chose us a spot on a rocky hill. In the failing light all the surrounding graves and dead dudes weren't immediately apparent. We slept soundly to the sounds of donkeys and coyotes.

Matt and I parted company in Bullhead City, Arizona after four great days together but I hope that we'll stay in touch, we seem to get along really well. I headed on my way to the Hoover Dam, Vegas and Death Valley, he went to see family in San Diego. It was 102º F. Oh what a change over the last few weeks. So near sea level and much further south. I pulled in to Matt's Motorsports in Bullhead for an oil change and found them all drinking beer because it was Saturday. The oil change was gratis and they sent me away with 2 litres for the next change! Good ole boys! Most of their work is on jet skis and speedboats because of the location on the great Colorado

River. This is leisure pursuit city where every big boys toy is available to rent or to own so that you too can do your bit to wantonly waste resources.

I shall pretend that my own ambling activities with an internal combustion engine are somehow more valid because I'm not going round in circles, and because I can think of no other reasons, but I probably just want to feel aggreived about rich people having fun.

The Hoover Dam, completed in 1935 and a 726 feet high wall across the Colorado River, created the now rapidly shrinking Lake Mead and without it there would be no Las Vegas and no perfectly green lawns and golf courses like those in Boulder City, where I saw two signs on a junction: to the left, the Veterans Home and to the right the Veterans Cemetery. Handy. Lake Mead, which has lost a third of its capacity in the last five years, enables California's agriculture to exist and lets every household in three States use a dishwasher, except those in Palm Springs who prefer a little Mexican. It provides green grass where there should be none and permits people with no dress sense to play golf under a perfectly blue sky, which I'm sure is never what was intended when the Scottish thought the whole game up. There was meant to be challenge, battling against a force nine and driving rain. Good sport for a God fearing sinner on a bracing day.

Worryingly, in this time of heightened terrorist paranoia, the dam is protected by Wackenhut private security guards, all of whom were playing cards in the shade, having instructed the scared looking YTS kid to inspect the traffic. No one was stopping for him, and it looked like no one else cared. Security must clearly be their number one corporate goal.

I stayed the night in a casino- well when in Rome- and made my choice because of the eye catching 50 foot neon sign outside saying "God Bless Our Armed Forces".

And perhaps because of the little one beside it that said all rooms $25. I parked Peggy up beneath the big sign and removed my pannier that had a sticker saying "No US War In Iraq". You know, it's just diplomacy. And survival.

Time was spent wandering the floor watching the various games and trying to work out how they were played. Roulette I get, but Craps? And who thought of the name? The lines upon lines of one arm bandits seemed to be attended almost exclusively by late middle aged to positively old, women, apparently mesmerised by the lights. All the gaming machines take credit cards, as do all the machines that are set into the counters of the bars, which I feel I should be morally outraged about and thus pen a strongly worded letter. I spent a long time trying to fully understand the machines, but they appeared so complicated. Holding lines 1-10, or playing a multiple of lines, or betting on lines, or doubling options, I really couldn't work it out, and given that without fully comprehending all of the possibilities and therefore completely engaging with the game, there was the risk that I may lose my quarter and not actually win the jackpot. Those sorts of risks are too much for me, so my 25cents stayed in my pocket.

I was up before the sun and looked out my window to the blackness of a desert only 28 floors below. While I was loading the bike I met Mr Vanishing Point, about to set out for another day on the road. Just like in the movie, he moves cars around the country for people who would rather fly. He was on his way to Houston, Texas from Portland Oregon, driving 17 hour days. He'd been doing it for a while, that distant look in his eyes gave it away.

I hit the glitz of Vegas before the sun rose, to see the lights and the monstrous vulgarity of the buildings. 5000 room hotels, built to ape castles and pyramids and innumerable Disneyesque structures that just screamed "tat"! It's ugliness didn't disappoint and neither did the people. It's a 24 hour city and I met the stereotypical gambler in a petrol station. 5am and a little bit pissed, drinking black coffee from a styrene cup, he had slick back hair, was slightly over enthusiastic, and had a mad glint in his eye. He directed me to the main strip, the safest street in the world. Apparently my picture would be taken 1000 times as I moved along it, though I'm not sure of the safety correlation. He had obviously never been to Britain and walked down any High street on a Saturday night. All those cameras seem to correspond with an increase in violence if anything, or at least an increase of the recording of violence, which is great for the programme makers on Channel 5. My local guide explained that if I turned left I would be robbed, and if I turned right I would be murdered, "Just stay on the strip and then get the hell outta this town while you can". Local knowledge really brings a place to life don't you think?

I followed his advice, rode the strip but ended up mesmerised rather than repulsed at this insanity in the desert, and then headed for Death Valley to keep up the violent theme. I followed a Hummer with the registration number "zerompg". Oh our American cousins, how they embrace environmentalism! After the previous days' high temperatures I was bracing myself, so it may surprise you, as it did me, that I rode into Death Valley in my waterproofs and at 20 degrees off the vertical to cope with the wind. Flash floods had closed some of the roads and it was a particularly game Ranger who opened a gate for me to go to Dante's View, a peak 5000 ft above the valley. He warned me that he would not acknowledge my existence and if I was caught would have to say I had come in on the 35 mile dirt road from the south. Good man, that's the spirit! The flash flooding had certainly caused a few wash outs, but I'm sure most of the 4x4s and SUVs could have coped with the inch or two of gravel I encountered on the road.

Dante's View although incredibly windy, offers the most amazing panorama of the whole valley, the salt flats on the valley floor, the tiny strip of tarmac that appears as little more than a thin pencil line on a massive modern art canvas of whites and the palest of browns. Since the road to the viewpoint was officially closed I had the whole thing to myself for as long as I wanted to just stand there and stare down on land that is 282 feet below sea level and sinking. Only a month ago I was slithering up Pikes Peak in Colorado trying to climb about 13,000 feet at the wrong time of year and now here I am, about to ride deeper into the earth than anywhere else in the western hemisphere, which I presume means west of Greenwich. Whatever you think of America's politics or dietary habits, you've got to admire the diversity of the landscape.

By lunchtime the rain was gone, all trace of it, and the heat was getting intense. I cannot for a moment imagine being here in the summer. There is nothing living here naturally, except a few tiny moluscs in the semi-permanent waterhole at the valley's lowest point, the aptly named Badwater Basin. Like riding through Nevada earlier, or Utah, or Arizona the desolation is amazing, only more so. What a place.

Just think, there is tarmac which offers the pretence of security and survival, next to the most harshly desolate landscape. Here but for the grace of an internal combustion engine go we. I'm sure people aren't meant to be here, and we take it all for granted.

I get on the bike and press the button to start the engine, then just sit there dumbstruck at the amazing parched landscape, doing everything possible to not visualise that little piston beneath me, banging up and down in its own harsh environment, ingesting air full of sand and dust, being cooled by fluid last checked in the factory (if I'm honest) and lubricated by oil designed to work well anywhere but the heat of the desert. And all the while explosive power is turned into motion and transmitted to a rear wheel by a chain that is coated in a grinding paste of oil and dirt. Yet it keeps going. The air stays in the tyres, the tubes don't explode, the bearings don't collapse and the desolate landscape rolls on for mile after mile after mile.

Groups like the 49ers come out here for parties, and the crowd of bikers I met in Furnace Creek come out from LA just for the ride. So much is taken for granted. No, perhaps it's blind faith and let's face it there aren't many countries with as much of that to go around. The bikers were a run of the mill bunch, who spent most of the conversation berating the EU and Mexico. Mexicans will all stab me if I'm stupid enough to go south of the border and Europe is the same as a communist State, stealing the individual's right and freedom to carry guns and 8 inch knives, (in a bid to stop stabbings perhaps?) but there seemed no conflict in the two statements. In Europe they've even banned TV to keep the populace stupid, so maybe that's something I should check on the BBC website, but I'm disappointed none of you thought to write and tell me.

The 49ers are a merry band of RV owners keeping alive the history of those who travelled to California for the gold rush of 1849. Many prospectors came overland and some even managed, unbelievably to cross Death Valley and then get over the Sierra Nevada mountains. It is a story worth reading if you get the time, one of arguments, madness and human indecision, as wagon trains split into smaller and smaller groups, risking everything and with no guides, to get to the West. Many more went by boat to Panama and travelled the 80 miles overland before catching another boat back up the west coast. However they got there, what is interesting, is that with all the new found wealth, California was invited to become the 31st State just a year later.

Crossing the mountains to leave to the west, I finally saw a coyote and stopped for a picture. Having never seen one before I was amazed at its size and quite bushy tail. More than that, I was stunned by the fact it wasn't timid and turned to approach me. The nearer and faster that it got, the quicker I realised that it bore an uncanny resemblance to the taxidermied wolf I had studied in the Roadkill Cafe.

My Italian winged steed Pegasus whisked me to safety, whether the danger was perceived or not.

The temperature dropped dramatically as I headed due north to Bishop up the Owen Valley in California, a depression maybe three miles wide between two rows of mountains. Sun from the west behind the Sierra Nevada lit up the lower mountains to the east. All the peaks of the Nevada range appeared to be smoking like unsettled volcanoes with the sun from behind illuminating the snow being blown off them. It was a great road to watch the dynamic nature of the landscape canvas. Loads of colour was slowly being stolen by the shadows of the higher peaks to the west and as all the tinting was finally taken with the setting sun, I was left with black and white and only the sky in technicolor. I rode for Yosemite.

Damn. I awoke next day and realised I'd caught the weather again. Yosemite was closed and so were all the roads over the mountains towards San Francisco.

The return south had the more majestic Sierra Nevada on my right and bathed this time in morning sun, so I could see how they soared from the 4000 ft valley I was in. Soared? Eagles soar, mountains don't soar, not least because that suggests movement and these peaks hardly move. Well, hardly move is probably right, because the mountains round here actually do. They are all slowly rising, forcing Death valley to tip up and continue to sink on one side. The point is not the movement, it is the soaring. I must remember to avoid cliches, like the plague. They make people incandescent with rage. No, what I could really observe with the sun hitting the mountains directly, was that they were as naked as the day they were born, smooth as a baby's butt on their lower reaches, yet as sharp as an axe higher up. The road was as straight as an arrow. Maybe you can tell, I was bored.

It was a mistake to have gone north the night before and now I was paying a dead straight 200 and something mile penalty for not thinking. Come on, if it was raining in Death Valley, surely it might have been snowing at 11,000ft in the Sierra Nevada? But all was not doom and gloom by any means. From leaving Bishop, where bizarrely, autumn appeared to be just beginning, the route back down the Owen Valley took me through a change in vegetation from some trees, to scrub, to absolutely nothing, to cactus as I rose away again and finally turned west. The change was slow but definite, though when I began to climb in earnest and crossed my first pass (Walkers Pass, for those following at home!) the change was dramatic. Scrub and funny little half cactus, half pampas grass trees on one side of the pass, became a mixture of vegetation and loads of it, on the other. Just like that. The difference between the west and east slopes was like chalk and cheese, day and night... oops it's happening again. These Sierras are so big they can create precipitation and yet completely control the climate and landscape either side of themselves for hundreds of miles.

Still, aside from that, the road from Isabelle Lake due west for 52miles was heavenly, a gem that I have never read about before and perhaps one of California's great riding secrets? I know I've said it before about roads in the north but there was never a moment I was on the crown of the tyre. Just grinning from ear to ear (uhh, cliché!) I tried to avoid the odd layer of sand and gravel that appeared where a stream had been incapable of holding the last few days' torrential rain and burst over the road. It was a fantastically technical ride and in the 52 miles I met one bike and a farmer in his pickup. That was it. The last few miles wind their way gently through the rolling hills of yellow grassed farmland, which is a nice way to come back to reality. The only things paying attention to me were the cattle, all of whom stared with that bovine curiosity and intrigue they are so famous for. They had added a liberal quantity of their own technical challenge to the road surface in places, so no doubt were just checking to see how I'd cope with the slippery brown obstacles. I told them not to stare and that they should be grateful they weren't living in Wyoming or Arizona, even if their grass was yellow.

And then I was in pure productive California. Lemons, grapes, olives, walnuts almonds and peaches as far as the eye could see, all liberally watered by the runoff from the mountains and with arrow straight roads between.

Tomorrow is election day! The making of History?

The man with no face in beautiful British Columbia

Canadian Prairie

Sunrise, Salton Sea, California

Photo—M. Stevens

Lake Tahoe, California

Positively prehistoric bison

Two in a bush

Moose on the loose

Damned mosquitoes

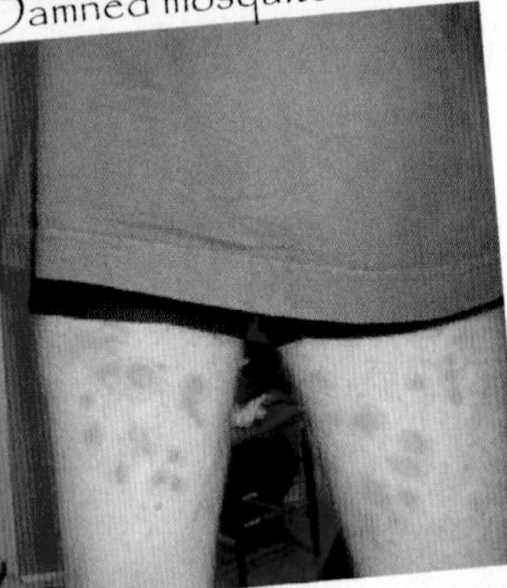

What's his name then?

Home from home

Mark and his son Joey in Halifax,

Uncle Charlie and Aunt Adele

Glenn and Gwen

Jon and Penny

Freddie, Elois, Brigette, Baptiste and Paul

Jane, Will, Ducie and Maeve

Ian and Angela,

Mexican sentiment?

Everyone's sentiment

American sentiment?

My Sentiment!

California sunrise

Mini moto

Now this is riding corrugations!

Lake Atitlan, Guatemala

Sierra Madre, NW Mexico

Ometepe Island

Blue Creek, Belize

My mate Matt

Jessie, Michael, Ciska and Sammy

New Years's Eve

Such a charmer

Pure Mexicana

Love from Honduras

Indigenous women, Chiapas

The ubiquitous CG125 Honda

Zapatista country

Freshest beef I ever had

Guatemala smokin'

Pacific sunset

Costa Rica

Tikal, Guatemala

With Matt and Jason in Guatemala

Copper Canyon,

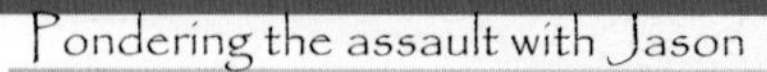
'Crasher' Matt strikes again

Pondering the assault with Jason

Glorious mud

Look mum, it's a gang!

Mexican Jungle

Shopping in Guatemala

A Celt in the sun

Fixing that very first electrical gremlin

The diners never noticed, Belize

Incoming dust storm– Guatemala

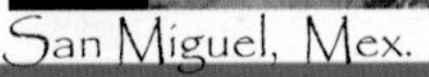

San Miguel, Mex.

San Christobal, Mex.

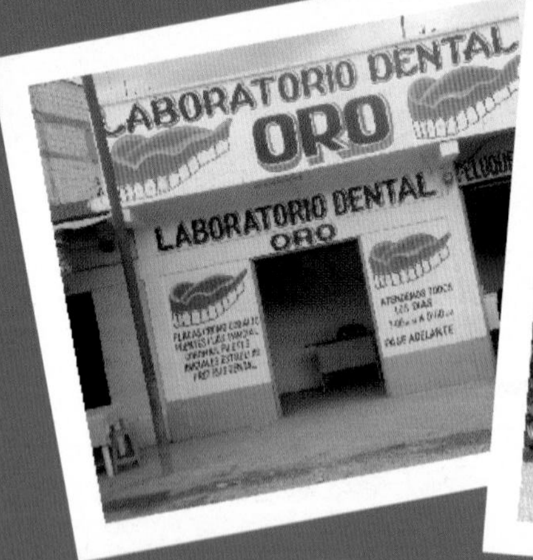

With Lee, Baz and Matt in San Juan

20 THE GLORIOUS 4TH OR A PILE OF POO?

Californ eye ay! Home to beach bums, surf dudes, vineyards, alternative living, liberal thinking and gang violence, (but really only in LA, and Oakland). There is one way to reduce that feeling of all round general Californian grooviness though: intermittent sleep due to the severity of the rain on the tent, and getting up with the dawn to discover that Chicken Lickin was right and that the sky really had fallen down. It seemed to hover immediately above the trees, just out of reach yet ready to engulf my little encampment at any moment.

Bummer. Dude.

I was only at 500 feet yet due to climb to seven thousand into Sequoia National Park, to see more giant Redwoods, but this time the super fat ones. The rangers let me in, but said there was a slight snow dusting in the upper reaches of the park. The road immediately climbs steeply and in no time I was through the low cloud and fully embraced by the medium height cloud, which was trying hard to regain altitude by depositing its contents. It was a futile activity because the medium cloud was hemmed in by the upper cloud layers which were full of snow. By the time I got to 6000ft I was jolly cold and meeting vehicles which had wiper shaped holes in an otherwise uniform suit of deep snow. Getting onto more level ground and starting to cut my own tracks in the snow on the road, my sodden gloves cleared enough snow from my visor to let me read that the next open visitor service/toilet was just 27miles. "Bugger this for a game of darts" I thought, and headed back the way I came.

It was by no means a disappointment though. I got to re experience some giant redwoods and saw a pair of young teenage black bears that were really brown, looking like they had been left out in the rain. Which, of course they had. Their mother was nowhere to be seen which is just typical of the irresponsibility and lack of guidance shown by single mothers today. I informed park ranger Jim at the lowest visitor centre, who assured me they were Black bears, just brown ones and not to be confused with Brown bears, which are brown. He also denied that there were any mummy bears that were of questionable moral or ethical standard within the park, so she would have been somewhere close at hand. Although the Californian flag features a Grizzly bear, they are of course extinct here, leaving only the brown black bears. Rather like the American Bald eagle which only now survives in Alaska, and Canada. It's good to hunt! On my descent I also had particularly close encounters with various creatures of the deer kind. One poor unfortunate felt trapped between a rock and a void place, given the way the narrow road wound round the mountain. In a state of panic it chose the void place. I stopped and peered over the edge but couldn't see through the misty gloom to establish whether or not it possessed any feline attributes.

I had a word with a fellow motorcyclist near the entrance and told him that there was a lot of snow up in the Park, after the rain cloud layer. He looked at me as though I was quite mad and said he'd driven all across the valley this morning and there was no sign of rain, so he was quite sure there wasn't any snow in the park. He even did one of those infuriating little arrogant snorts. I suppose

I can't blame his superiority complex, it comes with BMW ownership. Bitter? Who, me?

I was soon barrelling across the flat agricultural valley inhaling pesticides and getting sleepy, so I took a dirt road for 40 miles to cross the last range of lower hills next the Pacific. Uppy downy twisty roundy (don't you love my descriptive prose?) through the treeless, yellow grass and dust landscape, I got a bit of a surprise rounding a corrugated corner in a valley to find a river. My first good ford of the trip. Disappointingly it was only about axle deep and there were no crocodiles to liven things up.

I headed north to Hollister. Famous for not very much except when a slow weekend of news in 1947 led to the press embellishing a story about a gathering of motorcyclists, Hollister eventually gave us the immortal line "What are you rebelling against?" to which Jonny replied "Whadda ya got?"

The "riots" that tore up Hollister that 4th of July weekend, and ensured that for the rest of the twentieth century bikers would be viewed with fear and suspicion, did involve the arrest of some bikers, but only for speeding and drunkenness. Oh the creation of cultural legend. What would we do without a slow news day and Hollywood? Other than a mural of a young Marlon Brando on the side wall of 'Jonny's Cafe', there seemed to be as much about Hollister now that was wild, as there probably ever was.

In failing light I cruised into San Francisco at the end of rush hour and headed for the radio tower that is a landmark near Jane and Ducies house. Cold but happy and full of apprehension of the coming night's election results, I arrived to a house in darkness.

"Bugger, they aren't home yet" I thought, so set to and brewed up a cuppa on the doorstep.

Siobhan texted me from home with some early

election results, so I called to see why she was still awake on the other side of the world. She decided to phone Jane for me and see where everyone was. You see every time I had tried her number, I got a man who was becoming a little irate at being called Jane. It always makes me feel like Ewan and Charlie when expedition headquarters in the UK sorts everything out!

I got the message to break in, which I duly did, hoping that the dogs wouldn't lick me to death, or the neighbours call the police. It was all just in time, because I could feel a stirring and a rumbling down below that wasn't an earthquake, even if the world was about to fall out of my bottom. Then there was one of those moments that only ever happens in someone else's house. When it transpired the first flush wasn't enough, I left the cistern to refill and thought I'd try later. What I had to do immediately was get some laundry in the machine, get showered and try to generally improve my personal hygiene the time my hosts returned home.

I was against the clock.

It didn't help then, to return to the loo for flush number two and discover that cute little puppy dog of computer cable chewing fame, had beaten me to it. It appears I'd left a veritable feast in the bowl. Now there was poo on the floor, on the toilet seat and all round the bathroom and his little feet were walking it around the house!

Aarrghh!

I hoped I had it all cleaned up and was able to exude an air of serenity by the time Ducie came home. I think I carried it off too, even when he said, in that wonderfully base, colonial way, “there’s a weird smell of shit in the living room”. Had I missed some?

And then we settled down to watch the election. Did you hear about that? Some guy from Chicago won it.

Tears? Wow, what a thing. To put it in perspective, Ducie's parents had been denied the vote, refused college access and queued to get on the blacks only bus. A generation ago! Now that is why this country is such an enigma. It gives you hope, well it gives it to me anyway, though I'm still apprehensive of going to Texas...

I went for tyres in the morning and tried a new approach when it came to paying the bill. It was already a cheap deal, primarily because the boss saved on any kind of customer service. Nowhere to wash hands after taking out the wheels, no waiting area and an intercom that he used to scream abuse and obsenities at his staff. My tactic was this:

"So what's your name then?" (note, I wasn't wearing my hat)

"Whaddaya wanna know for?"

"Oh just for the book about my travels"

"You're writing a book eh? Joe, bring me over that check for our Irish friend."

Yes, a $30 saving. It works! A pair of Bridgestone Trailwings fitted for just over 200 dollars. Compare that to my painful experience in Winnipeg. On a roll, I headed off to find chain and sprockets and a few odds and ends. This time the chaps at SF Moto threw in a free set of brake pads! Now I had a dilemma though. What do I do, what do I say? Do I take the freebie gratefully, or do I speak up?

"Awe thanks very much, that's really kind of you, but they're the wrong ones"

"What? That's what the book says."

"Well it's FA 213s or 208s that she takes" says I, as obsequiously as possible.

"Oh, alright then, I'm sure you must know that bike well by now."

And that was it! Can you imagine telling a bike dealer in the UK that they are wrong? I headed back to begin work, and to give Peggy a good clean. In this cosmopolitan metropolis, she was feeling very self-conscious, surrounded as she was by gleaming Italian Ducatis and Moto Guzzis. Frankly my Latin lady was embarrassed at what she had become and I owed it to her to improve her jaded appearance.

The next few days I had a ball, using Jane's Vespa to scoot around the city. I love it! I want one! Unfortunately the seat lock is broken and Jane said they wanted 200 dollars for a new one, but it will have to be ordered "that's the problem with running an Italian bike in the US". Oh yes Jane, it's so different in Europe! Not.

Alcatraz was nice, and that's not something you hear everyday, but it was. The audio tour was excellent, but that'd be why they call it "award winning" no doubt. I also had a walking tour with Ranger Lori, who told us about the 100 prison guard families that lived on the island while it was a prison. It sure seemed idyllic, even the way she told it and she was certainly knowledgeable, so when she asked if there were any questions, any at all, I did think about how spiders make that initial leap when they build their webs, or where humanity might be if we didn't have opposable thumbs, but kept them to myself.

I saw the breakout cells of 1962 and the birdman's isolation cell as well as where the riot happened, which the marines broke up with grenades and shells- just like in the movies!

The view of the city must have been the most cruel part of incarceration on the island. There was no glass in the windows, so apart from the cold, the inmates could hear city life when the wind blew from the west. You could also see the incredible currents that surround the island which, combined with the icy temperatures, made swimming impossible. Did you know that only those who broke Federal law went there? Murder isn't a federal offence, but nicking stuff is, just like tax evasion. Now there are priorities. The only murderers who made it there went because they broke lesser prison rules in a different institution!

You'll not be surprised to hear that what I found the most interesting was the exhibition about the occupation of Alcatraz by the Native American student activists in November 1970. They managed to stay 15 months on the island and in so doing rekindled the concept of Indian identity as well as reversing the 'Termination Laws' among others, which were designed to remove all Indian reservation land and renege on all the previous agreements the government made with the indigenous population. Well I had a great time anyway and learnt a lot, which I followed by a ride down Lombard Street, that famously well kept steep twisty street in the city where hundreds of Japanese tourists took my picture. I like this town.

Using the underground one morning, I noticed that at one station, only young men got on and what's more, they were the most neatly coiffured and best dressed men I had ever seen. Almost absentmindedly I found it was way too easy to make eye contact and felt briefly unnerved. We'd just passed through the area known as Castro, and there is no gayer area in no gayer town. Then I caught sight of my reflection. With my hat, shorts, t shirt and borrowed shoulder bag I suddenly realised I looked as camp as they did, though perhaps in Village People terms, I was slightly more builder. It really wasn't what I needed because I had finally come to terms with my skinny white legs and had enough self consciousness to deal with. I had decided to embrace my whiteness. Dammit I am a Celt. Yes, I am reflective, but in these days of ethnic identity, I'm trying to learn how to be proud of it, and anyway, with enough factor 50 the sun burn doesn't really hurt all that much.

Castro is at the very heart of liberal California and it was here that the first openly gay man was elected into Californian political office. Unfortunately Harvey Milk was then assassinated and probably not for the reasons you might imagine. He was incredibly popular, successful and fought for all minority groups, but was shot by a jealous, unstable fellow politician in 1978. After all this time and development I was witness to the rebirth of gay political activity as California voted in the election a few days ago, to overturn the laws granting same sex marriage rights. I wonder if a figure as charismatic as Harvey Milk will emerge to unite the movement.

I then had a mad night out with Ducie and friends, culminating in dancing in the "Boom Boom Room" to a band called Papa Mali, who manage to seamlessly meld blues, jazz rock and hardcore trance. And it was San Francisco. I was really in San Francisco and for a while I felt I was in 1968 at the cutting edge of youth culture and it was groovy. Everything was groovy. Man.

Perhaps more amazingly though, I met James Connelly's great grandson, not surprisingly called Che, and he is a policeman, with SFPD. Now that is mad. James Connolly was one of the executed revolutionary leaders of the Easter Rising in Ireland in 1916. Che and I had a whale of a time, talking about Irish and South and Central American politics, until I lost my voice (and he was relieved). But his maternal family is from Honduras, so I may have more people to meet. Yippee.

I will buy my anti malarials on Monday, depending on the price and head for the border. I must say I am getting a little pissed off though with the number of people in the last month who have been warning me about Mexico.

"Watch those Mexicans", well that's not going to

hard, there's 250 million of them!

"They'll get you" etc etc, and always from those who've never been themselves. What is concerning me is the distinct lack of roads and bridges due to the flooding and landslides all over Central America. And if I'm honest, perhaps I'm a little apprehensive about the resurgence of Shining Path in Peru, the impending civil war in Bolivia and the riots in Ecuador, but I'm sure it'll be fine...

For now, I'm having a great time, with great hosts, in a great city, and Obama is President!

Yee Haww! Me Partisan? Who said that?

21 ALICE'S RESTAURANT

I'm sad to be leaving California. It has fantastic roads, incredibly diverse scenery and the people don't seem to harbour the same fear and paranoia that the rest of the country does. It does however, feature the same infuriatingly inconsistent characteristics. While California State has just managed to get the amount of the carcinogen Acrylomide reduced (but not removed) from fast food, freedom fries and Pringles snacks, in an attempt to improve the health of the people, and while it leads the nation in renewable energy and environmentalism, it has just slashed it's education budget by 2.5 billion dollars, following last years cut of $3 billion. Staff are being laid off, classes increased and colleges "restructured". While it is a consistently Democratic and green state, it has a Republican Governator in the form of Arnie who owns millions of gas guzzling vehicles, and while being sexually liberated, has just voted to repeal its same sex marriage laws.

This country as a whole seems to think it is in love with its veterans. There is a Veteran's day (though it used to be called Remembrance Day), Veteran's highways in every State, Veteran memorials and an acknowledgment that it is the Veterans that make America great and safe. It is just such a shame then, to go into any large town or city and see many of those veterans, discarded and on the street. The amputees and the homeless and the addicted and the traumatised, all still with their flags, all still proud to serve the nation that now steps over them. I was fortunate to chat with some of the homeless vets in SF who were selling the 'Street Sheet' which raises awareness of the homeless problems. This is the reality of those veterans that keep America great and free and safe, and are then spat aside at the end of their useful time. Of the 2,213,000 vets in California, 47% have no income whatsoever according to a report I read in the Los Angeles Times. You see, for society to help these people they are so indebted to, to actually pay that debt, would be something akin to socialism, and heaven forbid the government should get involved with that! Unless it's called a corporate bailout of course, because that is apparently so very different. But the nation has been involved in various forms of socialism before, especially when it has found itself in a financial mess and I, as it happens, have been the grateful recipient.

Surprised?

Well so many of the fantastic roads that I have ridden in the last 3 months, through stunning landscapes, previously inaccessible and remote, were built as public works during the last depression to provide work, stimulate the economy and install a much needed public infrastructure. With the mass of physical labour and the minimum of machinery, many of these feats of civil engineering had to follow many of the contours of the earth, and I am so, so glad. Highway 1 down the coast of California is a great example and what's more, for the architect in me, it has some great period 1930s concrete bridges which just ouse late art deco style! If this economic downturn turns into the full blown recession that has been threatening to materialise for a couple of years, I wonder how many scenic road building projects Obama will instigate!

I have experienced an election with a truly historically significant result in a period of tremendous economic flux, even though the votes haven't all been counted yet and probably won't be until December 2nd. 2.7 million still to be counted in California and it's certainly not alone. This is a great type of democracy!

While the stock market continues to tumble there have been some rallying shares: McDonalds and Tupperware, which kind of says "Junk food for dinner kids, and the left overs for breakfast"

There is physical evidence of the failing economy around though too. Obviously there are a lot of houses on the market and even more that are just lying vacant. Ebay witnessed a house sale in Tennessee close for $1.65 and yes, the decimal place is in the right place. Everyone seems to have a vehicle for sale at the end of their drive, and as for the numbers of homeless I am witnessing, I have no idea what the norm is, so can't comment. There are an awful lot of Estate Agent shops for sale or let though, so it's not all bad.

I am being warned daily about the risks of travel to Mexico, (mostly because they've never heard of Guatemala or Ecuador), but this is a country which has so many homicides and shootings they barely make more than one line on page 10 of the papers or a 20 second snippet at the end of a local news bulletin. I'm told to be aware of all the diseases in Mexico, but there is plenty of bubonic plague, typhoid and rabies in the US too and I don't recall seeing that in all the holiday brochures.

A jogger in Arizona was bitten by a rabid fox at the weekend. The hospital is certain it was a fox, because the woman jogged the two miles to casualty with the fox still locked on to her arm!

Yes, it is an amazing place, with some of the smartest minds in the western world and clearly some of the dummest (no b intended). It has some of the richest people on the globe and a wealth disparity possibly matched only by Zimbabwe. They spend a colossal amount on personal cosmetics and yet I am staggered that some can afford the acres of material necessary to get dressed in the morning. I know I said I'd lay off the obesity, but there's time for just one more wee story. I watched a Mitsubishi Spacewagon approach me the other day while I waited to cross the road. Now those of you who know your motors will be aware that this is not the hippest of vehicles and certainly not something often chosen by the well wicked kids on da street for to slam inta da weeds. Ya get me?

And so I paid this Spacewagon some attention as it approached, almost scraping its undercarriage on the road. It was then that I noticed it had but two occupants....

So yes, I left San Francisco and my wonderfully accommodating hosts with some regret. It is a city like no other both architecturally and socially. The climate is generally stable, though there is such a thing as autumn when it finally arrives. This nation is so big, with so many climatic variations that it is possible to chase the seasons in a day or two. No leaves on the tress here and just starting to change colour there. San Fran has a lot of eucalyptus though so it always maintains some green.

Riding south along the coast on the famous Highway 1, I headed back inland after about 50 miles and made my way through the coastal mountains on great twisties to Alice's Restaurant, "where you can get anything you want.... excepting Alice." This restaurant is perfectly positioned at the confluence of four great riding roads and is, as you'd expect, terribly popular with motorcyclists. I had heard that the burgers were nothing to ride out of your way for, but I dispute that heartily.

The menu has a motorcycle theme. The BMW

burger, though looking robust and coming with a long list of optional extras, seemed a little culturally misplaced with its Worcester sauce option. I settled for the Honda, primarily because they couldn't get the ingredients for an Aprilia burger… It was a succulent, huge, perfectly cooked piece of chicken breast in a wholemeal bun, with loads of fresh ingredients dressing it, plus Swiss cheese and sautéed mushrooms. What's more, the tea was hot. They used boiling water! First time on the North American continent.

I chose the Skyline Boulevard south from Alice's and rode the ridge. To my left was the whole of San Francisco bay area and to my right lay the Pacific. It was perfect riding and perfect sightseeing in perfect weather in perfect California. Camping beside the Big Sur River I noticed ample proof that there had been some very big floods in the area, but the iddy biddy river looked so sweet, I camped on its banks anyway in complete denial of the possibilities. There weren't actually any signs that said it was a flash flood area, but then that may have been because they had been washed away....

Riding the stunning pacific coast I passed the famous sign that has graced the pages of many a motorcycle magazine. It says twisty road, next 74 miles. I had to keep stopping for photos though, what with my surroundings and the fact that Peggy just looked so shiny after her makeover in San Francisco.

I was so impressed with the shiny object, 'my precious', that I forced her against her will to pose in front of some cliffs for a picture. The rugged coastline, with blue Pacific surf crashing on the small golden horseshoe beach in the bay below and the stunted pines seemingly clinging on to sheer rock, was the idyllic backdrop. But like a recalcitrant child, she got the hump and promptly threw herself to the ground.

Her new headlight bulb blew, her right hand mirror

broke off leaving an ugly stump and the bars bent in the yokes. Bloody kids! I was so angry with myself that I straightened the bars in my own fit of pique.

All angst subsided though with the sight of a huge Elephant seal colony that was so relaxed it was possible to get really close as they lay in the sand. There was some argy bargy as males proved themselves at one end of the beach, and I must say I am sure these creatures move with the utmost grace and fluidity in the water, but boy do they look stupid trying to chase each other on land. I cut inland again towards Palmdale and read with delight, "road not suitable for trucks, semi trailers or large RVs". Yes, good choice for bikes then!

It led in the end, to oil oil oil around the towns of McKindrick and Taft. Derricks stood everywhere, nodding their heads in continual agreement and stainless piping passed all over the desert floor. The smell of crude was pervasive and ironically I ran out of petrol for the first time on the trip and had to use my spare can. Then seamlessly it was fruit and nuts again, even derricks interspersed with vineyards, before I climbed again into the hills north of the LA metropolis and through that distinctive vanilla smell of hot Ponderosa Pine trees. With more great twists I headed up to 6500ft and to the town of Idylwild, which is a beautiful, heavily Christian town in a beautiful forested setting south of San Bernadino and on towards Palm Springs.

Over more mountains and a couple of days later I was rolling down into the valley of Palm Springs. With every bend the temperature rose until it was truly oppressive. 99 F and out of the desert came this town with perfectly manicured roadside verges and flowerbeds, tended by an army of Mexicans. Gated communities everywhere and a kaleidoscope of rainbows as the sprinklers worked overtime to claim this piece of dirt from the surrounding desert. It was obscene. Really. True, it looked amazing, not a blade of grass out of place, but what a waste. No one even enjoys the temperature, they hide in air conditioned buildings and move around in air conditioned cars. What is the point? And this is the winter! I took advantage of a great photo opportunity at the city limits where the sprinklers stop and the desert starts. It is environmental lunacy and not a bit wonder that Lake Mead is shrinking at the rate it is.

It's a town that a lot of millionaires call home, most famously the big tipping Frank Sinatra. I didn't stay very long. The Bauhaus and Art Deco architecture of many of the properties appealed, but the heat, the displays of wealth and the million dollar reconstructed faces sported by so many of the pensioners, really didn't.

I was pointing southwest and due to meet Matt with whom I had ridden the 66. He'd made a decision, and his cross country trip to see his Mum in Vermont for Christmas, was to be put on hold. We'd shared a few beers on the 66 and I do believe that one night I had alluded that Vermont would mean more of the snow he left behind in Alaska, while Mexico meant tequilas, beaches, sunshine and beautiful olive skinned women. It appears that I put forward a convincing case, I only hope that he hasn't been influenced by my hat....

We agreed to meet at Slab City, a huge free camp community in the desert, built on land vacated by the military and now populated by snowbirds in the winter and every type of drop out hippy and alternative living beatnik for much of the rest of the year. There are a few hardy souls that survive all summer in temperatures that consistently get into the high 40's C, but I was interested in seeing the place because it featured quite heavily in the film 'Into the Wild', a really moving story about Christopher McCandless travelling as a vagrant throughout the US discovering the beauty and joy that exists in the simplicity of everything, and the huge importance of human relationships. It seemed as though Matt and I were about to embark on something that would combine the importance of friendship, with just a bit of our own vagrancy, so it was apt. We failed however, at the first hurdle, and met up 50 miles away instead. A good start.

I waited to hear from him in the biggest dump of a town I had yet seen. Niland. If things weren't already broken they were boarded up in readiness for the event. Every second vehicle was either police or border security and I can't say there was a freelove and happiness aura to the town, so I finally met Matt near one of many immigration checkpoints and we camped a few miles down a sandy track on the side of the Salton Sea. At 220 ft below sea level, this was almost as low as Death Valley and right on the San Andreas fault. It only formed in 1905 when the Colorado river was in flood and breached some dykes but it is now little more than a collection point for all the drainage from the overly irrigated agricultural land to the south. We walked in the moonlight to check out the beach and choose a spot to camp, crunching over the sea shells and gravel. Until I turned on my torch and realised that it was in fact dead fish, as far as the eye could see. Concentrated sunlight and all the pesticides and fertilisers that the farming community add to make this corner of the desert productive, create a toxic soup in the Salton Sea. Good choice for a campsite.

We chatted like excited school kids about what we'd been doing and what might lie ahead. After my taking the piss out of his toolkit and sundry other items in his luggage, Matt had made some big changes and sent home 30 pounds of stuff. His toolkit had certainly been comprehensive when we met at the Grand Canyon, it's just that it comprehensively fitted some other bike.

I can't knock him (though I did), because he was very much learning on the job. He'd even sprayed his bike black so that it didn't look so conspicuously extravagant which is certainly in the spirit of things, though he did use hairspray instead of paint. It hasn't rained yet. While I was getting parts and servicing Peggy in San Fran, Matt had been doing the same in San Diego as well as trying to arrange his health and other insurances and get documents essential for border crossings, posted from Alaska. Normal people spend months planning a trip like this. I think we'll get along just fine.

The sunrise was beautiful, with the moon still in the sky. The colours and reflections in the poisoned Sea filled us with a serenity that felt good. Together a new chapter was beginning in this trip. Serendipity had got herself involved and I was glad. Then Matt fell off before we began.

We headed for slab city and also to see a guy nearby called Leonard Knight who had been flying across the country from San Diego in a balloon 40 years ago, when he crashed nearby in the desert. God found him and he has never left the area. Instead he has painted the desert. Literally. This is a thankless task, because the desert doesn't seem to take kindly to his work and weathers it somewhat, trying to reclaim the area and wipe out the Jesus Loves you slogans. He has built what can best be described as a building, out of the detritus he has found, and old hay bales that have been gifted to him. Inside it's pleasantly cool, and as a shrine to Jesus, I'm sure He's grateful. Leonard is a joy to talk to and full of enthusiasm for his project. The painted logs and adobe walls are certainly colourful and all the scrap vehicles covered in slogans brighten up an otherwise very sand coloured part of the world. However; God may well have found him, but I think the sun got there first.

On the way north to see Leonard, I had stopped for fuel and some kids came up to ask about my travels. The Hispanic kids down here near the border may be some of the poorest in America, but they are friendly and always wave, it's just the authorities that are scared witless by their own propaganda. Anyway, after telling the kids I was going to Mexico I walked into the shop passed an old Mexican guy sitting on the curb. He barely looked up and spoke from under his Stetson, keeping the sun from his eyes.

"You going to Mechiko?" Yes, I beam, full of excitement and expectation.

"Well, I ding you nee to durn a rown. Meh-hee-co ees behine you".

How very spaghetti western.

22 HAZARD COUNTY

Well that's not very fair is it? I leave California and they declare a state of emergency. I'm sure it wasn't just my departure, though no doubt I broke a lot of hearts. No, they seem to be having a bit of a forest fire over there at the minute and I'm missing it! I passed through the remains of many, both recent and historical, I even saw that the visibility in certain areas near LA was worse than even smog could achieve, but I didn't manage to see an up close, really out of control fire disaster. It's just so unfair.

I even jumped up and down as heavily as I could on the San Andreas fault and nothing. Nada. Not so much as a tremor. This whole earthquake thing is blown way out of proportion, probably because in California the seasons don't really change, there aren't ice storms, floods, hurricanes, tornados. Just glorious sunshine and a bit of a breeze off the Pacific to cool things, should an unsightly moisture mark appear on clothing, or a bead of sweat taint an otherwise civilised brow. There is really nothing to complain about, it's all too lovely. It's almost like they need a bit of a disaster, or at least the threat of one, to fit in with the other States.

"Well you know it isn't all perfect vistas, idyllic landscapes, temperate but dry weather, glorious beaches, wonderful fruit and veg production, heavenly vineyards, fantastic roads and an open caring, tolerant mindset here you know. We might have an earthquake at any time, it could be a living hell."   "Like Iowa".   "So there."

Matt and I rode towards Arizona through the Mojave Desert, past sand dunes and the classic tumbleweed and rock desert landscape, feeling, though perhaps not looking, like Easy Riders. In the Imperial Dunes, an area 45 miles long and 5 miles wide, we stopped with a gathering of dune dudes near Glamis for a chat and a cooling drink. Dune dudes are kinda like surf dudes, or mountainbike dudes, or paddlers, with the cool shades and the right matching labels, but without the same implied underlying embrace of their environmental surroundings. You see, instead of wave power or the harnessing of gravity to get their kicks, these people use 1000 horse power fire breathing dune buggies with paddles for back tyres that create 60feet high rooster tails and reshape the very landscape they use. They are at least, strictly confined to one area of desert as the authorities try to manage the whole region for all people and wildlife. The surroundings are so very fragile, they still bare the marks left by every wagon train of settlers that crossed the area 150 years ago in search of a new life and modern thrill seekers have managed to destroy ancient Indian desert art or 'intaglios' with their 4x4s. Having said that, there are nine military bases in the Californian desert, totalling some 3.2 million acres where they aren't immune from chucking the odd exploding rocket about, so the environmental protectors have a difficult job.

The buggy racing looked like loads of fun, but nobody I asked was prepared to lend me their $70,000 toy, so we were forced to leave and continue east on highway 78, which was first built as a plank road over the sand in 1915 to shorten the route to Yuma. It's an incredibly unforgiving area and certainly isn't over endowed with trees, so every plank travelled miles before it was used. It was about 15 miles the east of Glamis, (which is really just a big Dune Buggy and RV shop), that we passed a man walking along thumbing a lift. I've no idea from whence he came, or where he was going, but that's the desert for you. Maybe it was a mirage.

This close to the border with Mexico it really seemed like every third vehicle was either police or border security. The 1950 mile land border is now patrolled with helicopters, 4x4s, nightsights and every type of modern surveillance and detection equipment, and while there was always condemnation of the wall that divided Europe for so long, the US is in the process of constructing something similar to that which Israel is illegally building. It could be said that both are the result of wanting to protect stolen lands, it's just that the theft is separated by a century. It was after the war of 1848 that the USA got half of what was then Mexico. The areas now known as Arizona, California, Nevada, Utah and a good amount of New Mexico, all used to speak Spanish and it would appear, in a neat twist of fate, soon will again, regardless of a border policy that spends millions holding back the workers that the US economy can't afford to be without. For Native American nomadic tribes, like the Kickapoo whose lands straddle the relatively new political line, a wall is going to be somewhat problematic. It's interesting that there isn't talk of building a wall along the 49th parallel to keep the Canadian immigrants out.

All the police and border agency checkpoints reminded me of growing up in the border region of Ireland and even though the initial sight of them briefly knotted my stomach, passing through seemed to consist of rolling up to the stern looking men in uniform, lifting my helmet to reveal my Caucasian pinkness and thereby securing my onward passage. It appeared that being an alien wasn't the issue, just being a tanned Spanish speaking one with a thick black moustache was.

That was until I discovered that Hazard County is

in Arizona. Well it certainly must be, because it was a real life Rosco P. Coltrane that pulled me over in a flurry of lights and sirens. In short, an idiot with a gun and a badge.

Officer E H Simpson demanded to know where and why I had made such a stupid license plate for my bike and where my real one was. I explained that I wasn't from Arizona and that I didn't have an Arizona plate because I was passing through. I concurred that it was a stupid looking plate.

"But there aren't no gosh darned way you can ride that motorsickle in the United States of America with that mickey mouse license plate."

I explained that there was, and that I had been travelling in the US for 3 months, and that there was such a thing as a carnet de passage temporary importation document for travellers passing through a foreign country with a vehicle, but that as a European, North American countries didn't require it.

He demanded to see my permit to drive. I showed him my international driving license.

He demanded to see my permit to drive in the US of A. I pointed to what he was holding.

He screamed that this didn't show nuthin' and wanted to see my permit as he threw my license at me. I wanted to show him the page that was written in English and contained my photo, but he grabbed his gun.

Matt grabbed the camera.

I caught my tongue.

He called his base and they told him he was right, it was illegal and he was to take my number plate and give me a $600 citation. I asked what a citation was. He as good as spat in my face. I tried to show him my insurance, but he didn't want to see it because it didn't "have a damned thing to do with him whether I had insurance or not" which is odd given that it did. It's the law.

I offered him my registration document which he

accepted, until he saw it.

"What'n the hell is this boy?"

"My registration document."

"Don't you try bullshit with me, I've bin in this job fur twennyfive years and there ain't no registration looks like this"

"But this is a British one, showing my ownership entitlement, address and the number of the bike."

"Like I said boy, this ain't what registration looks like. Don't mess with me boy I know my job"

So I asked if I should have a Montana plate since that was where I had entered the country. He wasn't one to engage in rational argument, but (perhaps) realising what he had previously said led to such a conclusion, said yes. I said no one told me at the border. He said that Border Security and customs wouldn't know road laws. I wanted to say that they may know a thing or two about imports and exports though, but didn't, the gun was being fingered again. He wanted to know who had told me that I could enter the States with my bike. Rather than mention things like the internet, which we all know is the work of Satan, I said that the US Embassy in London told me.

"Damned Federal government don't know my job" (and you don't either asshole)

For such a tiny mind he had a huge attitude. Things continued in a similar vein for 15mins until he screamed, and I quote:

"Don't you not never feed bullshit to a bullshitter, son."

I was stumped. That many double negatives take a moment to process, but I wondered if I should point out what the statement implied about his own storytelling? Alas I had no time, because he continued that no one takes motorsickles across borders anyway, and there is no such thing as anyone having the right to drive in a different country.

I suggested travelling Canadians and really shouldn't have. He called the office again and I put on my hat. Well you never know, but it may have worked. His attitude softened marginally. I explained that when he took my number plate off I could never leave the US and travel onwards. He couldn't understand why, but in this paranoid border area the thought of his being responsible for the existence of an illegal alien may have scared him. Perhaps the office had found out they were wrong after all and he needed an exit strategy, which is unlikely as they aren't very fashionable in the States at the minute.

He put away his gun and told me not to make up crazy stories about documents that let you cross borders and permits to drive. He told me I was lucky that he didn't call for my bike to be towed and that I wasn't arrested. He then explained that I would never be able to enter the US again if I got the citation. Hell, I wouldn't be moral enough!

It's good to know that George Dubbya is passing another 90 laws before he leaves office, most of them handing more powers of arrest and surveillance to twits like this, though some are to relax laws protecting endangered species and the environment. It said on the side of the patrol car "endeavouring to serve". Perhaps, but there's still a long way still to go.

Matt was terribly apologetic on behalf of his country for the appalling behaviour he had just witnessed. I explained that no trip of mine passes without some engagement with the Repressive State Apparatus. He thought of the road ahead and I could see in his eyes thoughts of us getting royally rogered in a Mexican jail.

Rather than go to Tucson and register Peggy with the Arizona authorities as instructed, we headed for the mountains to get away from the police and the heat, 'cuz we is villains now' and because after a few days in the desert we were both almost salivating at the possibility of a couple of corners. Do you remember I asked what Arizona was for? Well there's a town in the south called Why, so they really don't even know themselves. As for the town of Superior, I can confirm there is one thing that it's not.

Frank Lloyd Wright the world renowned architect, designer of ergonomic homes as well as dramatic houses like "Fallingwater" in Pennsylvania (constructed over a river), built himself a house near Phoenix and founded a school that is still generating forward thinking architects to this day. Unfortunately very few of them seem to be practising in the area. Taliesin West was a new start for Wright when he moved here a few years after his lover Mamah, her two children, the gardener, one of his draughtsmen and two workmen were killed in his house by his butler with an axe, which you could say was a lucky escape for him, or a serious game of Cluedo.

All Wright's students started their education here by building their own accommodation from the resources available to them in the desert, giving them a grounding in what may be possible to create, which must have saved many a punch up in the future when they were tempted to present unachievable plans to the builders. He never really made a lot of money or gained the recognition he deserved when he was alive, which must class him as an artistic genius. Interestingly the open plan 4 bed house he built nearby in 1951 for his son, is currently on the market for £3.5m. Oh the fickle nature of the property market!

We had a tour of the place, even though there was a graduation ceremony going on and then we seemed to spend a few days on the Phoenix ring road, which is bigger than the M25. A huge sprawling metropolis, most of Phoenix was built after 1980 and there is subdivision after subdivision to pass, before heading higher into the mountains to camp. For three days straight we wound our way towards New Mexico in the mountains and forests and camped above 8000 feet, which was incredibly stupid. Every night we wore everything we had and slept with the cooking fuel to ensure it didn't freeze. The water containers were actually frozen solid and I couldn't get my roll matt to deflate in the mornings because the spittle inside kept freezing the nozzle. Another first was having ice form on my woolley hat, while I wore it!

The second or third night, as we set up camp by a small lake (that was frozen over in the morning), I did the dishes after dinner and they froze while I was trying to dry them. Later in the evening our precautionary camping arrangements behind a small bank of earth, paid off when first the police and then possibly concerned locals came up with searchlights and scanned the area for vagrants I suppose. As we held our breath and kept low we were grateful for their concern. It made us sleep more comfortably knowing there weren't any vagabond travellers about!

The thing is, we were stuck each morning until the sun was high enough to warm the batteries on the bikes because neither of them would start, which was quite embarrassing when passers by stopped to enquire and were regaled with stories of possible adventure to come, just as soon as we could start the engines. Another camp spot was by some hot springs in the Mogollon Range and I felt terribly Finnish sitting starkers in a steaming rocky pool, save for my woolly hat, with everything around me frozen solid. Of course it meant we could have tea for breakfast, (leaving our water bottles and butane in the hot water overnight) while discussing all the wolves and coyotes that were hanging around through the night in this rabies ridden part of the country. (There are more cases in Arizona this year than ever before). We were joined by Jim from Vermont who had been on the road for three years with his dog Amigo. He moves around the country in his VW van working with disturbed kids and chaingangs, but much as he'd love to head to Mexico for the winter, doesn't feel brave enough! He rehabilitates criminals and violent adolescents for goodness sake, there are few jobs that are tougher. Oh what stories about Mexico have entered the American psyche?

After we both posted some more things back home, (another 15lbs for Matt) which was terribly exciting for the lady in the tiny San Lorenzo post office, because she hadn't done international before, Matt announced he now had room to carry a spare tyre.

"Why"?

"Because your bike looks so cool and my bike doesn't. Everyone talks about your tyre. I need a tyre. Then I'll look like an adventurer."

"You don't you fool! You're doing it, you are an adventurer!"

"No, I gotta have a tyre too, it's hardcore"

"If you really want hardcore, you need a grill over your headlight"

"You reckon?"

"No. Lets ride"

Playing in the mountains took us into New Mexico and up over Emory Pass and through Black Canyon, really great roads where Matt had his first ever footpeg scraping experience. He thought my two highside attempts were great when the usually sliding tyres gripped, jettisoning me out of the saddle, so I just said "oh yeah, but don't try them till you have more experience....". Play it cool, he beats me at chess and pool all the time so it's only fair...

This is Apache land and we explored the Gila Wilderness Area (the first declared wilderness in the country) where Geronimo was born, but from Emory Pass there is a great view of much of the old tribal lands, the lands that also contained gold and copper. The Apaches weren't to keen on the European invasion, and there was a bit of a skirmish. You may have seen the movies. Anyway, the Warm Springs Apaches were forcibly removed to Florida in 1886 where the damp climate killed loads of them almost as efficiently as the small pox coated blankets that used to be handed out as gifts by the military. It was 1911 before any of them were permitted to return to New Mexico and to what had now become privately owned or government land. The government then went on to use their land to develop the atom bomb, so the Apaches got a bit of a bum deal all round.

We climbed through old Pueblo Indian cave houses from around 1200 and sat in awe as the setting sun transformed the landscape by lighting the rocks in a different colour every few minutes. There are lots of Pueblo Indian settlements in Arizona, New Mexico and Colorado all of which were abandoned between 1250 and 1300 AD. It would appear there was a prolonged drought, not dissimilar to that which the region is currently experiencing and life was no longer sustainable. They hadn't yet mastered the sprinkler system, or built a dam they could name after a vacuum cleaner.

Then it was south towards the border at El Paso, passing field after field of chillis. The town of Derry is just a chilli processing plant surrounded by Mexicans bent double in the fields under an unforgiving sun, which is just slightly different from its Irish namesake. I had a chat with a bus load of workers in Arizona who were deposited at a gas station to buy hot dogs crisps and coke. This was their daily 30 minute break between 6am and 6pm cutting lettuces in an irrigated patch of desert. Most of them seemed to be in their 50's but were so weathered it was hard to tell, as they hobbled towards the shop. No-one would tell me what they earned, they weren't allowed. The gang master stood by the bus, which towed a porta loo.

We luncheoned south of Derry in the town of Hatch, New Mexico (chilli capital of the world) and I know I was probably taking a risk, but chose the restaurant that said it catered for all tastes. Matt promptly fell off outside to entertain the diners.

One bite of a 'super mild' burrito and I thought I'd entered my final moments. How can anyone pretend for even a moment that chillies are good? What is the point of blowing your head off and killing all of your taste buds? How am I going to get through Mexico without loosing too much weight? The chef brought me cheese and ham and a bowl of salad. They'd never seen anyone go that colour before.

And so to Texas, "Proud home of President George W Bush" as the signs declare. We hunt for bike spares, water purification tablets and assorted other goodies in preparation for "the crossing". Having done an oil change yesterday my oil light is now flashing on tickover, but we found some black sticky tape to cover it, so everything is fine now. Although El Paso is a thriving city, generally the border region of the US is not. There are 48 counties in four states bordering Mexico and officially 27% of the population lives under the poverty line. Water supplies are generally regarded as "suspect" which I wasn't sure how to interpret until I drank some. I'm still a little gurgly.

We had some border experts demonstrate their complete lack of knowledge: "You must pay for your tourist card at the border, with your credit card." I told them I didn't have one.

"You must have one, otherwise you will be charged a bond of $400 or $600 dollars" Well, which? And why? And if it's a bond, what's it for and when do I get the money back?

"Because the guards are corrupt." So I give them my credit card details? That sounds like a plan!

"The bond is because you don't have a credit card and you get the money back when you come back to the US" But a bond for what exactly? And I'm not coming back to the US so can I get it back at the border to Belize?

"It's just a bond, and you must be coming back, everyone does" I am going south.

"Yes, but later you will come back, how else do you get back to Ireland? Well if you don't come back to the same entry point you lose your money".

What a load of nonsense. She also wanted 350 dollars for insurance that had no medical cover and had 33% excess on theft if the bike was stolen for good. For good? No ambiguity there then. "No, we may still find it, so we can't pay out yet, the police are still looking" Great. We decide to drive on and buy some insurance over the border. Even the bank tells us to buy Pesos in Mexico because we'll get a much better deal on exchange and charges.

I've just read in the El Paso Times that between January and September this year, the US authorities dumped 35,546 unaccompanied children in the Mexican desert in contravention of every international child welfare law that the US is a signatory to. A further 8,000 non Mexican children were also dumped there. If all these children have no papers, how do we know who are Mexican and who aren't. Also, surely the US is complicit in child trafficking if 8,000 aren't Mexican and are being placed in a country other than their own? Just a thought.

As I write this, from the bed beside me all I can hear is: "Amigo", "Friend"

"Amigos", "Friends"

"Mis Amigos" "My friends"

"Companeros".... etc

Matt has a Spanish programme on his Ipod. Now that surely is committed preparation and something I admire. Learning the language the day before we cross the border! I'll write to you all from the other side...

23 U S A(DDENDUM)

An addendum on the USA was never the plan, and I know my last mail was long, so sorry, but there's just so much to bore you with. I know I said I'd write from the 'other side', but Matt's having some documentation issues so now that I'm still stuck here in El Paso, I'll write a little more.

My motel is a beautifully preserved piece of late 60s kitsch. Everything from the foyer to the exposed stone cladding inside the room is genuine retro (?). The pool and the space for the chairs, the layout of the blocks of rooms, all pure resort, like a stylish Butlins with a huge Palm tree in the middle. There aren't any blokes with drainpipe suits walking around in dodgy cine 8, nor ladies in mini skirts, but there really should be. There is a sign at the front desk that says the management doesn't condone the trafficking of illegal aliens, which brings it all up to date, and a notice that sidearms are not permitted on the premises, which is timeless and rather comforting.

We were given a key, but I'm not sure why, given that the door has been kicked open so often we are able to unlock it with the "Do not disturb" sign that hangs on the handle. It's a bit of an irrelevance, because the sliding window has no way to lock it and anyway it's easier to just lift it right out. Everything was originally fitted in 1967 and untouched since, just like the threadbare shagpile carpet, the orange curtains, the broken circular table I'm balancing the computer on at the minute and the paper thin walls and ceiling clad in something the fire dept would love if they saw, but which provides some level of sound insulation. Not much though, which is why I can testify that presently there are two men in the room to my left watching cartoons, one woman with a cough to my right and a couple above who are currently expressing their affection for each other.

When we came back in last night after an Italian meal that Matt sent back and wouldn't pay for (he's clearly never been to Britain and learnt to bow his head and say everything is fine. Secretly I'm so proud of him!) what struck us both immediately from the aroma, was that someone must have broken in to our room and taken a dump and left. It's not beyond the realms of possibility

Luckily there are no bodies floating in the pool today. But then there shouldn't be, it's been drained.

So while I have some time and a power source I just thought I'd present something to ponder.

Why don't Americans have nut allergies? Everything that you can buy on the sweet stand has peanuts in it. There is no need to spend anytime choosing a chocolate bar, just grab anything and go. They all have peanuts in and all taste the same. The cereal bars contain peanuts, almost anything processed has peanuts in it. Surely it can't all be due to Jimmy Carter? My flight back from San Fran to Heathrow in August had a nut allergist on board (and I don't mean someone engaged in academic research) and no one was allowed crisps, Pringles, crackers, or to open a packet of anything made anywhere, which makes me wonder what kind of a holiday they had had in California.

When I was in a supermarket the other day trying to get some tea bags, I noticed an aisle marked Latino food, so went for a wee look. It would appear that Central

America is sponsored by Nestle. Latino Food seems to just mean Nestle products, which may mean I have difficulty sticking to my boycott....

While I'm on processed foods, I had often read about the beef industry using finishing pens to fatten cattle for slaughter for the fast food industry. Until you see them there is nothing that can prepare you for the sight, and smell. As far as I could see back from the road, and for 2kms on my odometer as I rode passed, there were caged pens, probably a few hundred feet square, stuffed with cattle standing exposed to the sun but for strips of canopy roofing. Some pens even had enough room in them for the cattle to lie down. Not too dissimilar to the cages that are on the back of the border patrol vehicles and used to pick up illegals, which is all very civilised.

The cattle get grain, steroids and antibiotic feeding by conveyor. Yumm, what a splendid thing the burger is. Of course the fast food industry isn't just beef, it's also fowl (foul?) and one of the biggest processors of all meats in the USA is Tysons. How's about that then? I first had my attention drawn to them in Nevada, where 3-trailer trucks rumbled passed emblazoned with "Have you had your Tyson today?" and I thought of Siobhan all alone at home and was grateful I didn't have a brother who might have felt the need to comfort her...

I've been warned that there are no drink drive laws in Mexico, but I'm not sure what they are in North America. I saw people barely able to walk in Canada struggle to get into their cars and drive off, and the southern region of the US is littered with roadside memorials and don't drink and drive signs where the witty locals have painted over the "don't" bit. I presume so many of the deaths are caused by the rural nature of the area. If no one comes along for a few hours and you have a mobile contract with AT&T there is no way you can call for help. Guess which (no) service provider I'm with?

I watched gangs of inmates picking rubbish from the side of the highway, under signs that said it is illegal to litter. Isn't there something ironic about that? Free citizens brazenly breaking the law and convicts clearing up after them. Or is littering an imprisonable offense? This is Texas after all.

If anything differentiates Canada from America, apart from the lack of paranoia and the geographical knowledge of her citizens, it has got to be books. Every village in Canada can support at least one book store, in the way that an American town seems able to support a gun store. In fact apart from the odd Barnes and Noble or Borders, outside San Francisco there don't really seem to be any bookshops, which might account for a great quote from Matt:

"Americans can maintain their incredible opinions because of their incredible ignorance."

Remember, he's American, so has more right than me to his opinion....

The US does churches like nowhere else as well. There are of course your main protestant denominations, Methodist, Baptist, Presbyterian, Lutheran of every type imaginable, and Catholic, especially now near the Mexican border. There is the Reformed Church, the United Church, the United Reformed Church, the Reformed United church (splitters), but it's the evangelical crew that really surprise. There are little power hierarchies in every town. Churches who've clearly been set up by individuals to serve their own power hungry egos. And the whole God Bless America thing is a tad overplayed I feel. I saw a woman in a t-shirt that had a picture of the Presidents in Mount Rushmore, overseen by an alabaster Jesus and the slogan, "The ONLY country where God Rules". Not sure what Dubbya would make of that undermining of his power, but as a born again he may well believe it. However it's interpreted, I feel there are one or two other theocracies that just may disagree. As you know, I have nothing against Christianity, but it seems that this is a nation that is obsessed with God, but not terribly sure of the principles of Christianity. Well come on, Jesus was a Capricorn. A sandal wearing, hippy Marxist one.

Creationism is being taught in lots of States, indeed there is discussion in the papers at the moment about Texas starting in the next year. Not surprisingly that doesn't seem to wash with those States like Wyoming and Colorado that base much of their tourism on Dinosaurs and geological formations, but it is an insight into the literal reading of much of the old testament that leads to such amazing intolerance.

I watched some nutters on the telly explain that the seven things that the Old Testament said would happen are now happening. They discussed where Ezekial writes about Russia and China having a pact to geographically extend their influence to Iraq where the US will defend the world. Where Iran hates the Jews and only the US can protect them and where the EU will govern the finances of the world. The Jack Van Impe Ministries have their own TV channel, but they aren't alone. Remember Billy Graham? Use the fear for whatever fundraising you want.

I understand that some US army recruits and Chaplains are now even trying to save souls for Jesus in Iraq and Afghanistan, much to the disappointment of senior command, who fortunately seem to have a slightly better grasp of the PR implications.

The TV here is fantastical and used for selling more than just religion. Take the adverts, from those for male enhancement and every type of drug for every type of disease you didn't know you had, to one I saw for waxed paper plates in the home. Feed your family and just throw them away. No washing up so more time for you! For watching telly I presume. What's landfill anyway?

But the news as I leave this great nation centres around whether or not the Big 3 car makers should be bailed out by the government. They have until Dec 2nd to put forward a good case for financial help and GM has already said it is prepared to sell five of its executive jets if the government will help. Five? That's certainly commitment to change. The credit crunch has really taken its toll on the auto industry. I see that the car companies are no longer offering 110% loans for their vehicles, but instead asking for 5% down payments before you drive away. Fancy that. The cheek, asking for you to actually pay for your new car, though Saturn is doing an introductory cash bonus rebate that can be used as a down payment.

What's even worse is that the American car buying public has begun to buy from the Orient, primarily I believe, because they don't break down. I'd buy Oriental on styling alone, because the whole American auto industry appears to have been used for work experience since the 1970's, with automotive stylists attempting to work out the concept of scale and proportion, before moving to Europe when they've got the hang of it and can get a proper job. There are some truly awful looking cars here and no matter how long I am exposed to them they just don't seem to become attractive, and this is coming from someone who once had a Skoda.

The Japanese and Koreans are providing vehicles capable of 40mpg while the big 3 still seem to think that 12- 25 is acceptable. The ubiquitous pickup truck is a classic. Reading the stats on the new F150 Ford, 'America's favourite vehicle', I see that the entry model, 4.6V8 and 250hp can carry 1300lbs, and the big one, 310hp 5.6V8 long wheelbase can carry 2010lbs. Economy from 15 to 19 mpg. The payload of the entry model is fractionally more than my 1.3 Fiat van used to carry, returning 60mpg! Why? They all have European arms making efficient engines in efficient cars. Please people, there is no penile correlation!

Oh, after that rant I just don't know how to wrap up. I could talk about the changing architecture as I went south through California, with the increasing Spanish influence introducing red tile roofs, spreading to southern Arizona and New Mexico where styles again alter to reflect the increasing severity of the sun with flat roofs, adobe coated walls and small windows to shield from the sun.

If I did that however, you'd switch off. Oh, you already have? Well I passed a mountain lion lying as roadkill a few days ago, ever seen one of those? And I had a Roadrunner run up the road in front of me in New Mexico. Beep beep!!

More cartoon capers to follow.

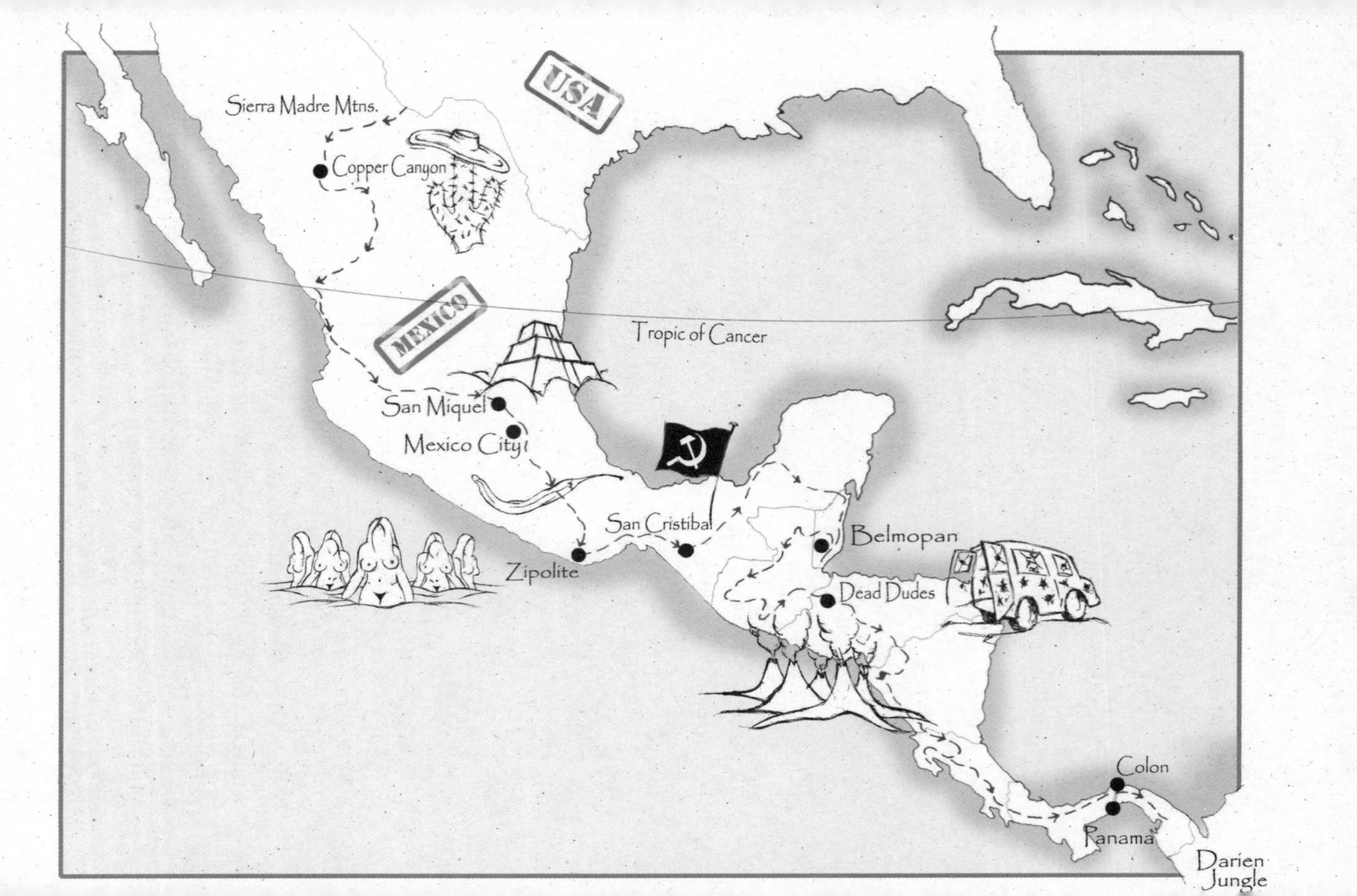
USA
Sierra Madre Mtns.
Copper Canyon
MEXICO
Tropic of Cancer
San Miquel
Mexico City
San Cristiba
Zipolite
Belmopan
Dead Dudes
Colon
Panama
Darien
Jungle

PART III

Latin America. Terra Incognita?

24 DOS CERVESAS POR FAVOR

Mexico waited for us, tantalisingly close beyond the Rio Grande. Which was neither rio nor grand. More stream piquente, though it had been very grande last month. So grande in fact, that the whole area was under water and the border closed to all traffic, literally. First however I had to leave the US, which seemed a little odd to all those officials I went to talk to at the border. Finally the fourth office I was directed to took the remains of my green card from my passport, to prove that I had left the US, but it was beyond comprehension that I wasn't coming back. They wished me luck. The Mexican consulate had wished me luck. The woman in the local chamber of commerce office in Presidio, who did our photocopying wished us luck, but then that might have been because Matt fell off outside her front door.....

The reason I had chosen this crossing, a very minor one, was that the lack of traffic would hopefully mean a lack of queues and hawkers on the other side.

"They're all mad you know, watch them, they'll steal everything you've got and be unhelpful."

We carried everyone's best wishes and, full of apprehension, we set off over the bridge.

As soon as we were through Mexican customs (a wave of the hand) I missed immigration entirely and rode on into town until Matt flagged me down. We returned, customs laughed. We parked up and immediately met Alfredo who was coming out of the building. Talkative and helpful, he said if we needed any help to call him in Chihuahua. Also to call if we wanted anything in the city when we got there. He wished us luck...

Then the helpful cleaner took us to immigration and the helpful polite and courteous immigration officer took us through the forms we needed. Round the corner for vehicle and personal permits a nice young lady with perfect English asked if we needed any help with translation. We didn't, yet. When we didn't have enough photocopies we were guided to a woman at the photocopy office who copied things for free. Manuel, who had befriended us by this time and wished to shine our shoes, offered to take my passport away to get it copied for me. To save me some time apparently. Then we ran into the only real bureaucracy of the whole day. The vehicle permits (not bonds) meant leaving our credit card details with the nice officers. Temporary importation assurance. If the bike doesn't leave, then $300 will be deducted from the card. Hmmm.

Good. So I can call upon my Carnet de Passage, bought for £3600 for just such an occurrence and the internationally recognised document that enables the crossing of borders and temporary importation of a vehicle. To which Mexico is a signatory.

The disadvantage of using a small border crossing is that no one has ever seen a Carnet before and won't accept it. Great. All in, the formalities take us two and a half hours, and could have been quicker, with fluent Spanish and a credit card, but not to worry, we are on the road and in Mexico, passing those segura cactus, the ones with arms that look great in a sombrero.

A police check of our papers and chassis numbers 30 miles later was followed by a military check on a bleak desert hillside. It was all very light hearted as they pointed their guns and got us to count from one to ten in Spanish before asking to see our pistols and drugs. "Pistoles y drogas?"

About 100 miles of mountainous desert later and we were in Chihuahua, home of revolutionary leader Pancho Villa and silly small dogs that yap.

Matt's first experience of driving in the rest of the world. He adapted really well after I just shouted follow me and look only ahead. I let all those dispatch riding tricks come to the fore and getting in the groove was a lot less stressful than stop start riding in the heat. Like everyone else we ran red lights, went round roundabouts the wrong way and went for every gap between the belching trucks and buses, our eyes streaming from the fumes.

We got an 'economico' hotel in the city centre that had secure parking, but also had blood splashed on the wall mounted telly and up the wall between the beds. There was even a shower rose which was promising, until it blew off onto Matt's head.

I had a mission in this town. Nestled deep in my trouser pocket was a 10 peso coin that my friend Sean had given me back in Bedford 6 years ago. He found it in his change one morning after the night before and passed it on with the words "there's more chance of you spending this than me." Sean was going to buy me a beer... And I think if I'd got here sooner he could have, but they cost 14pesos now. Inflation just ain't what it used to be!

We walked around, Matt's eyes on stalks at the age

and style of the old colonial buildings.

Even with the filth, there is great colour, so many of the buildings painted either with adverts, murals or political slogans. Then there's the bustle of markets, the mad vehicles with no lights (fitted) and crazy oversized wheels. The tyres are so fat it would appear replacements are out of the question, so the smooth shiny look is definitely "in". What's really funny though is when only two hugely oversized wheels are owned. It doesn't have to be an axle choice, though front seems popular for some bizarre reason. No, we even saw a pickup with one side bigger and fatter than the other. It was clear that the driver was having difficulty keeping it in a straight line, but I bet it looked good from the road when it was parked outside the house.

A tour of Pancho Villa's house, which became a museum when his wife left it to the State in 1982, was quite a macabre experience. The car in the courtyard is the one that he was assassinated in, in 1923 and there are pictures of the scene and of his corpse. From every angle. The exit wounds are particularly gruesome, showing all of his inside bits as rather more outside bits. We spent a couple of hours piecing the history of the revolution and the war of independence together from the notices that although translated into English, reminded me of a menu that I read in Spain once, that had me actually crying with laughter and left a very embarrassed waitress getting the manager to take our order.

Note to self- must read more about the Mexican revolution.

Chihuahua State is also home to 50,000 German speaking Mennonites who left Manitoba in the 1920s after falling out with a secular government that decreed schools should teach in English and after WW1, suggested that military conscription may become a reality. For a faith that has at it's core the belief that Church and State should never mix, this was unacceptable and so a whole people packed their bags and set off to transform the northern Mexican desert into productive farmland.

The further we drove into the country the more exciting it all became, though the language barrier is a stumbling block, it's not a huge one. At least not nearly as huge as the topes, or speed humps that are used to calm traffic and just occasionally have warning signs. These things are either about 8" high ramps which demand respect, or are made of big balls of polished steel set in the tar and about 3 to 4" tall. As difficult as these balls are to negotiate head on, (there are no gaps between them), they are sometimes used as lane dividers which is going to be interesting when it rains!

Walking round Creel the night before our assault on the Copper Canyon, which is larger and deeper than the Grand Canyon, we pop into a restaurant for food. The hostess informs us we can have chicken (pollo) or burgers.

"Pollo, por favor"

"Dos" pipes up Matt. She smiles and we sit. The man reading the paper with the eye patch and scars looks up. It'll be grand, I assure Matt, just some kind of chicken dish. The slamming of the machete on the counter seems ominous, but the smell is good. We wait, and are rewarded first with a pot of salsa, some limes and then a container full of tortillas.

"You see, some sort of chicken thing we can make up in the tortillas" I say, full of confidence.

Then the chickens arrive. Dos. Two chickens, on a massive plate, delicately carved in quarters with the machete. Holy shit! They tasted fantastically fresh and should have, they'd been running up the road when we pulled into town. KFC family bucket it was not, and all for a couple of quid. We ate till well beyond suffice and took enough with us to feed the first four dogs that we met on the way back to our room. There are literally hundreds of dogs of every hue, everywhere, but so far only a handful have thought us easy prey and given chase to the bikes.

A cold night was spent as the only guests in a really nice hotel and we awoke to the sound of rain, which was a little ominous because we were due to make the descent into the Copper Canyon, which is steep and loose. Or rather now, steep and muddy.

First though we had planned a 45kms trip along the rim of the canyon to Divisadero, due to be followed by a visit to a beautiful lake and waterfall, but after the run to Divisadero I lost Matt. I'm not sure how, since there is really only one road, but then I ran into a Federales Police road block. These are the guys that everyone fears and I can see why. High on a mountainside, their black para-military uniforms are foreboding, as are the guns and the way that most of them wear balaclavas or neck warmers pulled up over their faces. I was directed to a bumpy dirt track and then questioned. The questioning seemed intense enough, but the majority of my answers were simple.

"No entiendo."

In the end they gave up, trying to maintain their tough demeanour and though a giggle, one of them finally said "tang you" and pointed for me to leave.

I waited for an hour at the main road junction and then went to the lake to see if Matt had headed on without me, but the bloke taking money said no motorbikes had passed today. After seeing the 'Federales' head back into town in their pickups with all their guns pointing up, like in the movies, I headed back out to Divisadero to see if he'd crashed or broken down. I took all the gravel side roads to views over the canyons, but couldn't find him anywhere, so went back to being the only guest in the hotel. I explained “mi amigo es perdido” (lost) and hoped he'd come back to the hotel since we deliberated for so long in the morning as to whether or not to have another night here and just explore the immediate vicinity. The most worrying thing is that he has next to no cash with him, or water, but he does have the chain lube and air compressor! It's dark now, so I'll have to hope he's somewhere safe and I'll go and search in the morning.

25 THE TRES AMIGOS AND LEE

Wandering around the town of Creel, wondering whether or not Matt would come back to the same hotel, I let all of my western prejudices choose a restaurant, with dire consequences. No more shall I let aesthetics play a part in my choice, but instead shall follow the ancient law of eating where the locals do. From 9pm to 9am I painted the hotel room, every orifice explosively evacuating every ounce of substance from my body. Occasionally I would almost fall asleep with exhaustion after a bout of convulsing, only to be sharply awoken with the next one. Every twenty minutes, like clockwork, my stomach would inform me that there might be just a little bit left, but not to worry, it was keeping up the fight against any remaining microbes. I fell asleep for nearly an hour at 9am and then tried a sip of water, before getting the man from the hotel to help me get the bike off the stand and I wobbled off southward to Batopilas in the base of the Canyon and hopefully towards Matt.

Almost immediately a white pickup runs me off the road from the other direction and I can just manage to hold the bike upright as I sit astride it, stationary. The pickup turns round for another go, but stops beside me.

"How are ya doin' there?" says Mark Brady from Navan, who comes from Ireland for 6 months each year to work with indigenous Tarahumara Indians, and who had seen the Irish flag on the front of the bike. I did my best to hold up a conversation, but was working harder to hold up the bike, and hold down the glass of water. There are times when you curse your fellow countrymen and their friendliness! At least I knew I had found a friend (with appalling driving) to help if I couldn't find Matt today. I decided to cut short the chat and head out of town, in the rain and fog, amid warnings of the impending snowfall. It just gets better! One of the appeals of Batopilas, apart from the famously challenging "road" to get down there, is that being almost 6 thousand feet lower than Creel and the rim of the Copper Canyon, it's nice and toastie, even when winter has arrived around the edge.

With thickening fog, which still managed to produce heavy rain, I overshot the unmarked turning to Batopilas by 20kms. For some inexplicable reason my body had now started to sweat profusely, no doubt because it had realised there was one more way of expelling liquids that it hadn't thought of before, and I started to feel even weaker.

Turning in to the correct mud road, I had slithered barely a mile and was wondering whether Matt would really have come this way on his own, when I got a corner completely wrong at the same time as I met the only vehicle for an hour. I'd like to think that I scored points for style and grace, as my wheels swapped ends in the rutted quagmire and I remained upright, coming to a halt next to the passenger window.

"Hi, there! You must be Paddy" said the Canadian girl in the front seat. What? Had my pirouetting reputation gone before me?

"Your friend is down in the village. He's worried about you and asked us to look out for you. He's at the far end of the village. Take care on the road, it starts to get steep and slippery ahead."

Starts to?

It's funny, just how big an impact the wave of relief had. I knew Matt had no money left, no spare fuel and no water and that he was only on his way to Vermont when I met him, with no plans for foreign adventure, so I felt somehow responsible for him as he now sat at the bottom of a huge hole in the ground, thirsty and broke. But more importantly, he was carrying the chain lube, the little electric tyre pump and the biscuits.

The first few miles didn't seem too bad and I picked up the pace, letting the bike slide around beneath me on the relatively smooth surface. Then I got to the construction zone. There were no cones, or lollipop ladies, no stop signs or diversions, just lots of heavy machinery in the mud trying to cut a road from the canyon walls and workers huddling around fires to keep warm. The smoke was hanging in the air between the pine trees, where the fog had lifted, but the going became properly stupid. The puddles were sometimes like trenches, so I adopted a "hope for the best" style of riding, as sometimes they were deeper than the bash plate, but the ever-falling altitude and slick surface meant that actually stopping wasn't really an option. I just plunged from one obstacle to the next, be it a fallen tree, semi submerged in the mud, or a recently carved culvert. Then, perhaps carrying 15- 20mph, I got in a big slide with the bars turned full lock, and held it, feet up for almost 5yds, to the accompaniment of a huge cheer from one group of workers who were huddled round a fire ill dressed for the cold. I don't know who divinely intervened for that moment, but I just sat there and held on!

I began to enjoy the ride in the mud, as crazy as it was and as weak as I felt, on this road that seemed to have a propensity for falling down the mountainside. Mud splashes and boulder negotiation paled into insignificance when I rounded one corner to find a Caterpillar busy bashing part of the cliff face and in so doing, had created a rock and gravel landslide that covered the track. I waited behind a pickup, while the Cat pushed some of the debris and the largest rocks over the edge into the abyss and then we were called forward. The available route, about half the track width and of course the edge beside the void, was covered in maybe 2 feet of loose rock and gravel at its shallowest. The remainder of the way forward had debris piled at a slope of about 30 degrees, increasing towards the rock wall of the mountain. It was going to be a very long way down if I screwed up and looked just like those pictures of the Peruvian Andes that you see in real adventure books.

The 4x4 pickup took a run at it and bounced precariously across spewing stones and mud at me as it went. The dozer driver looked at me through the broken window on his cab and waved me on. It was one of those times when you just quietly and resignedly, say 'shit'. In for a penny, it was adventure I was here for, but I had no strength to stand on the footpegs so just opened the throttle....

Peggy and I made it through, even though it wasn't dignified, but buoyed by the experience, I really enjoyed the rest of the 65km descent. I came out of the rain clouds, the track dried, and became barely the width of a car in places as it clung to the edge of the canyon, and wound its way down. Most of the road is single track and the surface is one of broken rock, bike breaking corrugations or sand, though occasionally all three at the same time. The scenery though, is truly stunning. The vegetation changes dramatically with altitude, so the pine forests at the top give way to cactus and palms by the bottom. After all, it's only a few degrees north of the Tropic of Cancer, which accounts for the big increase in temperature too. Boulders the size of every sporting ball you can imagine littered the track, there were washouts everywhere and more than once I caught the centre stand cross brace on rocks. It was the kind of situation that led to laughter- what an insane road.

I loved it.

Bridges with huge planks, though not all present and correct. Water splashes, hairpin after blind hairpin cut from the rock and all liberally interspersed with boulders and wildlife. Big wildlife; donkeys, oxen and goats. Then, as if by magic, a town appears! Nearly 2kms long, it is the perfect village, strung out along the canyon floor and with no obvious reason for its existence. The road down the canyon was only built in 1975, yet here it is, with a couple of little squares and one or two streets off the main one, a combination of slab concrete and cobbles.

Waiting with a line of pickups who are trying to get past a digger whose jib has just accidentally felled one of the few trees, a man comes over and tells me my amigo is waiting at Juanita's Hotel on the big square. It's that kind of place, everyone knows. Matt looked more relieved than I felt, and he couldn't stop talking. What's more, he'd done the road, and he's been riding for 6 months. He only got his licence before leaving Alaska. That's the spirit! Juanita, a real character in her 60's, insisted that the bikes be kept in the courtyard for safety, which just left the final ride, through the dining room and the kitchen to get there.

News came later of another pair of bikers arriving in town and we found Jason from California and Lee from Vancouver unloading Lees bike from a pickup. He had crashed over a cliff, but was saved by a couple of bushes and a small tree, so with block and tackle they had winched the bike back up to the road. All of us were too exhausted for civility, so we agreed to stay in town a few days and prepare for the trip back up and out together. Matt produced a spare watchstrap for me when he saw that my own had broken, which was very touching, but led me to believe there may still be excess baggage on his bike! That first night I fell asleep to the sounds of Mexican accordion music from next door's rear patio gathering, and the occasional burst of small arms fire from the surrounding hills.

We were staying in the south end of town, which, although more prosperous, and with gaily painted houses, definitely had the greater percentage of pock marked buildings and vehicles peppered with bullet holes. One Ford truck down the street from Juanita's place had five bullet holes in the windscreen on the drivers side and interesting staining on the seats. This was drug baron territory, and the kind of place where you can meet pickups three at a time. The first and last contain heavily armed young men and the middle one usually has a covered load, what ever that may be... This area has seen almost 4000 homicides this year, but that's rural life in the mountains for you.

Post recuperation the three Amigos; Jason, Matt and I, set off for the ride out of the valley. Lee couldn't face it after his cliff excursion and got a lift in a pickup, which it turns out, had a more expensive cargo than just his bike on board. Hence the accompanying riflemen. We agreed to meet up later and waved him off.

Then we had a blast. Jason even filmed some of it from a fancy little camera mount he has on his bike. Matt only crashed twice, but luckily neither of them involved plummeting down a mountain, so we all kept grinning through the filth. I can't believe the pounding that Peggy got without (serious) complaint.

We had a real "sense of achievement" moment at the top and decided to stick together for a while. Guys are really simple like that.

Generally Mexican tarmac is pretty good when you can find it, though you never can tell when it'll deteriorate, or open up as huge potholes, but that all adds to the fun and the policy for resurfacing seems to be just that, resurface without any preparation, which means perfect black top for a couple of months. The twisting sinuous canyon rim roads were perfect, but the variation increased as we headed south towards Durango. Having met up with Lee, the four of us got a room en route instead of camping in the sub zero temperatures, but were still faced with the cold start problem again.

"What? Your bikes have kick-starts?" asked Lee, following some glib comment.

"No, we just kick them a few times in the morning and that usually helps".

He looked confused...

Days of dirt riding and manly bonding followed. Riding tracks, crossing various streams and spending spare moments fixing Matt's bike after each subsequent little crash, filled the next week. We seem to be stopped at least twice a day in military checkpoints, though apart from some searching of panniers and pointing of guns, everything passes peacefully.

Jason has a huge 50 litre fuel tank on his bike, so it's typical that it was his that ran out and needed to get a fill up from a vendor at the side of the road, which just goes to prove it isn't size that matters. (I tell myself). The fuel was siphoned from a big container and probably should have been strained through a t-shirt. This was all becoming the real deal, proper adventure riding, and proper adventure catering too, cooking and eating what we could get, like the freshest beef I've ever had, dead less than an hour. We talked Manuel into dicing us some of the meat he was butchering from his cow at the side of the road. It went very well with cactus of the Mickey Mouse ears variety, which is a little bland, but a great bulker when you haven't got spuds or rice.

We spent a couple of days in Durango, a beautiful university town, with great colonial architecture and a maze of markets, while Matt recovered from a particularly nasty spill. Holding nearly 40mph on the dirt, which reflects white in the high sun and is really hard to see properly, he failed to notice that a small cattle grid was missing most of its bars on one side. His side.

His evasive action at the last minute turned a huge accident into a not quite so huge one, and we had the bike going again in about two hours, but he was badly beaten up. That didn't daunt his spirit though and as Lee moaned about whatever he could think of, Matt was raring to go again and attempt the next challenge, with swollen (broken?) ankle, bruised and cut chest, shoulder, arm and thigh.

I can't imagine what it'll take to piss him off, but I hope we never find out, cos I'll surely not cope with the size of that challenge. I've never met someone with such spirit and couldn't be luckier with my travel companion. We even bicker like a comic duo and Jason threatens to take away our handbags. It must be love!

26 BROTHELS AND TEQUILA

Oh Meh-hee-co, like so many countries, is a land of contrast. One that wants to half emissions of CO by 2050, shaming much of the West in the process, yet is proud of recently opening the worlds largest outdoor ice rink. Outdoor ice rink, in the tropics! If they want to clean up emissions there will have to be a hell of a change in attitudes. Take the automotive world for example.

At the lower end of the socio economic spectrum there are vehicles that are kept going on a wing and a prayer. Trucks that are so overloaded and under-serviced that they crawl along at pitiful speeds through the mountains. On a bike they pose no immediate threat because it's possible to smell them well in advance, even before your eyes begin to sting and you enter the dense black cloud of diesel smoke on an incline. On descents, the piston rings are so badly worn that the blue haze of burning engine oil warns of their presence. Many of them are parked up for what the British bike industry used to call "roadside maintenance". It is not uncommon to see even relatively new trucks sitting precariously jacked up on locally sourced tree trunks or huge boulders, with the driver and a local mechanic doing a quick gearbox rebuild in the dust. The other common failure is collapsed suspension, especially when a Toyota or Nissan pickup is asked to carry about 5 tons of bricks, fruit or timber just once too often. I'm not sure though, if that is any more environmentally damaging than the educated rich, and there are millions of them, that choose to flaunt their wealth with tricked up Hummers and the like, all air-con and power everything.

Mexico is interesting for that. The north may be poor, like every non Mexican will tell you, but it exists alongside a lot of money. Some of the towns I've passed through (like Durango) seem to have an efficient public infrastructure and lots of civic pride, while others, like El Salto, deserve the accolade "shithole". Please excuse my eloquence, but it is a dreadful timber town in the mountains, with mills belching smoke, and every tin roofed shack and hovel burning wood against the cold, while dogs displaying their skeletal form scavenge in the sea of waste and discarded plastic. The plastic that is the scourge of the globe, but that is most clearly visible disfiguring any developing nation.

I wrote last from Durango, with Matt recovering from his earthly magnetism, and with all of us united in putting Lees boots outside on the hotel windowsill. He blames the material they are made of… Oh, but here is some justification for all my previous invective toward mildly drizzle proof motorbike clothing. Both Lee and Jason have bought Rev-it suits. Lee, like me, had to buy waterproofs about 100miles after leaving Vancouver and the first time it rained. Jason lives in California, so wore his for 6 months without experiencing rain, but then washed his jacket. 12 of the seams had parted when he took it out of the machine, but Rev-it told him to bugger off as he had mistreated the jacket. Mistreated? I wasn't aware that Whirlpool was more abrasive than Tarmac! We shall just see what customer service says to me when I get back, they have a right to reply. Am I being libelous or slanderous now? Well I suppose that depends on whether you are reading this yourself or having it read to you...

Either way, you can probably see that I still seethe.

So, yes, leaving Durango, an old colonial town, with fantastic squares, parks, universities and millions of tiny Hyundai taxis, I also left behind the northern drug baron and mafia zone. (Well I thought I had, but I've just read of 11 killed in gun battles in the south...)

The attitude of the people seemed to change from Durango onwards, not that they had been unfriendly before, but there was a certain reservation and almost fear in the eyes in some areas. The drug trade is powerful, but the rewards of the US market are huge, so it's not surprising. Two weeks before I arrived in the country the Interior Minister, Moriño, had been killed in a mysterious plane crash, just a fortnight after announcing his plans and funding to tackle the drug barons head on. Isn't coincidence terrifically coincidental? The numbers of military and police checkpoints are reducing as I ride south, but the splendour of the buildings and vehicles that the Federales use is undiminished. It's part of the government plan to bribe the Federal Police so that they don't bribe everyone else.

Anyway, we headed out of Durango, bound for the coast at Mazatlan, and travelled the truly stunning and entertaining Route 40 through the mountains and down to the Pacific coast. The road stays at around 2000 metres above sea level, (you'll notice I've gone metric again) and weaves around canyons and along ridges, through pine forests and the odd tiny village. We couldn't help but play on the twisties until about 40 kms of liberally sprinkled pea gravel spoiled our fun and led to an awful lot of "ohmegawd" moments. It is as though Matt and I have now been riding together for 10 years and can sense what the other is going to do. Except when he tries to knock me off at petrol stops and traffic lights. Oh how we laugh…

Then we crossed the Tropic of Cancer! If ever there was a seminal moment in any road trip, an imaginary line, the crossing of which symbolised achievement, surely that's gotta be it. As lines on a map go, I think you'll agree that it's pretty significant, even if it is usually dotted and doesn't carry quite the gravitas of the solid equator. True, the water in the sink didn't start spinning the other way and I didn't begin to get a bit of an upside down feeling, but it's still a bit of a trek from Northern Ireland, and dammit, Peggy and I were officially in the tropics! Right on cue and as if to celebrate the fact, we began to descend into intense humidity and thick, thick vegetation. Villages used banana leaves and the like as roofing material, and fruit hung everywhere. We stopped at a little shop, run by Carolina and her family, next a truly disgusting river ousing through paradise with a full load of plastic bags and other detritus. Jason struck a deal. We'd buy a load of her bread, biscuits and beer if we could camp in the yard behind her shop. Job done. We set up camp with her eight dogs, ten chickens, four (bloody noisy) cockerels, two horses, three cats and a tremendously hard done by donkey that told everyone about it all night. Still, it was all preferable to gunfire and those damned engine Jake brakes that the trucks use and which shatter the night. Even the fact that the cats were a little put out that we had camped in their litter tray didn't daunt our spirit and the sense of achievement of sleeping in the warm tropical air.

The town of Concordia is where you go to buy furniture. It may be where all of Mexico goes, because there seemed to be no other businesses within 5kms of it. Beautiful chairs, all artisan made but in various states of completion, lined the road and filled every shed, until we at last hit the coastal highway and the fruit and veg stalls near Mazatlan.

On the run south from there I experienced, possibly for the first time since Nova Scotia, thick green vegetation right up to the roadside and not a blade of yellow grass anywhere. There were huge fronds of unidentifiable vegetation and banana plants all covered in thick creepers and vines. The creatures who found themselves somewhat compromised by the traffic were squishy lizards and iguanas instead of furry squirrels, but there were still the dogs, alive or dead.

More old colonial towns with beautiful squares were separated by dense forest or intensive agriculture, until we headed back inland and climbed again, finally rolling into the town of Tequila, set in the semi arid desert which is perfect for growing the Blue Agave plant. Where better to try your first ever shot of Tequila, than in the main square of the town itself, under the arches next to a 17th century church? You see I'm just an authentic kind of guy. If Tequila doesn't come from the State of Jalisco, then technically it is Mezcal and a poor quality relative. I sipped. I savoured.

It was horrible.

The agave, a spikey trunkless plant, of the sort that garden centres sell to commercial developers to adorn the patios and fountain areas of a thousand office "work zones", grows in abundance in these parts, and it is the ball root from which Tequila is made. It is not technically a cactus, though is often mistaken for one, and maybe I had a horrible glass of the regional delicacy, but it reminded me of a bottle of poteen that I once shared in a hostel in Dublin. Like developing a taste for English Ale, one day perhaps my palate will find spirits enticing, but for now...

From Tequila to Guadalajara the land supports two crops staple to Mexican cuisine; corn for the tortillas and agave for tequila. I am now attempting to avoid both and looking longingly at roads that lead towards Belize, potatoes and tea. In the meantime I am enjoying all other aspects of Mexico more and more, apart from spicy meal times and I had previously viewed it as somewhere to cross on the way to Central America. To date I have met no one unhelpful, and the only truly infuriating thing is the Mexican use of the left hand indicator. Remember we are driving on the right here. The left indicator is used as an invitation to pass. It is also used as an indication of intention to turn left. Occasionally.

Confusion? Near misses? Oh yes. I only wish the horses and donkeys and carts were fitted with indicators too, and that people actually turning left on a busy highway didn't indicate right, head for the right edge of the road and then sweep in a huge arc to the left. Still, it keeps you on your toes incase the random speed humps, potholes, children and livestock don't.

The traffic in the cities is mad, which is a buzz, and Matt has now fully embraced the cut and thrust. I can see a career for him in London as a courier. The hawkers that work the traffic lights and intermingle freely with the traffic sell everything imaginable, but in Guadalajara one very enterprising young man was juggling fire as he walked between the cars and the trucks with the leaking fuel tanks, trying to earn a few pesos.

We parted company with Lee before Guadalajara, Jason and he seemed to have a lot of irreconcilable differences, and then we had a particularly entertaining evening, not that the two are related. We'd seen some Motels that had secure parking in the form of an individual garage beneath each room, and regularly advertised prices of about 100 pesos a room (about a fiver). Because of this, we just rode until it was almost dark, before selecting a particularly tidy one and pulling in to the reception area.

"She wants to know how many hours we want the room for", said Jason.

"What?"

"And how many complimentary services do we need?"

Good old Catholicism. These shiny, well tended motels, with secure, unobservable parking, situated throughout the country, served a thriving industry for the well healed, hypocritical, family oriented client. Our room was great. The shower was all travertine tiles and plenty large enough to accommodate friends, or workers. There were 10 porn channels and a menu that included imaginative and some truly unimaginable items to make our stay more enjoyable, and pizza. In truth, it was the cleanest, nicest place we'd ever stayed, with the best mirrors, but also with a fantastic place to work on the bikes. True, all the staff looked at the three of us oddly, and much as we were tempted to order some heavy-duty grease to see the looks on their faces, we didn't.

As we head farther south, Matt and I have decided to go undercover. Since more and more people are now looking at me in an inquisitive, "who's the pink guy?" kind of way, I have decided that a disguise is in order and to that end have grown a big Mexican moustache and chin adornment. Just a little black hairspray and I should blend right in. Matt on the other hand, has been riding his bike around without headlight, clocks, screen, license plate or mudguard after the last crash, and of course who needs helmets? He really fits in.

We are holed up in San Miguel de Allende, about 250kms north west of Mexico City. The climate is cooler, the town a wonderfully restored colonial masterpiece, with cobbled streets and every service imaginable. The gringos are in plentiful supply too, as this is the upper middleclass American's southern gettaway of choice. It started with artists and hippies in the 70's and is now somewhere that 200,000 American dollars will buy you a two bed flat. I'm staying in Jason's mum's house, with seven bathrooms, (I thought there were six but found another one yesterday) and three roof terraces. How lucky am I? But really, you must understand this motorcycle travelling is really tough. Honest.

We've been recuperating in opulence, enjoying fine dining and tourist strolling, whilst at the same time using a welding workshop that belongs to a man called Abel, to rebuild Matt's broken bits. I've made a mark 2 version of my fuel can holders, adding small skid plates to further protect the cans from any unscheduled dismounts. Chasing each other a few days ago in the hills led to one scary moment too many, so better safe than sorry. I may have the diamond smile and boyish charm of world champion Valentino Rossi, but it would appear that I have marginally less talent. Overtaking and leading both the amigos through a long lefthander, they got to witness a just recovered highside, at very close quarters when I overstepped the adhesive qualities of my tyres. We all slowed down.

But I've found a new rear tyre here in San Miguel. What's more amazing, is that I found it in an Aprilia dealer! True, Alberto had only sold three Aprilias in his time, and didn't actually have any for sale at the minute, (or any spares) but he was proud to be a main dealer and even had a sign to say so. He invited us in to do oil changes and whatever we wanted, blowing out my air filter for me and offering tools and the use of his workshop. What a star, just like all main dealers?

This is a wonderful town and the ideal location to while away the time. The weather is beautiful, there are so many restaurants I want to experience, as much for the architecture as the cuisine, and little bars and courtyard cafes, all set on cobbled streets which are predominantly pedestrian, with just the odd 125 Honda or horse passing by. There is a Starbucks too, but apart from that it's great.

It's like the middle class ideal of Mediterranean living, without any of the European health and safety nonsense. And there is more guacamole and avocado than you can imagine. Avocado is so common it is added to the Aztec Burgers (yes really) in the way Australians use beetroot.

I really love it here, even though I have just cut the top off my index finger on a rusty bit of metal in Abel's workshop. C'est la vie.

Now I just have to decide what country I'm going to spend Christmas in. Perhaps Belize on the Caribbean coast. Oh, how rude of me. I forgot to ask. How is the December weather in the UK by the way?

27 ALBERTO- HERO OF THE HOUR

So I'm still in San Miguel. 11 days now and counting. Matt and I were all set to go, with the route all planned and a determination to be in Belize for the festive period. A white sand tropical beach, the Caribbean gently lapping the shore, a palm frond roofed bar (say that after a few!), and the possibility of a soothing hammock. That was until Jason decided he wanted to come too, but he needed a couple of days to get himself together, so we waited. Then Peggy's lazy starter motor finally decided to join the ranks of the terminally unemployable and signed on the sick for good. I considered everything and even cleaned all the oil and grime off the engine to make sure all the electric connections were sound, putting Vaseline on all the shiny bits (Jason had a jar...), and I bought her a new sticker of Che Guevara to celebrate getting to Latin America, but it has made no discernible difference. She still refuses to start, which I think is a little ungrateful.

Rescheduling particularly messy jobs to an indeterminate future date is something of a forte for me, and I now have justifiable reason. Four hours later and with the whole bike cleaned and reassembled, it didn't make the slightest bit of difference.

Now I hear you all, your voices ringing in my head "You're taking an Italian bike?" "Well, er yes, but that old Italian wiring gremlins thing, is just folklore. This isn't the

1970's and things have improved enormously. Haven't they?" There must be something else, some rational factor, but in truth, it's harder to justify Guiseppe and Franco's famously laissez faire attitude to production line assembly, when I tell you that the charging circuit has become a little random again; 14.2 v at idle and 11-13.5v (variable) at higher revs. Perhaps when I also tell you that the temperature gauge reads 120ºC with the kill switch in the off position, (unless the side lights are on and it's a Sunday), and reads 50ºC at most other times, you'll see that I'm out of my electronic depth. The neutral light pulses when the engine is finally running, but it's taking longer and longer anaerobic workouts for Matt as he pushes, before we can get to that stage. Luckily for Peg that Italian styling means she still looks a million dollars even stationary. I'm just keeping the faith.

So another day is spent going from address to address following advice and recommendation in search of a reliable auto electrician, and exploring more of the beautiful and intriguing San Miguel in the process. It's almost like courier work, in as much as following random addresses lets you discover areas that you might otherwise avoid: Swindon, or Grimsby for example.

In San Miguel though, there is a pleasant surprise around every corner, and they aren't all wearing spray-on jeans. There is the colonial architecture and the way that there is a small entrepreneurial enterprise seemingly in every front room. You'll find a mechanic between the wedding dress shop and the bakery, or a cabinet and coffin maker next a silversmith or restaurant. The men in their white cowboy hats standing chatting and on every corner or unoccupied doorway there sit the indigenous people in their fantastically coloured multi layered robes, selling handmade dolls or bead necklaces, their snotty nosed kids quietly playing in the dirt. Just as everywhere else, the indigenous population here is somewhat sidelined.

The cobbled streets and potholes play havoc with the worn out suspension and steering racks of the taxis, but the friendly cabbies pass on their wisdom over the top of the mechanical racket, in the way that cabbies do everywhere. The music blaring from shops and vehicles, the ringing of a thousand church bells, the screams and yelps of the always smiling kids in their inappropriate t-shirts ("kiss me I'm Irish", or "Nestle, for life"), and the barking of dogs all adds to the cacophony that is Mexico. The old man with the milk churns and bags of maize on his donkey, does battle with the 125 Hondas and their helmetless, sandal shod riders, or the overloaded pickup trucks, brimming with produce and liberally topped off with a human cargo that adds and subtracts itself seamlessly at the appropriate spot without interrupting the traffic flow. The smells of the cooking from the street side stalls next to the 4 star restaurants and the pungent aroma of raw sewage, all intermingle with the incense from head shops, the scent of the blooming arrays of flowers and the nauseating diesel fumes.

This is Mexico and I love it all.

Then there is the sheer hilarity of seeing VW Beetles adorned with antlers and red noses and fat cheerful snowmen lining the roofs of houses, as carol singers parade the streets with stories of Good King Wenceslas peering out at the snow. It's the tropics! I don't believe there has been a single flake of snow in these parts this side of the last ice-age. It's a kind of madness. Fair enough to indoctrinate, by force if needs be, a whole continent with an alien religion, if you feel strongly enough about it and have the arrogance that is necessary to ignore and belittle what the population already holds dear. But what's with the northern European cultural identity transfer?

"Right, from now on we decree that your concept of deities to be utter nonsense. No longer may you believe in the power of the sun to give life, nor that the cosmos has geometric laws you fully understand or that your calender is accurate to 0.000069 days in a true year, unlike the crap Julian and Gregorian ones that we use in Europe. Furthermore, we feel it is barbaric that you sacrifice animals and people to your gods, and if you don't listen to us, we'll kill you in the name of our God."

"Instead we want you to believe in a god you can't see, that lives in an indeterminate place up in the sky that you have so accurately mapped, who metamorphosed his own son into a human figure who he then sacrificed for the good of all."

"Oh, and even though He lived in the deserts of the Middle East, we feel it's necessary that you celebrate His human birth with horned horse like creatures you've never seen that fly through the air and with a pointy green tree that you should bring inside your house and cover in shiny ornaments". Most people, on pain of death, seemed to buy the reasoned argument as presented and the thing I really like about the Christmas decorations here, is that the electricity supply can be so random and pulsating, the fairy lights look great!

While I'm having a pop at organised religion, why is it do you think, that the Virgin Mary only appears to people in devoutly Catholic countries? Are Prods not worthy of an appearance, or does she think their patriarchal social structure would preclude anyone from taking her seriously should she show up?

I ask, because the last week has coincided with the celebrations of the Virgin of Guadalupe, when she came to a shepherd (nice touch eh?) outside the town and told him to go to the mayor and tell him to build a church in her name. (I can't believe there wasn't one already). He did so, and the mayor told him to bugger off back up the hill and not eat anymore of the fungi that was growing there. However, Mary came back and told the shepherd to take the mayor a bunch or roses (though not in any homophilic sense), because it was December and not rose season, a ploy she was sure would sway a powerful local politician. The shepherd put them under his coat (?) and when he got to the town hall and opened his coat, found that the petals had stained the lining in her Caucasian image. Absolute proof, the politicians believed and so the church was built. And Mary only appears in the Bible, what, three times? If it all happened to a shepherd in County Antrim it might be more like "There was this woman appeared in the field the other day and told me to go and build a church in her name. I told her to get inside and finish the dishes."

The upshot of Mary's appearance, is that bangers and fireworks have been going off almost continually for seven days. They start at 4am and usually finish at around midnight, only giving the town's dogs four hours of peace a day to communicate with each other from the roof tops. Thankfully there aren't that many Mexican dogs in San Miguel. The majority here, are well fed, north American and go places on leads or in the front seats of SUVs. You can see the local mutts staring distastefully, or possibly disbelievingly at the pampered pooches in their collars. A good percentage of dog owners are Canadian, though all the ones I've met are, not surprisingly, from Alberta.

Disturbed sleep aside, I've been having a wonderful time here, relaxing in splendour and meeting other travellers. Ingo and Birte from Hamburg started travelling with their campervan in Nova Scotia in January and had some great stories about their time in the Copper Canyon region. They went hiking and stumbled upon a huge growing operation, complete with large numbers of armed henchmen. It took them all their powers of diplomacy and dumb tourist ignorance to get away unscathed. I feel rather sheltered to date. They were great cooks so we let them use the kitchen and they prepared dinner while we provided stimulating conversation. I think. Or was that the wine?

I found somewhere providing food without jalapenos or any other chillies, even if it was in a place called El Infierno. Ominous, I know, for someone with as sensitive a palate as mine, but the translation is not “the Inferno”, rather it’s “Hell” and just maybe, culinary hell for a Mexican is no chillies! However having visited the loo, I can confirm that the establishment’s name was aptly descriptive. Not only was it, emm, 'choice', with it's low surrounding wall, but I could see and smell that the ultimate destination for the ingredients of any meal, ran perilously close to their initial preparation area. This was never meant to be a description of sanitation systems, but now that I've started.... I hasten to add however, that many are wonderful and would easily shame the services provided by petrol stations across Britain.

One quite upmarket restaurant had lots of signs leading the way to 'Sanitarios' that turned out to be anything but, and I entered one swing-door saloon bar and thought that I'd entered a sewer. The barman seemed delighted to see us, being the only customers, though he regularly rushed out to serve passing motorists it seemed, or maybe it was for a breath of fresh air. Then, as we sat at a table with some dead cockroaches who obviously couldn’t stand the smell, we noticed that the sanitary facilities were in the corner. Actually in the corner, where all your business was carried out. We hadn't initially noticed given the gloomy lighting. It wasn't dimmed and moody, it's just that the solitary bulb couldn't light the whole place very well.

I had a haircut down in the local market and attracted a small audience. Jason and I sat together, everyone believing we were brothers, and our blond hair fell onto a sea of black. I think the hairdressers quite enjoyed the novelty, not often getting to deal with balding heads or minor celebrity status. Perhaps the best news to date though, is that I found Jorge's little health food shop, with fresh yoghurt, mouldy pesto, and pure, organic Ceylon tea. I bought out his tea stock and took a box of Roiboos too, just for the evenings. Bliss! It's the little things that make a road trip. Like freshly laundered underwear or the possibility of fresh milk, a bit of cheddar or bread that's still warm to the touch and just so tempting that you've hollowed it out before you get back from the shops. The cleanliness of my underwear I have some control over, the other small joys remain merely a possibility, a comfort in the recesses of my mind that I can call upon to override reality in nations that don't do dairy and sell only yesterday's loaf. Speaking to various bakers, they seemed horrified that they should be selling the bread they were making that day. It appears to be the only profession that doesn't start work at sunrise, instead the shops open at 10am and the ovens are fired up to begin the baking process, which will be completed in the afternoon just before closing time, ensuring that the shelves are fully stocked for opening time next day.

Tomorrow, mechanic brothers Carlos and Hector are due to come around at 11am and tackle Peggy's wiring loom and they're bringing a new 19" front tyre with them. I can hardly contain myself!

28 WHAT I DID ON MY CHRISTMAS HOLIDAYS

Not surprisingly, Carlos and Hector didn't show up when agreed, or at all, so we went looking for them and got nowhere. It turns out Hector isn't due in to work until next Monday, and no one has seen Carlos. In the words of John Priestly "A good holiday is spent among people whose notions of time are vaguer than yours" and the rest of the staff at the garage were certainly that. They really didn't get my frustration, this being the land of manãna and all that. They explained, in that big moustachioed, golden toothed and spittle strewn smile kind of way, that I would just have to wait until they were ready. So I showed them a thing or two about consumer power, they weren't going to mess with me! I decided not to buy that 19" front tyre, even if it was an incredible bargain and if the chances of finding another one were close to zero this side of Panama City. That'd show them where the power really lay in this relationship. I think I may even have harrumphed. Quite loudly!

If they weren't quaking in their boots at that display of consumer potency, it at least made me feel marginally better, though I'm not sure how smug I'll be when I watch the tread slowly vanish from my front Bridgestone. I went back to see Alberto, of Aprilia main dealer fame, and explained my problem. Well if anyone had a good diagnostic system and all the Aprilia factory tools and diagrams, it was going to be him. Wasn't it?

"What, are you joking?" said Alberto "I bloody hate wiring, but here are the keys to my truck, take my trailer and get the bike back here, then we'll think about what to do". There. Now isn't that exactly the sort of behaviour you'd expect of a main dealer?

Jason and I took off down the road in a truck with Texas plates, that had last seen road tax in July 04, towing a trailer registered in Minnesota, with no functioning lights except the one for the oil pressure which came on with amazing regularity and was only extinguished with a sharp tap of the brake pedal. I'm not sure if it was the oil surge forward in the sump, or the whole vehicle lurching to the right, but it acted as a cure for a few hundred yards at a time.

With the bike back at his place, Alberto proceeded to call Mexico City before handing me the phone to discuss the intricacies of my wiring symptoms with a Frenchman at Aprilia headquarters who spoke some German as well as Spanish. I'm still amazed that the call lasted as long as it did!

Then it was off to see Romualdo at the top of the mountain, who was a highly recommended wiring whizz, (even Carlos round the corner in the cafe had mentioned him, and Carlos had a 350 Suzuki as well as the ubiquitous Honda which definitely qualifies him to make recommendations). The poor old truck wasn't entirely happy with the slog up the mountain, but made it in the end, and Peggy was entrusted to Romualdo who worked out of the corner of a yard, surrounded by bikes piled high creating narrow passageways for access. There wasn't a clear spare inch of space on his workbench and I marvelled at his working model, but still left him with a few printed sheets of wiring diagram in English, badly translated from Italian, which I hoped would help.

I spent a difficult night; well, leaving one's child with a stranger is never easy, especially one who works in such disorganised surroundings. Next afternoon we all rode up to see what was what. Not surprisingly, Romualdo said there was nothing wrong and Peggy had started up straight away, but he'd put the battery on charge just in case. Then he gave me one of those looks that only mechanics can give you when they are sure you are being over dramatic and there's nothing wrong that they can see.

Nothing wrong? Not a thing? Started straight up?

Cantankerous Italian piece of …

Then Matt casually said, "What about these wires here that are all shiny? Should the inner bits be showing?" Bless him, my hero. Rom quickly tidied them up, wrapping them in insulating tape, before charging me $2 for his diagnosis.

Yippee!! I rode away full of relief even though the bike was stripped down to its barest essentials and managed nearly a mile on the cobbles until the speedometer cable bracket fell off, getting caught on the way and thrusting the speedo cable into the front wheel, where luckily it lost the battle with the spokes before I was jettisoned over the handlebars. Good old Alberto was so upset that he didn't stock any of the right spare parts (I tried to seem surprised), he took the cable off every bike in the shop until we matched a possible from a Chinese dirt bike. After some bodgery it was on, and I was back on the road south, leaving San Miguel behind and trying desperately to do the maths in my head that was necessary to work out my speed and distance. No matter how fast I went, the speedo wouldn't cross 80kph, and for 15 miles on Matt's bike I had registered 11.5kms. As the day went on and I sank further into mathematical mayhem, I gave up on cracking the equation that could describe my new arithemic conversion. By lunchtime, I was still keeping up with the lads, but managing to register only 6kms in an hour. At 44040kms the odometer finally stopped functioning, and I've been waiting almost a week now, for the fuel light to lie once again and force me to use that spare can of fuel. For those of you only drive, Peggy doesn't have a fuel gauge. On the plus side of course, not registering any miles is going to be great for the resale value when I get back to Britain…

I got away from San Miguel with a full stock of Ceylon tea, a new rear tyre, fresh oil and my first Christmas present: a sheepskin seat cover from Jason. But staring at the stationary speedometer was sad, rather like the first acceptance that Peggy was beginning to fall apart and would never be quite the same. Heaven forbid that she is mortal! We headed towards the ancient Mayan city of Teotihuacan 60kms northeast of Mexico City and used the good, but very expensive toll road to make up time and distance.

These "cuota" roads have the most ingenious charging system that I am yet to fathom. In short, at some time in the journey, say 50miles in, you come upon a tollbooth and pay someone who hates the job, an extortionate amount of money. You then proceed on your merry way and may be stopped again in 10miles, or in 40miles, for a sum twice what you previously paid. The booths may be near junctions, or not, close to bridges or not. I can't figure out the significance of their positioning at all. However, the fee includes insurance, so for those miles travelled you know that everyone else around you has some form of road insurance. It's the only time it happens. What is nice about the tollbooths is that, because of the unhappy workers and the huge traffic bottlenecks, there is an impromptu market at each one where you can buy anything you want from the comfort of your vehicle: clothes, drinks, food, bedding, wives, parrots and tortoises.

The mayhem also provides enough distraction for

three toll weary motorcyclists to decide that they aren't going to pay another £3 for an unspecified distance and instead shall cut across 12 lanes of traffic and vendors, mount the central reservation, ride between some trees, descend into a small gully and remerge on the opposite carriageway, before crossing that, finding a conveniently sized gap in some barriers and disappearing down a donkey track that eventually joins an urban street. We turned right and found that we had discovered "Crufts al fresco". No, even at dog shows there aren't as many canines as we encountered in the next harrowing 40 miles of urbana and there certainly aren't as many copulating wherever the fancy takes them.

According to the map, we were way, way outside the yellow splodge that makes up Mexico City, but I am fast realising, with plenty of cross referencing, that maps of Mexico are purely schematic. Battling mile after mile of speedbump-infested, signpost-free, dog and donkey littered urban tarmac, we fought with possibly the worst and most aggressive drivers I have ever been unfortunate enough to meet. The State is complicit in the carnage though, operating a "no road signs at all" policy, including those indicating priority at junctions. Gone is any of the rural or small town politeness that permits side road traffic to take advantage of the speed bump system to enter and exit the main highway. Here, everyone has an equal right to be a victim and when three, four lane highways meet at a single point, with not so much as a white line or a give way sign, your average biker gets a "high" similar to that which most people buy in a back alley. Never a dull moment and I thrived on it.

We called a halt to the madness by ducking into another "Motel", with secure garaged parking, intriguing menu and huge shower area, but this time with complimentary beer too!

Teotihuacan, or 'Place of the Gods' is somewhere

that I thought Peggy might feel at home. It is one of the ancient cities of the Maya and is shrouded in as much mystery, as it is smog. It is not certain exactly when its construction began, and many of the structures, like the pyramids of the Sun and Moon were built over older cave systems. They and the Avenue of the Dead, were actually named by the later Aztecs, but Teotihuacan is believed to have been home to 250,000 people around 500AD and as such was the biggest city in the Americas for a time. The archaeological finds are some of the world's most impressive and the whole city, temple and pyramid complex is one of Mexico's most important tourist sites. The new town of Teotihuacan is built right up to the sides of the complex, and having climbed the 70m high Pyramid of the Sun, the view was fantastic. It took a while to reach the top though, what with the steep steps, strong sun, already high altitude and aged legs, so I permitted myself a very long, contemplative moment, to absorb my surroundings, and enough oxygen to make the descent. The steps were constructed so steeply to ensure that the corpses of those lucky enough to have been slaughtered in sacrifice to the greater good, didn't get stuck when they were rolled over the edge.

There was a little friction over lunch about the best route around Mexico City, with Matt reluctant to take the main multi lane ring road in case he fell asleep through boredom. As it turned out, sleep was the last thing he would achieve on that road. There are basically three lanes each way, but the bridges when they appear, are only two or one lane wide. There is of course, absolutely no prior warning, but this is generally not a problem, because urban Mexican drivers have found that one clearly demarcated lane is ample to hold three or occasionally four vehicles abreast. The excitement is compounded by the location of businesses right up to the very edge of the highway, thus making the hard shoulder somewhere to display goods, cook, dine, park, mend vehicles and catch a bus. With none of the hindrance of rights of way signs, it becomes possible to move from business to business in either direction, so some of the lanes become two way, the junctions are free for alls and in the middle of the mêlée are reversing vehicles and a large number of horses and donkeys being driven to the edge of their miserable lives, pulling massive loads in homebuilt carts. The poor creatures are skin and bone and in much worse condition than their rural counterparts.

VW bay window vans and minibuses are everywhere and the primary means of transport for the capital, making the whole place look like a Vee Dub festival. They, as most minibuses and taxis the nation over, drive everywhere with their hazard warning lights flashing, just as the police drive everywhere with their blue lights on, making it impossible to discern whether or not they mean it, or are about to execute some random manoeuvre. Whilst passing one such minibus, I noticed a woman on the roadside wave and looked in my mirrors praying that Matt wasn't following me as the van slewed to the right to grab another fare. He was, and I watched him get pinned to the kerb by the van, collecting both the side of the van and the woman's bag in the process, before I looked ahead to see a Beetle come across the central reservation to turn left in front of me. I managed to lock up both wheels and stay upright until the bug just cleared my path, at which point Matt reappeared beside me and we both shook our heads, grinned inanely, our eyes streaming from the fumes and filth, and nailed the throttle.

In all we battled the ring road for two solid hours, there never being a quiet moment till we stopped before Amecameca for a drink and a session of "Did you see the.... and the bloody.... what about that idiot in the...."

There are no drink drive laws in Mexico, like most of the world, but it is worrying to see billboards that say

"Have a happier journey with XYZ special beer", and scary to see truckers pull in, buy a case of beer and crack the first one before they've got back to the cab.

Amecameca is at the base of the 5465m volcano Popocatepetl and has a wonderful marketplace and a little hotel where the only power socket in the room is in the shower cubicle. Like Drink- drive laws, Mexico doesn't really entertain building regulations either. Even though the volcano erupted dramatically twice in 2000 and was clearly smoking heavily from its snowcapped dome when we arrived, we thought we'd try and cross the high pass between it and its not quite as active, but truly unpronounceable neighbour, Iztaccihuatl.

What a difference a day on the road can make. After breakfast at Martha's stall, which has operated continuously for 48 years on the same spot with the same family and sells the chewiest cheese in the bluest tortillas, we climbed and climbed and climbed to the Cortes Pass and rode above the incredibly distinct thick brown atmospheric soup of the city environs. If Mexico wants to shame the western world in the next few years with its environmental progress, it's got a hell of a job on its hands.

The light powdery lava dust made the going pretty tough, with treacherous tight hairpins occasionally coated in maybe 6inches of the stuff, obscuring the rocks below. Where any small streams crossed the road, there was a resultant slime that finally caught out yours truly. First time off in ten years but it made Matt feel much better. It was a slow speed crash and Peggy was fine, but the left pannier was ripped off smashing the lock that I had just replaced in San Miguel! No doubt that box was never meant to be secured.

After only a further 60kms we were back on the tar and having a ball through twisty mountains on the way to Oaxaca, (pronounced Wahaka) passing pickup trucks as overloaded as any I've seen. These ones though, were full of Police. 25-30 per vehicle, clinging to the roof and each other as they stood in the back or on the lowered tailgate, with weaponry pointing every which way. Something heavy was going down for Christmas.

Preparing to camp on the banks of a river beside a tiny hamlet, we met four likely lads in matching white cowboy hats. All of Aztec origin, Fortino, Pancho, Lucas and Victor, wouldn't hear of us camping and insisted that we follow them to the farm of their 86 year old father, Alphonso, where we would be their guests and eat heartily. But first, beer, the international communicator. After more than anyone should have, we saddled up and followed them up the road, noting, that although Fortino wasn't drinking, it was the very pissed Pancho who was driving!

There was something very biblical about that evening. We were taken in to the whole family like lost relatives, given loads of food that all came directly from their land, and the three of us bedded down in the half covered barn just before Christmas eve with the chickens and turkeys, donkey and dogs, biting spiders and bed bugs. The three wise men? We were lacking gold and frankincense, but after my little accident I was at least carrying a mirror, which, if you say it in a northern Irish accent, is murr. No, you're right, it probably doesn't count.

Breakfast, prepared by the 80 year old Esperanza and her niece Concepta, was more of the same incredible hospitality, and as we settled in to a feast of cow cheese, made on the farm, with beans grown next the corn for the tortillas, and just up the valley from the orange trees that provided the juice and the grasslands that gave us the fried crickets, Pancho tried to foist more beer on us. Turns out that beer is all he consumes, much to his family's dismay, since it's the only thing they don't make themselves and the intra-family dynamics were interesting, so it was good when he decided to show us around the farm and the river, including the old home that he grew up in until an earthquake took most of it down the hill and too far to walk from the farmyard.

It was a remarkably intense 24 hours or so that we spent together, and the huge character that was the 4'8" Esperanza, was moved to tears on our departure. They wanted us to be their guests for the next week, and two of the lads even disappeared in the early hours to get a goat for the feasting, but we really needed to do some miles, so sadly departed. With three of the sons working and living with their own families in the US, their time together here as a family is limited and to be so genuinely invited to become a part of that small community was very touching. Fortino proudly told me how he had a domestic gardening business and although he did very long hours, it still wasn't enough to make life all that comfortable in the States. I had a powerful flashback to the gardeners bent double toiling in the sun of Palm Springs.

We moved onward to the beautiful city of Oaxaca and watched the way that the Latin Americans really celebrate Christmas. It was a scene of joviality and colourful floats, with brass bands and dancers and puppets all liberally interspersed with fireworks, bangers and rockets exploding in and above the crowd.

I'm not entirely sure how more people weren't injured, but everyone seemed to be having a blast, quite literally. With churches gaily decorated inside and out and a mad cacophony, I couldn't help thinking that the church in the UK could learn a lot about boosting its popularity from this place. Another Mexican tradition is that every street and block involves all the kids in the run up to Christmas. There are evening parades, where the children walk up and down with lanterns looking for a place to stay for the night, in re-enactment of the birth. There are also games where a huge papier maché figure or head, is filled with sweets and hung from a string across the road. The children use sticks to bash it until the sweets fall out. Playing in the street is never a problem, because someone just parks a car across either end of the road leaving everyone free to party. No council requests, or health and safety formalities. Just close the road and get on with it. What great priorities.

We stayed a couple of days before heading south to the Pacific coast and the idyllic beach at the tiny town of Zipolite, after first stopping in the mountain village of San Jose de Pacifico which is famous for its fungi. Jason fancied turning his road trip into much more of a Kerouac experience, but it wasn't the season apparently.

Coming out of the hills was a shock to the system as the temperature and humidity climbed to what was, quite frankly, unreasonable heights. This little piece of Mexican coastal paradise has been discovered and colonised by New Age hippies and dreadlocked alternatives from everywhere, but most typically from France and Italy, and regardless of how unsavoury many of them looked, they had brought with them their national love of culinary excellence. The beach front and back streets were awash (tsunamis aside) with tiny, wonderful, European restaurants. No chillies. Rejoice.

I sat on the beach that first night, after consuming a delicious bowl of garlic mushrooms with a little more vigour and less decorum than I really ought, watching the waves crash on the beach in the darkness and marvelled at the repetitive patterns and the sound. With no distinct line between sea and sky in the blackness, I watched each wave break and then tried to guess where the next line of white surf would appear. I couldn't stop my eyes following the previous waves in, so each new breaker was a huge surprise, both in height and volume. I worked out the patterns of the breakers; left to right twice but small, then central once. Once more left to right before three right to left and then four huge central ones. It was a strange balance between soothing, mesmerizing peace and engrossing intrigue, but mostly what I gleaned from the whole experience, is that staring at the sea can drive you slightly mad and makes your tea go cold. Perhaps the mushrooms were organic and locally sourced...

Our hut on the beach, with no facilities save for a tap on a wall outside and a couple of hammocks under the palm trees, was perfect, allowing us to dip in and out of the warm sea at will.

All the young individuals wear the same truly individual uniform of faded baggy clothes, beads, Celtic or Aztec tattoos and beaded or dread-locked hair. I have to say that it's a look I quite like, but the other look I'm quite fond of is the one that many others sported on the beach. That of nature.

I, not surprisingly given my physique and general reflective qualities, didn't partake of such naked behaviour, but I did swim a few times a day and, em, people watch. It was hard though (no pun intended), to be there looking at beautiful bodies and be constantly reminded of Siobhan, so I only managed to stick it for four or five days, before heading on towards Chiapas the poorest state in Mexico and the one that is still technically having a bit of a war.

San Cristobal, the current centre of hot Latin American revolutionary activity and anti-globalisation resistance was to be the place to see in the New Year.

29 NEW YEAR PARTY OR REVOLUTION?

Having been nibbled on by everything that flew, crawled or hopped in Zipolite, it was pleasant to get moving again and head for the mountains, but first we had to follow the Pacific coast south east. In all the riding gear it was oppressively hot, like the Arizona desert crossed with a Finnish sauna. 'Only' 32ºC, but the tropical humidity was exhausting. The heat was radiated back by the tarmac so that it got me from below as well as above.

Although the military presence began to increase on the approach to Chiapas, it is the ingenuity of the police that is worth noting. Like many groups of children attempting to sell fresh fruit or tamales, the police use a rope lifted across the road, to stop you. They then present buckets for you to put money in if you wish. I have to say it is the most polite form of corruption I have ever experienced, and I was faced only with smiles when I elected not to help with their seasonal bonus. The military presence increased as did the wind, as we approached the insurgent State and we rode, admittedly at a precarious angle, past huge developments of wind turbines. Seas of the things, even more concentrated than in Canada, capitalising on the ferocious gale that comes down from the mountains. This is the narrowest part of Mexico, and the strip of mountains between the Caribbean and the

Pacific creates all kinds of air pressure variations and hence the wind.

We found a moderately sheltered place to camp in a small scrubby forest, but the disadvantage of that shelter was that the beasties had found it too. And pounced. It wasn't just me though. For the first time the lads started getting bitten too and what a racket of complaint. "Welcome to my world lads".

They both ignored my offer of highly noxious synthetically manipulated industrial DEET based repellent, choosing instead their natural, homeopathic San Francisco stuff. I'm not proud of coating myself in a poisonous toxic liquid, but I had to laugh as Jason liberally sprayed himself with the healthy, natural, alternative and was set upon by hundreds of mosquitoes who clearly adored the smell.

Of course the biting spiders still got me in the tent, one of them painfully, right in the middle of my back. Imagine my surprise when I reached round to swat whatever it was and squashed something large and hairy. I know it's pointless shouting "Aaahh" and jumping up after the event, half destroying the tent in the process, but I've watched David Attenborough and am pre-programmed for just such a reaction. Apart from leaving a bit of a welt, it appears that my hairy arachnid wasn't a people killer, which is a bit of a relief.

A nice early start saw us packed away and on the road by 6am to try and gain some altitude before the temperature got too high. I thought I was grumpy in the heat, but I've finally found Matt's one weak point and why he enjoys living in Alaska. It seems it is possible for him to have a bad day after all.

All the military activity abruptly ended with the crossing into Chiapas.

The war began on January 1st 1994, coordinated to celebrate the instigation of the North American Free trade agreement (NAFTA) upon which the Mexican people had not been consulted. The Zapatista movement (EZLN) led by the charismatic Sub Commandante Marcos, fought for indigenous rights, social change, land reform and against the neo liberal economic ideal of globalisation. They have been so successful, that although Chiapas is still the poorest Mexican state and definitely the most beautiful, the military no longer go there and there are government housing development and infrastructure projects happening all over the region. All over the place there are signs up declaring zones where the land has been taken and handed back to the dispossessed people to be farmed sustainably. There appears to be state wide support for the movement which is named after the 19th C Mexican revolutionary Emiliano Zapata, especially among the 300,000 indigenous peoples, though it is currently in peace mode, unless the Mexican government reneges on its promises and investment.

The New Year celebrations coincide with the anniversary of the start of the war but not surprisingly, getting to those celebrations takes a lot of forward planning if you are a foreigner, with a vetting procedure and passport examination. I hadn't thought ahead and it wasn't really the lads bag, so I just enjoyed the association of being close at such a momentous time and bought a T-shirt that is probably illegal to wear somewhere.

The regional capital, San Cristobal is another beautiful colonial city, but one that ouses revolution and sedition. From the dress of the youth, to the graffiti on the street corners, to the EZLN cafés and restaurants, it is a place with a wonderful feel of social cohesion and where anything is possible. Being a bit of a western champagne socialist myself, I got involved with the whole classless thing and engaged with the power of the proletariat, having a small boy clean my boots while I sat savouring a hot chocolate on the terrace.

San Cristobal also has more hotels and hostels than I think I have ever seen, and definitely more tourists than anywhere else I have been so far, so perhaps the economic opportunities of this whole revolutionary thing, shouldn't be underestimated. I mean, even Che does a pretty good line in t-shirts. I met 12 overland bikers from all over the place, but as usual, most were from Germany.

I also met the most incredible Dutch family who I ended up seeing in the New Year with. Michael, Ciska, Sammy (10) and Jessie (12), have been on the road for 6 years, with a couple of tandem bicycles and they are about the loveliest people you could ever care to meet. The boys are multi lingual and possibly the most well adjusted, balanced, sprightly and well educated kids I know. Life on the road certainly seems to be working for them.

We stayed three days in a great old court-yarded hacienda. Although there were no windows in the room, we could see when it was daylight through all the gaps in the roof. I believe it's called rustic charm.

The surrounding mountainous countryside is just stunning, like Switzerland but with litter and a wider variety of vegetation. The problem is that the roads are terrible. There were even signs which, literally translated, read "absent". What they meant was that the road was absent, having long since fallen down the hillside. There was no consistency in their use however but there was still the Mexican persistence in using bloody speed bumps with no warning. It's so unfair when there's so much beauty to look at.

Having gone over some really nasty ones which were hidden in the shade of trees, I was trying to be ultra alert and not get caught out unnecessarily, when another unpainted obscured one appeared and I had to scrub off some speed. Braking hard I glanced in the mirror to see Jason and his big red BMW gaining impossibly quickly. I tried to crack open the throttle again but I was way too late and after the initial rear impact threw Peggy sideways, picking the back end up into the air, I collided heavily with the tarmac and slid for an admirable distance.

It is because of that, that I'd like to recommend kevlar lined jeans. Proven to protect- or some such slogan, but let's just say it meant I could save all my bandages for another time. After everyone warned me about the Mexican drivers, it's the smiley Californians I should have been watching out for. With the poor, now reshapen left hand pannier tied on with ratchet straps, and the crash bars modified with locally sourced rocks to enable me to select gears, I limped on. Literally.

We did discuss the liability insurance he had bought at the border, and whether or not we could all get new bikes from the claim, and maybe some nicer hotel rooms. What really pisses me off though, is that he didn't fall off, and it was me that was expecting the impact! At least he bent all his crash bars and front fairing, so that's something. I think Matt felt left out…

Descending into the jungle again we followed signs to the Agua Azul, the blue water cascades and for the first time on the trip, (apart from New Brunswick) became celebrities. Crowds surrounded us, and as we rode everyone stopped what they were doing to stare. The braver souls engaged us in conversation, the rest just gawked. 6 year old Luis got the 5 peso job of watching the bikes and promised to remain vigilant, before wandering off to secure another contract. As with everywhere I've been in Mexico so far, the concept of childhood is really only embraced by the rich. Most of the small adults seem to start some kind of work, usually in retail, at about the age of four and the ones around here seem to have mastered the art of carrying all of their produce on their heads by the age of six. But what a beautiful place to work.

A huge series of waterfalls with the most amazing turquoise coloured water, surrounded by jungle, it didn't look real. There are some kind of minerals in the water that lay deposits on the rock, like stalactites, and mean that the falls are always advancing, but it also means there is a smooth surface akin to something created by Disney, or for the penguin enclosure at the zoo. Given the heat though, the pools of azure couldn't have been more inviting if Siobhan had been swimming naked in them.

We camped in the garden beside Toñio's house (a friendly bloke who worked as a water engineer and meteorologist and lived at the top of the falls), so we could watch the sunrise in the morning and be the first to swim in the waters, drinking from a coconut and pausing only to eat some fresh fruit. I'm telling you, it's tough being on the road and not managing to hold down a career.

Palenque is an incredible Mayan ruined city in the Chiapas jungle. Unlike Teotihuacan, the exposed city is over a smaller area, has controlled zones where the hawkers try to sell you junk, and is under constant threat of reclaim by the jungle. It is unbelievable that anyone even found it, given the density of the vegetation and in fact there are now nearly 2000 more unexcavated buildings and temples located in the vicinity. Some of the mounds are only excavated on one side, so that you can see how camouflaged the pyramids had become. The new discoveries are being made by satellite imaging and aerial photography. In the dense forest floor the slow decay of the limestone pyramids are altering the chemical composition of the soil, so determining what plants can thrive in the alkaline ground and making it possible to identify differences in vegetation that can then be explored more thoroughly. The whole place had a much nicer feel than Teotihuacan, and was awash with toucans and hummingbirds, monkeys and snakes all of which made it seem terribly foreign.

That night's hotel, at a cost of 33pesos (almost £1.50) was grass roofed and set in a tiny clearing. Sleep was only disturbed by the howler monkeys which make a truly indescribable noise, and I have never been happier to be woken, it's a sound like no other. Luckily they didn't nick or break anything on the bikes, but to be honest I don't really think I'd have cared, they couldn't do as much damage as Jason! We later met a French Canadian lawyer called Edith who had managed to get to the EZLN celebrations for New Year and I think it must have been her stories that so captivated Jason allowing Matt and I to have the room to ourselves

From there it was four days of jungle, traversing the Yucatan peninsula and towards Belize. This was an exercise that I still look back on with glee. Sleeping to the sound of cicadas, sweating profusely and waking on one occasion to two tarantulas on my tent, it couldn't have been more authentic.

Although constantly assured by locals that we were on the right track, we just couldn't believe it as we opened gates and rode up paths passing people's shacks, and chickens. Single width footpaths through jungle undergrowth, it continued for hours. I occasionally managed second gear, and the whole thing was hilarious, aside from the boa constrictor. We stopped for photos in a jungle clearing to remove all the vines that the panniers were collecting and to laugh. Adventure motorcycling eh?

The Yucatan peninsula in Mexico, the bit that sticks up into the Caribbean, is special in many ways, not least that a lot of the inhabitants still speak Mayan as their first language and the Mayan resistance to colonisation was so strong for so long that many of the white settlers actually ended up embracing the language too. It's a long and intriguing history of uprising, war and diplomatic manoeuvring as is all of the Mayan story, and given that so many of the people we talked to identify themselves as Mayan first and Mexican second, it is not over yet.

I'll be sorry to see the back of Mexico, with the incredibly industrious, friendly people and the kids in the villages that come out to make hand slap contact as we drive past. The colourful towns and the crazy vehicles, the blaring music that drives you out of the shops instead of inviting you in, the donkeys and all the military checkpoints where my zip lock bags of mixed herbs and powdered milk always lead to special investigation and the invitation for me to eat some there and then. I'll not miss the topes, or the chillies, or the flour tortillas I've grown to hate so vehemently.

There is a whole new country waiting just over the river from where I am now. One that may be every bit as engaging: a new culture, a new people, a new language that I hope I'll understand, and the very real possibility that I'll be able to find good tea and maybe even baked beans.

You see there are one or two things that I can't knock British imperialist colonisation for. And so to Belize…

30 THE BIG FOUR OH!

"Fifteen dollars"

"Excuse me?"

"Fifteen dollars"

"What for? I just want an exit stamp please."

"Ok. Ten dollars"

"How about nothing at all except a stamp?"

"Go and clear your motorcycle first, then come back"

Jason and I headed to customs and vehicular clearance to see if I could get the $300 dollars back that I left with the Mexican authorities when I entered the country, and Matt stayed to watch the bikes, beside Mr Fifteen dollars. Three crisp hundred dollar bills and a mild case of heat stroke later, we returned to see an exasperated Matt watch the last of a busload of travellers getting back on a coach and head into Belize.

"He's just stung everyone of them 200 pesos, and they had it ready to give him"

Maybe the bus driver primed them and takes his cut later.

So I turned to Mr Fifteen dollars. "Can I have my exit stamp now por favor?"

"Si." And that was that, a determined look and it was suddenly free. Funny how bureaucracy works sometimes isn't it?

If it hadn't been for all the military and the stifling heat we may have posed for momentous photos, but instead we rode over the bridge, under the very English "Welcome to Belize" sign and met Edward, who would show us where to buy mandatory insurance, and then guide us through the "nightmare" that is Belizian customs. We bought insurance from his friend ($30 for a month), and caused a small office crisis by asking to see a copy of the policy, but declined Edward's offer of "guidance" through customs. Determined to help though, he warned us of the road ahead.

"Wen you geet too Orange Walk, mick sewer you go too de leff side. If you go to de rite side you weel aff to stop at al de traffic lite. Wen day red you go stap and wait til dem green. Den the nex wan, if red you go stap also. Man, it crazy slow"

Thanking Edward for his time he suggested we pay him a little something for his service, so I gave him a dollar as did Matt and J.

"What dis? Is dat al?"

Well, frankly, yes. That's more than enough.

Further up the road we came to a wooden hut with four guys reading the paper, chatting and wit dem plenty Reggae musik playing. This'd be official fumigation then, and an opportunity for a conversation about Peggy's vital statistics.

"Wow- how fast she go chief?"

$5 Belizean dollars for Daniel to get some weed killer and spray the bottom half of the wheels. Clearly the top half couldn't be carrying any nasty Mexican bugs, and I'm sure they respect the territorial political boundary where so much of the two countries join anyway. Our half wet wheels then rolled on up to immigration and customs.

"Welcome to Belize chief. May I see your passport?"

"And how long do you wish to stay?" I tell him a

few weeks would be nice.

"I'll give you a month. Now you must go to customs chief".

Customs was sitting at the next desk, with big black shades helping to accentuate the gleam of the golden teeth. He asked if I wanted to declare anything so I mentioned the bike. He looked at my immigration stamp, saw the one month permit and gave the bike two weeks. And that was that. No queue, no expense, unless you count the £1.50 for fumigation, and no hassle at all. We'd heard from Gringos who were living in Mexico, that the Belizeans would rip us off at every turn. That the government were charging for visitors visas (like Mexico and everywhere else), that we'd be charged to bring the bikes in (like in Mexico and everywhere else), that all the officials were greedy bribe hungry bastards. Instead we got cheery smiles, offers of da weed, and best wishes in our travels, which I don't think is quite the same. But then everyone I met in the States warned about how dreadful and corrupt Mexico would be... Mr fifteen dollars was the only time and he didn't try too hard. Isn't fear and prejudice great?

Belize is about the size of Wales (honestly), but has only about 260,000 people, with a third of them living in Belize City. What that amounts to in essence, is somewhere unlike anywhere else in Latin America, and certainly unlike Mexico. There isn't anybody around! There is very little traffic, but that can also be attributed to the fact that Belize is much, much poorer than Mexico. The bulk of the population travel by bicycle, all of which are of identical design, with rear hub brake only. They are, of course, still capable of carrying a family of 6 and the shopping. For vehicles that do exist, the automotive fashion that everyone adheres to, whether private or commercial, is to sport at least one particularly soft tyre, though I'm not sure it'll catch on globally. The other dramatic national difference, apart from skin colour, is that the people this side of the border are at least a foot taller. This was an incredible relief since I was getting really sick of banging my head on everything in Mexico. All the market stalls and hanging goods in shops were placed at eye level. My eye level, leading to a permanent stoop during periods of retail therapy lest I suffer permanent blindness.

Being an ex British colony that only gained its independence in the early 1980's, Belize is English speaking and predominantly black, though with a significant Mayan population in the south and a (relatively) huge, new Chinese diaspora, that ensures there are more Chinese restaurants across the country than even in Northern Ireland. Belize never really shone as a jewel in the British Empire though, especially after it had been raped of much of its logwood and mahogany, so it's no surprise that at the same time Thatcher was fighting a war to maintain a distant South Atlantic island no one had heard of, she was happy to sign away Britain's only remaining piece of the American mainland continent, populated by what was left of the indigenous Maya and the slaves Britain imported to improve the rate of deforestation.

So what of it now, over 25 years after independence? Well, I've been here a week and I can't decide how to describe it culturally or socially. Physically it is green. Very very green. The north is flat, has a few sugar plantations, citrus farms and swamps. The west is virginal mountainous jungle and the south is recovering jungle. One of the national symbols, the Mahogany tree, is unfortunately in short supply, having been transformed into far too many dodgy fire surrounds and front doors in the 50's and 60's.

There are 4 roads. The Northern Highway, going

north from Belize City, the Southern Highway going south from Belize city, the Western highway, see a pattern yet? and the Hummingbird highway going diagonally to join the western and southern. These are mostly 2 lane, but not totally and not all paved either. Everything else is dirt track or footpath and this year's wet season was so severe that most of the country's bridges have been destroyed. I have been enjoying so many of the appalling roads that I am currently in danger of outstaying my visa. My never terribly good rear shock finally collapsed and has left me with an unrideable bike.

Matt urged me to try and use the warranty the shock came with and it was with some trepidation that I entered negotiations with Alf Hagon in London, given my experience of the British bike industry, and given that they supplied the wrong parts in the first place, after telling me in no uncertain terms that they were the suspension specialists, when I tried to request a stronger than standard spring at the outset.

Would you believe they replied to my email almost instantly, and requested an address and phone number so that they could ship out a complete replacement unit via UPS! I've now had quite a dialogue with them and they are building a special unit with heavier spring and different damping. They are sending fresh fork oil and stickers which they would like me to put on the bike, and want to use me for promotional purposes. My first sponsor? It's a shame that they didn't just build what I asked them for in the first place....

For a while there I was thinking that I had misnamed Peggy, and should perhaps have called her Christine, given that the odometer has started running backwards! I was hoping that the mirror would fix itself, the dents in the fuel can, the bent luggage racks and split in the pannier would all miraculously be repaired, but a collapsed shock has put paid to that theory. We all live in hope, and a little dream is not a bad thing to carry...

A guy called Mike who owns a bar in the capital city, Belmopan, has given us use of his lean-to at the back of the pub and his outside toilet. I can even get internet access if I stand in the middle of the next field. The only thing that could possibly be better would be to be able to get some sleep before 3am when the revellers finally leave. The shelter is such a relief because it has been raining constantly for 5 days now, and many of the roads are returning to their natural state. But lets go back to the beginning.

That first Belizean night was spent in the town of Orange Walk, not just because of the time of day, but because I was intrigued by Edward's warning of "all de traffic lite wot meak ya stap." I presumed it must be some huge metropolis, but there were in fact two traffic lights. Everything is relative in Belize.

The journey south from the border let me witness a new kind of poverty, and although there were still the smiles and waves, there seemed to be a lethargy that I hadn't seen in Mexico. The houses are a mixture of whatever, and many of them are constructed with at least one huge piece of tin purloined from the many vehicle graveyards. I've never seen a breakers yard before where every vehicle has had its roof cut off! Architecturally, the buildings are a mix of new world British colonial (all wooden, on stilts with balconies and verandas), and Mexican style concrete block but with thatch and car panels providing the roof instead of corrugated tin. The wooden houses seem to defy the laws of physics though, with bends and slopes and everything patched at crazy angles. Needless to say they aren't built quite like that, but the humidity, termites, carver ants and the odd hurricane rapidly reshape them, creating... character.

One near constant though, regardless of house

style, is the British obsession with a cut lawn, even if it is shaped around an old scrapped Mercedes. I don't think I'd even seen a lawn since Palm Springs. Our first retail experience had me yelp with delight. Not surprisingly Jason "big tank" needed fuel, so while he was filling up I wandered round the shop and found Heinz Baked Beans and Custard creams. My chance to introduce my American friends to the best of British cuisine!

Orange Walk, is, well, a bit of a dump really. The open sewers don't help, it has to be said, but the whole place just exudes, well filth I suppose. But it's not just that, there is the lethargy I mentioned before. No one can be bothered, the shops are all dreadfully presented, they all seem to sell the same stuff- a mixture of plastic Chinese tat, there being no concept of specialisation and certainly no idea of marketing. It's in stark contrast to entrepreneurial Mexico and what Belize sorely needs is a lick of paint to brighten it up and a signwriter. Of course I was never able to confirm the grammatical accuracy of the signs I'd seen in Spanish, but I feel that "Trespassers will be Persecuted" is a little harsh, especially for a first offence, and the official highways signs "drive slowly for your safetly" is demonstration of the nation's loose adoption of the English language.

Mr and Mrs Lee were very accommodating though, inviting us to put the bikes in the dining room of their Orange Walk hotel, and what's funny is that the old boy sitting reading the paper at the front door didn't bat an eyelid, or miss a line as we rode passed him and squeezed through the door. We slept soundly even with the intense heat, but awoke to discover that red ants had colonised all of our stuff. Inside the helmets, the lining of the jackets, gloves, everything. Oh, the tropics!

After a morning of dirt and single track broken tar we arrived at Altun Ha, another ancient Mayan city, but were confronted with a whole new sight. Coach loads of tourists, all from Cruise ships in Belize City, were given 45mins for a whistle stop tour of the sight. Interestingly many of them, especially the men, spent more time photographing and looking at our bikes than the ruins, and were easy to engage in conversation. Arriving in Belize that morning, on their 5000 berth cruise ships, they were seeing the ruins in the morning, Belize City in the afternoon and then they were sailing at 6pm. Another day another country. Each to their own as they say, but if I had a dollar for every time someone said "I wish I was doing what you are", I'd have been able to buy lunch. Just how expensive can a poor country be?

True, tourist nick-naks are going to cost, especially at a trap like Altun Ha, but everything here seems to be expensive, if there is anything you actually want. I heard people ask on more than one occasion whether there were any postcards available of Altun Ha and not just the classic Belizean beach. The reply? "Na man, dem all soul long tam ago". So would anybody tink of getting some more? The quality sales patter continued to an old man who was trying to decline the purchase of a carved wooden walking stick. "Wat you mean no room. I see dem big boat. Der plenty room for a bit of woood". What charm.

A road side cafe was where we finally found reasonably affordable food, and Hattie was proud to tell us that "Today our special meal, jus for you, is stoo chicken and we gat sam rice and we gat sam beans too". There being no written menu we settled in for the plat du jour a little sceptical that it was special for just today. The military across the way at the army barracks came over to see if we needed any weed. One stop shopping.

Then the road got properly rough. Tyre shredding, suspension breaking rough rocks interspersed with sand. Deep sand. I hate sand. It's official. I know all the armchair heroes say "just sit back and open the throttle, make the front end light". Bollocks. It's 35 degrees, the bike is fully loaded, not terribly powerful, has an extra 10kgs of water and fuel up the front and the patch of sand is 20 miles long. Don't give me "open the throttle".

A long, but exhilarating ride ended at night fall in Placencia, on the Caribbean coast. A little village on a white sand spit covered in palm trees, was where I would wake up and be forty.

Forty huh? Funny old age, and about the time, if pundits are to be believed, that I should be having a panic, reassessing my life, quitting my career and considering buying a motorbike and heading off on an adventure to unknown lands. I must say though, over the last few weeks I've been considering a nice job in accountancy. The good news is that forty is a time when you don't feel like you have to do something, just because it's expected of you, or is the "done" thing. So for breakfast I had a tin of baked beans on bread (couldn't toast it) and after a lazy read of the paper, spent much of the day repairing the damage that Jason had done to Peggy in the collision. I did all this surrounded by iguanas sunning themselves and strange colourful birds singing amazing songs. That night we took a small motor launch (I've always wanted to say that!) over to a gastro-bar on an island. Need I say tropical?

I had the added company of a couple from Vancouver on a BMW who manage musical acts and after realising that they did everything online anyway, decided to do it from a different place each day! We were told that the village would be experiencing something of a communal high over the weekend, given that two bales of coke had washed ashore that morning. I suppose that's one of the 'inconveniences' of living on a drug trafficking route, but nobody seemed in the least surprised. The bar lady, Tracey, kept lining up shots on the house to celebrate my birthday, but if we weren't paying attention or all present at the same time, she drank them herself or gave them to the next boat load of arrivals. What a mad place.

We decided to head back to the mainland where Tracey was going to organise a real night on the town, but instead I watched a floodlit basketball game played by shoeless giants and ended up sitting on a recliner with my feet in the Caribbean sea, just chatting under a full moon, with a cup of tea. You see that's the rebel in me, I just don't care!

Reading the local paper is always very illuminating and for such a small country it is incredible that there are seven nationals. In Placencia though, I enjoyed the paper of the coastal islands, so there wasn't quite as much mayhem and murder as there is in one that covers the goings on in Belize City. What there was, on the front page, was the story of an accident between a golf cart and a bicycle. The police were called because the cyclist was an American lawyer and she wanted to claim damages. The police said she was silly and should watch where she was going. The police couldn't prove whether or not the golf buggy driver had been using his mobile phone at the time the incident occurred. Heady times! Page 3 had an article and big picture of a runaway golf buggy that had gone into Mrs Percival's shop. I mean, these things are a menace, must we wait until someone is killed before they are banned? If only the Daily Mail was published here there'd some kind of campaign.

Between all the electric cart mayhem though, was the story that after Christmas the Belize Armed Forces and the Guatemalan Army did a joint exercise near the border in a show of good will after the signing of a new peace and land demarcation agreement between the two countries. They've been bickering for years about who owns what. Unfortunately the local villagers were none to impressed with all the noise and they took both lots of military hostage, holding them until they agreed to stop making a racket and buggered off back to base. The embarrassment didn't stop there though. The Belizean military forgot to write up the incident, and the first that the authorities knew, was when the Guatemalan foreign minister asked what the government was going to do about the upstart villagers.

Probably give them more weed so that they are as stoned as the soldiers. (Allegedly). That is the over riding thing about this country, no one seems to give a damn about anything. No one seems to know anything either, or at least refuses to impart any knowledge they have.

"Is there a hairdresser in town, or a post office?"

Blank looks followed by a "Me dunno man".

"But your town is only four blocks long, how can you not know?"

Similar discourse happens when ordering food in a restaurant. The waitress never knows what is on the menu and has no idea about what any of the dishes are. But if you press them long enough you discover "we gaw stoo chicken an rice an beans". Getting fresh fruit and veg is proving problematic as well, but there are more types of Spam and tinned vegetables in the supermarkets than you can imagine.

One thing to be wary of though, should you find yourself in a shop, is the sell by dates on all the goods. I needed to buy coffee for the boys, but couldn't find any that wasn't at least a year out of date. On another day Matt bought a Snickers bar in a shop that not only had no water, but where the shop keeper didn't know where to look through his stock to find any. Matt divided that Snickers bar into 5 that night to share with our co-diners (a couple from Surrey) after a most appalling meal. Not only did we wait 2hrs 45 mins, but the veggie tamales weren't, and my chicken and onion soup was bone broth.

The whole situation was comical. One meal came out at a time and everyone in the dining room had to try and identify it as the waiter didn't know what each dish was, or which table to bring it to. It was all so ludicrous that we thought the snickers would be a pleasant dessert. I'm sure it would have been had we eaten it before it's sell by date of Feb 2004. It was so old I was surprised it wasn't called Marathon. That was by no means the end of that night of service industry encounters though. We retired to our room after negotiating for the key and paying a deposit. We had initially thought that a key would be included in the extortionate $30 price. Silly us.

After retiring to our room we noticed an inordinately large number of ants, even for Belize. They were running over the pillows and sheets and up the walls. No amount of zen like acceptance was going to get us to nod off. Then Matt realised that the whole nest was under his mattress and thousands were caring for all the eggs. How very National Geographic and even more surprising given that we had had to wait hours for our room to be cleaned. Our new chamber only had big sticky frogs and spiders, but after a major chemical attack next door and lots of banging as bits of wood reigned havoc on the nest, a couple from Connecticut were shown the room, where I'm sure they slept soundly.

Anyway, I've got ahead of myself again. After Placencia we headed south to the beautiful Blue Creek, which is effectively the furthest south you can go in Belize. There is no open land border with Guatemala here, but the locals assured me that it was possible to get through. The road to the creek and a cave where the turquoise waters emerge from the centre of the earth was an enjoyable struggle and involved me losing some stickers as I scrapped the boxes on some rocks. Peggy was wider than the track in many places and with the drop offs to other creeks and damp slippery mosses under wheel, it was quite an exhilarating ride. The people in the area were 100% Mayan and although very poor, all living in one room wooden shacks with twice height thatched roofs, they seemed very industrious and definitely very friendly. Ignacio seemed to be the man in charge in these parts, and with his permission we set up camp by the side of the creek.

If anyone remembers the BMW adverts a few years ago for the GS series, where the posters said "Get there before Judith Chalmers does" that's just how I felt. The Holiday Programme will no doubt discover Blue Creek soon, especially with the current construction of a tourist lodge set deep in the jungle, but for now I can confidently say that I was one of the very first guests. When the builders went home we invaded the building and pitched our tents on the covered verandas, overlooking the beautiful waters that were so stocked with fish it felt like you could walk across the blue green surface. The workers showed up in the morning and didn't bat an eyelid at the gringos asleep on their carpentry.

The next day the heavens opened and the taps stayed on for the next five days, turning the dirt roads into a quagmire. Returning from the exploration of more Mayan ruins at Labaantun, I realised that I was suddenly guilty of terrible environmental damage. Peggy was sitting in the middle of the lush green of the jungle, the grass below and the leaves above all glistening with moisture in the bright sunlight, and I noticed a huge pool of rainbow organic compounds on the ground beneath her, signifying the bursting and collapse of the rear shock absorber as it finally cried enough. Now that is not something I'd hoped I'd ever see and I'm not sure which I felt worse about, being stranded in the Caribbean or leaving my oily mark so indelibly on this otherwise pristine landscape. I limped north to the capital city of Belmopan, which is little more than a regional outpost. It doesn't really appear to contain anything, though a few embassies have moved there since it was decided to shift the government from Belize City to somewhere that didn't flood every year and where homicide wasn't the biggest cause of death among people between the ages of zero and old age.

There are three stop signs in Belmopan and a couple of speed bumps, though there may have been more, but I didn't see them in the few days I spent there. There are two banks, five shops in the main parade, a bus station and about four Chinese restaurants. Occasionally there is a small market selling dreadful looking veg, manned by dreadfully disinterested people, and there is a phone box. Oh, and there's a Courts furniture store with a sale on. Honestly.

Camping behind the pub was great, and I'm eternally grateful for the generosity, but I could no longer stick the sleep deprivation of the late nights, (well I'm forty now you know) so I headed for the peace and tranquillity of a Mennonite Community. Der kline Germaine Mennonite Kolonie, like the Amish but with pickup trucks and I don't imagine you were expecting that. I know I wasn't.

31 NOT QUITE THE SHOCK I HAD EXPECTED

So Alf Hagon's warranty department agreed to post out a replacement rear shock absorber, even though I explained that I couldn't quite put my hands on the original receipt just at the minute. No quibble. A two year warranty is a two year warranty and they are terribly sorry for my inconvenience. Hurray! Fingers crossed I'll have my faith in the British bike industry restored. I wait.

And I wait. Then they tell me they sent it out on a 10 day super saver service, but gave me a tracking number so that I could see where it was. The normal post to the UK barely takes that long, but they apologise and assure me that it never really takes 10 days. I explain that 3 day express takes three days guaranteed and wouldn't that be handy?

I had more time to kill, but used some of it to arrange a place to do the suspension replacement when it finally arrived. Willie Penner at Motor Solutions agreed to let me use his workshop, and helped me with internet, phone and fax services. Motor Solutions have been the Capital city's official Kawasaki dealer for just over a year and they are expecting their first couple of bikes any day soon! They warned me not to underestimate the length of time customs may hold my part.

After staying a few nights with Leonard and Elizabeth Rymer on their Mennonite farm, we had to move for the Sabbath because other brethren were coming and they needed the room. It was a really soothing place to be though. Not just because of their "everything based on trust" ethos, but also because they had a parrot who spoke low German like the settlers, said "good morning" as though it was from Windsor, and had a fantastic party trick; calling in the cattle!

The Mennonite 'kolonie' arrived in Belize from Mexico in 1958 after falling out with what they saw as a corrupt, interfering government. A total of 62 families made the gruelling journey to the area called Spanish Lookout, and they settled 18,000 acres of jungle. 50 years on, it is an incredible sight. There are still some who use only horses and carts and wear matching Germanic dungarees, with the ladies in plain blue dresses, but many of them have embraced pickup trucks, baseball caps and mobile phones.

The cleared jungle landscape reminded me so much of the UK, all green rolling hills and standing old growth trees, cattle munching on the abundant grass and corrugated steel barns at all the farmsteads that nestle beneath steely grey skies. Lines of agricultural machinery working arable fields, manned by swarthy tall blond men with sunburn and hundreds of Salvadoran and Guatemalan refugees. And there is everything you could possibly want to buy in the spacious hardware and automotive shops that sit in their own huge plots either side of the main road in this thriving farming community. Everything that is, except a battery for an Aprilia Pegaso.

Spanish Lookout is situated right on the (still disputed) border with Guatemala, and when this was all a little piece of Empire, there was a constant fear of Spanish invasion. In fact, the Spanish were never really that interested in Belize and instead they just annoyed the hell out of the British by granting asylum to any escaped slaves that could make it across the border. All very honourable, but of course the old Spanish Empire wasn't all liberal enlightenment. They were, after all, in someone else's continent, nicking whatever they could get, but granting freedom for slaves looked good and cost the Brits another £50 for every replacement. Economic sabotage. The thing was, these rights and freedoms were only granted to the slaves if they converted to Catholicism. If they didn't, they were taken back to the Brits! Ah yes, humanitarian compassion with strings attached.

I took myself and Peggy the pogo stick, to the town of San Ignacio and holed up for what turned out to be a week in a wee hotel owned by an ex British army squaddie called Wally. The boys left me and went away to explore the jungle and various ruins and waterfalls down roads that I could no longer travel.

Now Wally wasn't alone. It seems that San Ignacio is the place to come if you are an ex British soldier with a nervous tick, an alcohol problem and a sack full of guilt on your shoulders. I was really surprised, given my own origins, with just how open and frank some of them were to talk about their time in the army, and especially time spent in Northern Ireland.

But I digress, which shouldn't surprise you. I got an email from Hagons saying the shock had finally arrived in Belize, but just in case it was a porky pie I checked the tracking number with UPS. Yes! It was scanned in at Belize, which meant that customs were now holding it until I paid the import duty. I high tailed it (bouncily) to Belmopan to tell Willie and Glenfield at Motor Solutions that it was in at last and just to warn them that I'd become a fixture in their workshop soon. Willie said I should give UPS a call just to be sure before riding into Belize City.

"Nah, me no gaw da pakidge heah chief. Sumtam dem jus scan em in case day is layit"

In case they are late? Which element of "tracking

emergency packages" is it that you don't fully understand?

I bounced slowly and dejectedly back to my hotel, but enjoyed a superb evening with Fabio and Simonietta in their (best in the country) Italian restaurant, Amore Mio. I'd become a bit of a regular, trying almost every dish on the menu and sampling all the liqueurs (on the house). This night was spent talking about Ducatis and pasta and Alfa Romeos and oregano and pizzas and time spent working around the world, until Simonietta went home and told Fabio and I to clean up and lock up, or words to that effect. Some of them were in Italian but were delivered in a certain tone....

I really grew to like that little town of San Ignacio and although there was a big shoot out at the bank a few days before I arrived, only three people were killed, so apparently it was nothing. There are gangs though, either side of the river, which is a fixture in most Belizean towns, but something the tourist can remain blissfully unaware of. There was a little second hand bookshop where I could stock up on English language reading material and it was good to catch up on titles that I probably should have read years ago, like 'Our Man in Havana'. There's a really poignant bit in it where 'Our Man' has to go to Jamaica and comments on the urban environment he finds, the sprawling nature of Kingston and the lack of design or order in the metropolitan melee. As a result he says, it has a physical character unlike any Latin American town, where the Spanish seemed proud of their settlements and ordered them around central squares, churches and markets. It was as though the English were in the area with no permanence, but just the desire to extract what they could as cheaply and quickly as possible.

That for me sums up exactly the difference between Mexico and Belize. It's true Belize started to enter British consciousness as little more than a place where her pirates, like Walter Raleigh could put to ground for a while and ride out storms or count their booty. It was as though it was an accidental colony that the British elite really didn't care about and still don't, Commonwealth member or not, but they do at least ensure a good supply of baked beans, tea and custard creams gets through.

With Matt's birthday coming up, Willie said he'd chase up the shock for me with UPS, collect it from customs and even pay the duty, so that I could go and meet the boys on the beach. All I had to do was get back to the workshop and fit it when it finally materialised, which couldn't be more accommodating. Glenfield gave me directions to Hopkins where the lads were, and I feel I must relay them to you. It may give you a sense of this little nation. Bear in mind we are standing in the capital city and where I was heading was on the other side of the country about 80miles away.

"Go dande rowadd and jus keep on goin. Den you gotta torn at de petril stay shon.

First dare iss noh petril stay shon, Den dare is wan! Dare you gotta torn to de rye it. (65miles)

Den is easy. Juss stay on de rowadd till you cum to de bustap. (10 miles) Iss not so big, maybe ...(he marks out about 6' by 8' on the ground) but it is wan off de nicest bustaps in all of Belize, you canut miss dis. Dare you juss torn leff and it maybe five miles more own lee. Ba de rowadd, oh man iss bad..."

And how big is Hopkins? Do you think I'll be able to find the lads ?

"Well, it mostlee wan street. You juss ask for de white guys wit de mota sykills. Evree wan will no".

I set off, confident that as a courier it shouldn't be too difficult for me to make one right turn and then one left turn. Then it started to rain again. Hard. That "Hoh, hoh" wet crotch moment, came after barely 5 miles and the heavy clouds meant the light was fading faster than normal. I bravely picked up the pace until the rev counter told me I was doing nearly 60 miles an hour, but it was all too much. A nearly uncontrollable Peggy bounced and slid over the whole road, so I slowed down and accepted that I wouldn't make it before nightfall, even though I had a black visor and no working lights. Ho hum! Well would you believe it? As the last grey of dusk was vanishing, there was no sign of a petrol station, and then there was, just like he said! Before I could see it, I couldn't see it. He wasn't wrong, it's just that it reminded of Irish people that start giving directions with lines like "Oh, you don't want to start from here..." Assessing ten miles in the pitch black, with no lights, visor open, rain on the glasses and no odometer, is quite difficult, but then I was confident that I would have no difficulty spotting one of the nicest bus stops in all Belize and everything would be fine.

I missed it, but I did follow a man on a bicycle who led me to the left turn and wished me luck. But the road, oh man! Glenfield's every word was true. I crawled along trying to wind my way between potholes that were occasionally axle deep, and trying to remain on the track and not fall off into the swamp on either side. The rear end banged and thumped and bounced and I had to laugh because I felt I could get no wetter nor ride more slowly. Actually I could. Peggy stopped at the edge of the village and all the power was gone. I started walking.

That was how I met Marlon and his three year old daughter Viv. He came out of the darkness to see why I'd stopped near his house (that I hadn't seen). He then gave me his quad to go looking for the lads, but I couldn't see a thing through the darkness and rain, so came slowly back to the house. I don't think it was meant to be four wheel steering, but every bump sent the thing crabbing in a different direction. I really didn't have the energy to rise to the challenge, so instead I spent the evening with Marlon and was finding the conversation all quite fascinating right up to the bit where, in tears, this tattooed, psychologically unstable, ex gang member from Belize city, fondled his knife and told me how he was going to kill his ex wife and the fucking Canadian that she had run off with. I didn't doubt a word of it and just hoped that the Canadian didn't look anything like me as I shared rice and beans and then lay on the floor and tried to fall asleep...

A place looks very different when you can see it, and the next morning I walked down the windswept beach until I found Matt and Jason in tents sheltering behind a makeshift cover of timber and tarpaulin.

Well happy birthday Matt! The poor guy had been down since he lost his "Life is Good" baseball cap in Mexico, so Jay and I'd got him a similar one before we entered Belize and found a Guatemalan woman who'd create a patch reading "Life is Good, Central America 2008/9". The quality personalised souvenir birthday present was meant to cheer him up, but I don't think the lady could read my writing, so I'm not entirely sure what the cap now reads, though it's definitely authentic!

Sitting and sheltering from the storm left time to watch the activities of some of the 523 species of bird the country has and to ruminate on why the locals use the beach as a tip, while simultaneously trying to expand their tourist appeal. Then the sun came out, the wind abated and we went along to a little beach hut bar where I had a really mad encounter with someone. I had read a book on the plane to San Francisco that I really enjoyed, called Deer Hunting with Jesus, about working class white America and the reasons why it always votes against its best interests. Well would you believe I met the author? Joe Bageant and I had a great time, putting the world to rights as it is always easy to do in a bar and he was a font of knowledge about Belize since he now spends much of his time here doing community development projects.

We got Peggy going a couple of days later and

after a terrific feed of fresh coconuts cut from the palms on the beach, which it turns out are more effective than immodium, I headed back to fit the recently arrived shock, which cost £100 in customs duty which was the sort of shock I hadn't expected! And they forgot to put the stickers and oil in the box. Is there a day I don't moan?

Over tea and a period of calm reflection, I picked up the Belize City paper and decided to do the word search since I've never really been a crossword person. There were 30 words to find but the editor was keeping it all very "local interest". Starting alphabetically with Arrest, Arson and Attorney, the words went all the way through to Verdict and Witness. Don't any of you ask why I gave the city a miss!

Back to my San Ignacio hotel where the suspension process started again and I took out the shock once more to adjust it properly, and fitted my new spare rectifier in a last ditch attempt to sort the continuing electrical gremlins. All this was done under the watchful gaze of Ricky and Hector the parrots who loitered around the hotel yard doing among other things, pitch, volume and time perfect renditions of smoke alarms. A little disconcerting when you try to fall asleep in your room, imagining how they learnt the sound. And that was that.

I was ready to leave Belize, described to me by Joe Bageant as an incredibly poor rich country. The Mennonites are creating vast amounts of agricultural produce, the country has its own oil and fantastic coral reefs and fish resources, yet the people stay poor. The last Prime Minister, Said Musa, is currently in court on corruption charges. Hugo Chavez of Venezuela presented Belize with $20m for educational projects. The former PM passed $10m of it on to the country, and $10 m of it to his bank account. In all, the PUP party who had been in power for multiple terms until recently is widely believed to have pilfered one billion dollars from the country. This is a country of 270,000 people. Imagine sharing that out!

I suppose I shouldn't be so surprised at the lethargy that the people exude. They were screwed as slaves, then left destitute when the trees had been cut down and sold. They were ignored by Britain when struck by hurricanes, and after they gained independence their politicians chose to invest heavily in Switzerland.

It seems to be a time of global hope, what with Obama fever and all, so all eyes are on Dean Barrow, Belize's first black Prime Minister to see what real change he can bring. I wouldn't say the population waits with baited breath, more just a long slow toke. I never experienced Belize's famously corrupt police force either, so perhaps that is another fallacy. All I ever saw was them providing a public transportation service with hitchhikers crammed in the back of their pickups, and my only direct contact with them was when they stopped to see if everything was alright and whether or not I needed any help or directions.

Let's see what Guatemala is like, and whether or not they have as much rain. Surely it can't be as expensive!

32 JUST TAKE THE KEYS

The crossing out of Belize was a good deal simpler than it could have been, had I not gone to the border the previous week to extend my bike's permit. It turns out that the two week allowance written in my passport was a complete fabrication, but was the simplest way, with the least amount of work, that the border guards in the north of the country could let me in. I was supposed to have been issued with a one month permit after I had fully read and understood the dire consequences that would befall me, were I to attempt to sell Peggy while in Belize. Thing is, that takes a lot of time and paperwork, especially when 3 bikes arrive at once and spoil an otherwise slow day under the Caribbean sun, so the good officers hadn't bothered. Had I left things to chance and just attempted to exit anyway, my bike would have been impounded for good. Which you'll have to agree, would have left me without one vital ingredient for continued adventure motorcycling. The three hours spent sorting it all out was worth it I feel.

So into Guatemala, with another quick fumigation farce and sooo many guns! All the officials were incredibly polite though, relevant photocopies were easily attained, and the shoe shine boys I hadn't seen since Mexico were back with a vengeance. No one had once offered to clean up my appearance in Belize, but here, everyone was concerned. I think the shoe shiners were the only unarmed people working the border though (and they were the ones who it turns out, need it most). At the border, if you needed your hands free for anything, side arm pistols were de rigueur, otherwise machine guns or shotguns, with holstered pistols just in case, was what everyone was wearing this spring. It's a little disappointing that everyone chose black, but I suppose it does match all clothing, uniform or not, and matches the majority of pickup truck dashboards, horse saddles and even looks well slung over a naked shoulder if you are busy working in the field or pushing a wheel barrow.

Yes, to say Guatemala is a violent country would be something of an understatement. The thing is, after twelve days here, I am more struck by the friendly industrious nature of the people, and the stunning physical beauty of the place, than I am by the violence. This little place has had a terribly harsh past and some things take a while to get over, so what is surprising is that it isn't more violent. True, I have ridden past three separate, obviously dead bodies, and I have had a look at El Neuevo Diario newspaper everyday and read some truly stunning stories, like five shoeshine boys getting shot dead in the town of Solola while I was staying 10 miles down the road, because they were working the wrong street, or that the price of an assassination is now running at 300 Quetzales, or about £27.

The perpetration of fear being what it is, and with all the guidebook and foreign office warnings about banditry and set-ups, it may well be the case that the 3 dead dudes I rode passed were just bluffing to get me to stop, but they looked pretty dead to me, so I didn't. After all, my telephonic linguistic skills aren't really up to calling the emergency services; should I know how to, or where my exact location is, notwithstanding the lack of national ambulance service anyway. And OK, I was a bit freaked out.

But this place is the size of Iceland (so clearly bigger than Wales), has a population of 13million, a third of which survive on $2 a day, and has emerged in the last ten years from a 30 year war which claimed the lives of nearly 300,000 people. 93% of the atrocities were carried out by the government and military and no-one has yet been held accountable.

When Bishop Gerrardi released his first report into government human rights abuses in 1998, he was killed two days later. The good news is that Bill Clinton apologised in 1999 for the US providing all the arms and training to the military during that time. So that was nice. Another prominent Human Rights and environmental campaigner Dr Yuri Melini, survived an assassination attempt but was severely injured, just last September so it's still not wise to be too vocal in this part of the world, though change is gradual and much of it began in 1996 with the signing of a peace agreement between the government and the rebels. That first instrumental step was taken by the then President, Alvaro Arzu, who not surprisingly rides a motorbike. Don't all the best people? He rides a Suzuki B-King, and I know that because I met him and had a wee chat about all sorts, including good twisty roads to the coast and rough steep ones that climb the sides of volcanoes. I noticed his bike wasn't actually registered, but then it is the only one of its kind that I've seen, and given the electronic tracking device he had attached to his chest, I don't think it is really that necessary.

I'm jumping around though like I did in Belize and that's no way to deliver a linear travel report, so permit me to backtrack to the border.

The border guard held up the last barrier so that I could suffer the ignominy of being pushed into a new country, Peggy's electrical gremlin resurfacing, as always, at the most inopportune moments. After she fired up we set off on the main highway from the east of the country, and managed nigh on 30 mph once or twice. The first 30 miles were worse than just normal, pockmarked, unpaved, hard packed clay.

Looking ahead provided some insight into coming road conditions, as vehicles zig zagged at walking pace between potholes. These things were anything up to a foot deep and often ran the entire width of the road. All I can say is that I'm glad it wasn't raining, because I met I guy on a GS from Colorado in Belize, who had come the other way in the rain and it had taken him all day. That included being towed out of the ditch by a horse after he had slithered off the road. One horse power eh? That's all you really need!

The first striking thing about Guatemala is that there are very few cars. Instead everyone uses scooters and motorbikes, and the ubiquitous Latin American pickup truck. For the first ten miles it seemed odd that there was no commercial traffic at all on the road, given that it is the only land connection between Guatemala and Belize, and that the whole eastern side of the country has no link to Mexico except through Belize. Then I met 11 trucks in convoy in the thick dust, nose to tail, and that reminded me of something else I had read about banditry so I concentrated harder on the road ahead.

The second thing to impress itself upon me is that the mobile chicanes are no longer dogs, but instead pigs and horses. I kid you not. They are everywhere, wandering free and yet clearly very important. Horses are used for everything including daily transport. Although there are regional differences in use, quality of care remains high, and it's really nice to see a little foal trotting along learning the ropes beside mum who is pulling a cart or carriage.

Poverty can take on a romance when it occurs

amidst a beautiful landscape. However this quaint romance can blind the observer. I was astounded to hear someone say how much more prosperous Guatemala was than Belize! Colourful certainly. Industrious looking people for sure. Smilier faces and more hand slapping through the villages, but naked children and parents attempting to bathe in mosquito infested stagnant waters next to houses that are little more than a thatched roof on 4 legs, may be photogenic in the right light, but it's not really a sign of successful economic development or of efficient municipal infrastructure. Much of Belize may have been a dump, but you could drink the water out of the taps, because there were taps!

Lunch was in the oft tourist frequented village of El Remate, because it lies on the northerly route to the Mayan ruins at Tikal, and because Peggy stopped again and refused to start even on a push, lacking enough electrical power to prime the fuel pump. She popped, died, popped again a couple of times and rolled to a halt beside an 1150 GS ridden by a couple from South Africa. Johan and Charmaine were in fact, the couple who had contacted me online when they heard about my rear shock failure and offered to bring one with them from Mexico if I needed it. What a small world it really is, and how very embarrassing that I should be able to say "Oh yes, I got that sorted, it's just the engine that doesn't work now".

"Aprilia- choice of global adventurers" not something I recall seeing all that often.

It was a fantastic place to stop though, Lake Peten Itza on the left, with its thatch covered fishing jetties jutting into the deep blue and thick impenetrable jungle to the right behind the single storey dwellings and businesses of the village. In a desperate move I changed the new rectifier for the old one that I was still carrying, and after a push we were back on the road. It would appear that the new spare rectifier/ regulator that I had carried all this way, neither rectified nor regulated!

Johan and Charmaine decided they'd like to spend the evening with us, so we found a little hotel in the beautiful island town of Flores, whose causeway permits it to jut into the lake from the south. We rode the bikes into the lobby as was becoming the norm. The hotel provided the perfect base to explore this colonial island town with its cobbled streets and plethora of cafes and restaurants almost all with stunning views of the lake.

Although Flores was an ancient Mayan settlement, the Spanish destroyed every building and last vestige of the past in 1687 when they took control, creating in its place what currently exists. The hotel was closing down as a result of the economic downturn, so we could have any room we liked, but services were a bit limited. Like water. The refreshing thing though, was that it cost £4 was clean and comfortable and we had a set of keys for the whole building. Our hosts were heading back home to their village in the mountains of the west and we were to drop in the keys on our way past! How trusting is that? Welcome to Guatemala! There was even Internet access from the fancy tourist hotel down the street if I leaned off my balcony. Leaning over the balcony wasn't something to be taken lightly, given some of the incredible cracks in the whole building. It may even have been a survivor of the massive 1976 earthquake that killed 22,000 people all across the country, but then again, they seem to have tremors in this area all the time. Either way, it certainly wasn't just a bit of subsidence; I could put my hand into some of the cracks in the walls.

Fortunately the Spanish never found the Mayan settlement of Tikal, situated deep in the jungle to the north of Flores, or if they did they chose not to destroy it. The ride up there was pleasantly peaceful, as the jungle closed in all around and the road signs warned me to watch for, well... Well apart from the snakes and big cats I'm afraid I didn't recognise any of the creatures, but if strange black 2-D monsters were lurking, I was ready for them.

Due to the low lying flat nature of the topography, the plan was to camp at the ruins and be there to explore in the morning, before the heat became unbearable, and the tour buses arrived. Oh I'm such a travel snob- but a place like that demands a bit of peace and quiet to enjoy, savour, absorb and get good pics. But snobbery of any kind can bite you on the ass as they say, and my camera died to spite me. It had long suffered when I was in an area of high humidity, it's circuit boards getting so confused it would open and close and randomly select which programme to use, but it doesn't get much more humid than this, so this time it cried enough. Which is all a shame really, because I would like to be able to share with you some of the strange creatures and birds that I saw, and was to continue seeing for days. What I wouldn't like to share is all the things that bite. From mozzies to those damned noseeums that hurt like hell and make me look like a measles victim. How do they do it? They are smaller than the human eye can cope with and yet they inflict such damage. Like daddy long legs, what are they for? That is what David Attenborough should spend time filming with all his amazing camera crew, if he is able to find them.

Tikal is possibly the most famous ruin in the region, in part because of its 3 main imposing pyramids that rise above the tree canopy level of the surrounding jungle. The geometric perfection of their construction is astounding and I could wax lyrical about the place but you all will have gathered by now that descriptive prose is not a strong point of mine so it's best I don't make an arse of myself or do the place an injustice.

The journey back to Flores the following day was going really well until it rained. It didn't rain much, just a sprinkling, but it was enough to reduce us to giggling idiots. With speed down to about five miles an hour we valiantly tried to keep the bikes upright on something akin to ice, but with much more muddy sticking power. Jay and Matt both fell a couple of times and picking them up was like some clown scene at the circus, as we desperately tried to get grip to even stand up. On one cambered corner halfway down a hill, I was trying to pick up Jason's bike when two little dirt bikes approached slowly, but couldn't stay up on the outside of the corner and at about 2mph they slid down for the unavoidable collision. Even reaching out to fend one of them off, I simply slid with him in slow motion to the hedge. With everyone laughing and apologising, another three bikes approached, followed by a 4x4 pickup that had less grip than any of us. Well, it's one way to meet people, but now I understand when I read about people riding for a whole day in the mud and managing 25miles.

A few days later we wound our way across the country to lake Atitlan, five and a half thousand feet up in the mountains, nestled between a host of nine thousand foot volcanoes of the 'school book conical' variety and recognised as being the most beautiful lake in the world. I hasten to add that even English poets (none of whom I can currently remember the names) have lyrically described it as more beautiful than Lake Como (or is that Garda?) in Italy. I know that beautiful is not a terribly descriptive adjective being a little subjective, nor is it good at painting a picture of landscapes that may be alien to many, but I'm afraid that is what best describes Guatemala. Its swamps and jungles are beautiful, its flat farmland with huge trees in blossom is beautiful. Its terraced fields on improbable mountainsides are beautiful, as are its pine and broadleaf forests, its river valleys and canyons and its cactus strewn semi arid hills.

Guatemala does however, suffer from flooding in the rainy season, wind in the windy season and earth tremors and landslides in all seasons. If anyone checks BBC online they'll see where half a mountain fell down on Jan 6th in Guatemala. It killed 36, or at least 36 bodies were recovered, but thankfully there were no houses or villages beneath it. That anyone was aware of. No, the casualty figure is because one road ran across the side of the mountain, and I can vouch for the fact that Guatemala wins hands down in the contest to see how many people can fit into a truck or pickup. The Mexicans can jam them in, but often with somewhere to sit, even if it's on the roof. In Guatemala, it is standing room only, with large frameworks welded on to give people half a chance to have something to hold on to, and extra frames to ensure a few fit on the cab roof and on the extended tail board.

The 36 bodies appear to have come from one pickup that was caught up in the landslide.

Coban is a cool mountain town where German settlers started coffee plantations in the near permanent drizzle. We arrived in drizzle and left in drizzle, rather like Ireland but here someone had set up a stall under every eaves or piece of shelter. Sell sell sell is the Guatemalan mantra, and after Belize, it's nice to know that everything you could need is available especially fresh fruit and vegetables.

However, over dinner I mentioned some of the history I had just discovered about the town and its German settlers.

"Well there don't seem to be any Germans here now."

"No, the US Govt threw them all out in 1942 because of apparent Nazi sympathies."

"Are you telling me that the US just marched into a foreign country and decided who could do what?"

Errmm.... Oh dear, I wonder when or if we should ever broach the subject of Honduras, Nicaragua, Panama, El Salvador.... I do hope they're winding me up.

"Lets try the local beer shall we lads?"

The road that had been destroyed was the one that we needed to take west of Coban, so instead we set off on a detour that had just been carved out of the neighbouring mountains, literally. I no longer have the words "I can't do it" in my riding vocabulary. At times the 30-35 degree slopes switched back on themselves every 50 yards with huge drop offs. Rocks interspersed with sand and fine deep dust offered little traction on such climbs and descents. The track was generally the width of a Caterpiller earth moving blade, though narrower in places, which meant we simply couldn't be on the "road" when there was another vehicle. We stopped to talk to some of the construction drivers and ask how the hell they did it. "With difficulty" was the answer and they pointed to the valley floor where one of them hadn't quite managed to keep his grip. I could see a small toy Caterpillar earthmover about 1000ft down.

The road was a real bike breaker, with every kind of obstacle imaginable and without stopping, other than to drink water and say "Holy Shit" to each other, the detour took us most of the day, but we did come upon one vantage point that let us see the whole landslide we were bypassing. I had read that the mountain had fallen down, and that is exactly what had happened. The mountain had fallen down and you could see the cutting where the road was on each of the neighbouring mountains and then there was just a huge gap. Sobering.

We stayed a night in Cunen where a fun fair and market had rolled in to town. Everyone was enjoying the Ferris wheel and other crazy rides, with all the usual screams and laughter, but something wasn't quite right. I realised that there were no power generators, no background noise, just men manually swinging whole families upside down on homemade rigs. The minimal, though effective lighting, was provided by a battery pack tied to the framework in random positions, supporting its associated strip lamp. An eco-funfair option for the middleclass?

The next morning, just beyond the village of Sacapulas where an overloaded minibus came past with brakes billowing smoke, the greenery of the east gives way to semi arid browns and yellows and the houses all adopt Spanish red tiled roofs. Just like that, the architecture and environment changes like night and day. What doesn't end though is the fantastically twisty roads with perfect surfaces when there is one. The other thing that doesn't end is that around every fourth or fifth corner we encountered a landslide or rock fall blocking part or all of the road, recent or ancient, with no warning and a makeshift single track through or round the obstruction. It was exciting, but what I've never encountered before is when a road has moved. Imagine you are riding perfect blacktop with a solid yellow line, absorbing as many beautiful vistas as you can while there is a road, and suddenly “BANG”, you've dropped a foot or more. The earth and road has dropped and there is no warning, the blacktop even looks seamless! I did three of these and am eternally grateful that they were all down ones and not up ones! Hitting a step a foot or more high when you aren't expecting it could be particularly damaging to a front wheel. Or a chin.

Guatemala has teams of road workers dressed in corporate green T-shirts that fight a loosing battle to maintain the mountain roads. Huge teams of these men fight to clear rockfalls without the use of heavy machinery, but more often armed only with hammers and chisels with which they break the rocks before carrying away the smaller pieces. Labour clearly isn't that expensive, but with a couple of JCBs I can't help thinking they may start to win the war.

Four days on the shores of Lake Atitlan was good for all of us, but it was dry season and the famous southerly winds made the dust get everywhere. It also made a good number of the town's corrugated sheet roofs make a bid for freedom from their captivity atop the walls. We lay in our room remarking, in a resigned fashion, that the view of the stars we would soon be witnessing, would be welcome relief after the incessant banging as our own tin roof began parting company with the building. We met up with the cycling family again and it was great to have people other than ourselves to talk to in English. We took advantage of the fact and subconsciously spent little time together as the three amigos. It was good I think, to recharge our batteries so to speak and to soothe any building frustrations. Michael, Ciska and the boys had come due south from San Cristobal in Mexico where we had seen them for the New Year, and apart from all having had a strange flu with a high fever and weight loss, they seemed fine. The boys had enrolled in a local school for a few weeks while the family waited for some parts to arrive from Europe for the bicycles, and they seemed to have become a big hit with all the local girls.

I sold Michael my lightweight zip off trousers, because he hadn't been able to get any and they were just perfect light weight luggage for the bicycle, but also because I couldn't resist some colourful patchwork baggy pantaloons off the market and had room to carry only one pair of trousers. I got a local tailor to sew a variety of internal pockets into my brown, copper and orange fashion statement. I'm still working out what that statement is, but at least I know I'm not a slave to conformity. Matt said I looked like a gunt, if I heard him right.

From there it was on to the old colonial town and former capital city, Antigua. Cobbled streets and packed full of gringos, it has an Irish pub (offering Irish stew made with beef?) and has three clearly visible volcanoes, one of which burps smokily every 20mins or so. There is also an alarmingly large number of amputees, but this, the western side of the country was worst hit by what has been described as the government's "scorched earth" policy. This region saw 450 Mayan towns completely destroyed and many thousands killed or maimed in acts of terror. It's sobering to then read that the guy who stood and won the Presidency in 2000, did so on a ticket of law and order. Apparently his past as a confessed murderer and organiser of military terror raids on civilians, put him in a unique position to understand Guatemala's violence!

The police are generally tamer these days than in the past and it's surprising, because they are forced to ride 125 Kymcos, often three up, I kid you not. The salesman who got that contract must still be enjoying his global cruise... While we were getting the framework and exhaust welded on Jay's beemer, two coppers rode in on a Kymco with a completely broken frame, bald tyres and no lights fitted at all except the headlight. They happily showed us where the other side of the frame had broken and been plated only a couple of months earlier.

A trip to the Pacific coast reminded me of just how bloody hot it is when you lose altitude, so there was a sharp retreat to the mountains that took forever. We spent one hour trying to track down the guy with the flat piece of steel that is laughingly called a ferry to get across one of the rivers. I've done a few river crossings now, using broken bridges, fording and by dodgy boat, but this thing really took the biscuit. Luckily we had turned the bikes around (slowly and gingerly lest we sink the craft) and were pointing the right way with engines running, when he rammed the opposing riverbank. A perfectly timed dumping of the clutch helped us be propelled up the steep earthen bank. Jay, the last one off, had to make a leap of faith as the craft made good its rebound into the river.

A full afternoon of awful mountain track riding led Matt close to a heart attack after some lads pointed a gun at him, but finally led all of us into Guatemala City. Five million people and Central America's biggest city, it was the place where we were sure Matt could get his desperately needed battery (I'd been push starting him for a week, which was only fair), and where Jason could get all the bits he needed too, this being the centre of motorcycling in Central America. More people use bikes here than any other country, though there is talk of legislation to ban the carrying of passengers, such is the problem with drive by shootings. You see, it's always a reckless few spoiling things for the majority.

Zona 4 in the city is known as the hub of motorcycling, where all the biggest shops are and I found out there was even an Aprilia dealer!

Jason got on the phone to track down some spare parts for me.

"What did he just say Jay?"

"Air filters aren't a stock item, but maybe he could order one for you. Might take some time though." We all just smile.

Oh Guatemala, what a physically beautiful country (apart from the bit to the east of GT City), and what colourful people. From Guatemala City to the border with Honduras, the terrain became much drier. Along the Rio Motagua valley the colours were browns and yellows. Gone were the wonderful lush greens, so familiar and comforting to a European, replaced instead by overgrazed dust bowls reminiscent of so much of central and northern Mexico and populated by disconsolate cattle feeding on any remaining vegetation.

It's such a diverse place, with colourful people who give you the keys to their hotels and smile in spite of their terribly sad past.

How wonderful it is go to a petrol station where all the customers are on bikes, and how frightening it is on a twisting mountain road, to be faced with one of the infamous “chicken buses”, overloaded with people and a roof full of luggage, brakes visibly on fire and with a young lad at the wheel who is convinced he is Michael Schumacher.

Maybe it's a government inspired euthanasia programme.

33 POTHOLES AND HOMICIDES

Filtering slowly past all the trucks, buses and pickups, we made it near the front of the mile long tailback, which wound its way up and down through the hills hoping we'd catch a glimpse of whatever the holdup was. An accident, another landslide? In a situation like this the traffic feels obliged to use all available tarmac and some of the grass verge, so what had been a single forward lane can be transformed into something containing perhaps 4 vehicles abreast as more and more decide to overtake the traffic queue and see just how close to the front they can get. Needless to say, when the traffic is free to flow again, it doesn't.

By dismounting and walking up to the obstruction, we got a perfect view of the new shiny black SUV with the pock marked windscreen and the neat line of holes down its flank. The bodies were all still there, being examined by the police and what were, no doubt, the forensic team. The corpse of the politician turned drug lord and those of two of his compatriots, were rolled from side to side on the road as the number of bullet wounds was established and as the world looked on. No white sheets or protective screens here. CSI it ain't.

Welcome to Honduras!

I'd entered Honduras that morning, the process taking only two and a half hours including the time it took to convince immigration officer Mendoza that my full name was not James Patrick Eireannach/Irish, as he had written on my bike permit, but instead James Patrick Tyson. Convincing a Central American border guard that they have made a mistake is not easy and perhaps even a little foolhardy, but he eventually wrote out a new form and settled on James Patrick Eireannach/Irish Tyson. At least the passport number is right, so we'll see what happens at the exit post.

Another few days had been spent in Guatemala waiting for Matt to get better and lose the temperature of 104 that he'd been running. In typically male fashion, we decided he should sit in the shower and then take paracetamol interspersed with ibuprofen and lots of water. Even though his nose wouldn't stop running, I don't think any of us actually considered contacting the medical profession. Well it was bound to pass, and we were sure it was just something he had caught in Guatemala from our cycling friends. He didn't seem to have malarial symptoms or anything, it was just a weird flu…

In the meantime Jason and I had time to arrange a laundry load and adjust chains and do all those other jobs that periodically need doing on the road. It wasn't the most successful laundry experience though. I'm now travelling with a total of two pairs of socks and Matt has two remaining pairs of pants. The male bonding, brotherhood symbolism as signified by the T- shirt swapping that Matt and I engaged in earlier, (similar only to cutting our wrists and joining our blood), doesn't extend to the sharing of underwear, so he's just going to have to go commando to Panama. Arguing about lost underwear in a laundrette doesn't seem to be covered in my Spanish phrasebooks.

I also attempted to start a shipping process out of Panama, so that I could prove I was leaving before I arrived, which is an over land condition of entry. Now Peggy the Pegaso, as you may recall, is named after the mythological Pegasus, transporter of the gods and all that and it may be a little pompous of me to suggest that by simple logic that makes me some kind of god, even if life on the road can create illusions of grandeur. However it was just a little surreal to get a one line reply from the shipping agent in Panama that said simply "What is your destiny?"

What a profound question. Should I know the answer? Surely at my age I must have some idea of my projected destiny, but even I, a god upon my mythical steed, can't predict the future with absolute certainty. I've read that they regularly change the rules of entry to Panama, but no one ever mentioned philosophy!

Honduran scenery is beautiful, like Guatemala, in a lower, less dramatic, though no less exquisite way. There is more deforestation though, with the resultant soil erosion and unstable hillsides and it is hard for a European to see all the hardwood cut and piled up for nothing more than firewood. To my middle class shame though, I can't help myself looking in a 'Grand Designs' way, at the beautiful woods that are used to make toilet cubicles and the like. The colours and depth of the grain, the natural sheen of roughly planed planks of slow growing hardwoods, dressed with simple ethnic fabrics in natural dyes....

Don't know what happened there, sorry.

But fuel for housing and cooking is an essential ingredient for life, and when a full days work on a construction site pays about $4, the environment will always suffer. Judgmental moralising from afar just doesn't cut it, as they say. In a similar vein, the way that Honduras is trying to acknowledge and protect its amazing biodiversity, is causing a great deal of friction. Realising the huge potential eco-tourism market is certainly concentrating the minds of the legislators who have now implemented 40 protected areas, but there is a history of conflict between environmentalists and local business interests in Honduras, not least on the Garifuna Caribbean shore, where in 1995 Janet Kawas was killed after campaigning to protect what has now become Punta Sal National Park. Similarly Antonio Rivas was killed after using his radio station to campaign against unregulated open cast mining. The government says it now recognises its responsibilities as a signatory to UN Human Rights legislation and to that end has prosecuted some 600 police and started investigating the cases of some of the 11,000 people currently detained without charge. I'm not sure just how efficient all the investigations will be, given that a UN report found that by 2006 the case of Janet Kawas was still to be opened. An interim report found that an investigation was needed because no one knew who killed her. Eleven years to work that out. See what I mean?

We passed the famous Copan ruins, the southerly limit of the ancient Mayan world and stayed in the town of Gracias. This was fate as opposed to design. Matt had managed to lose his fever as we left Guatemala, but I found it for him, and for three days I got to enjoy 103-104 degrees and eat painkillers between cold showers and sleep. I didn't get the phlegm though. Instead I got a cough, of the sort that almost makes you chuck, so whatever it is, the virus is mutating! The only thing I can tell you about Gracias is that the streets are in terrible condition. I mean, rutted, muddy disasters. Oh, and that on our arrival we had apples thrown at us. I stayed in bed the rest of the time, but not because any Granny Smith phobia.

With some strength restored we set off on the main road to La Esperenza and all I can say is that I'm glad it wasn't raining. It varied from rutted clay steep climbs to broken limestone pavement before becoming a fresh new road as if by magic, carved through the hills with perfectly cambered bend after bend. It's not as though we even rode through a zone of preparatory roadworks, it was just a rutted goat track one minute and then perfect black top the next. It was up on the broken limestone outcrops, high in the mountains that we met a little Hyundai Atoz, bouncing along slowly over the rocks. A tiny urban shopping car going where most 4x4s would never dare tread, it's nine occupants all waving and smiling as we met. Go on, tell me who can really justify a Hummer?

And if Guatemala wins the Central American competition for greatest number of people than can fit in and on a pickup, Honduras wins hands down for the worst urban streets. Even if a main highway rolls into town, the minute it hits the town boundary it becomes a rutted, washed out, potholed, rock and mud combo. Intriguing.

With 7 million people, Honduras is the most football mad of all the Latin American states so far. Where Belize has basketball courts, the Spanish countries have soccer fields, and everyone is mad about it, male or female. Our first weekend here witnessed a world cup qualifier between Honduras and Costa Rica. All the little tuk tuk taxis were draped in the national flag, and almost everyone was wearing a football shirt, but then at almost $3 I suppose they are affordable if you really want one. Makes you wonder how shirts of identical construction can cost £60 or more in the UK. If you have one, check the label and see where it was made.

I watched the game on telly in the hotel and you could have heard a pin drop when Costa Rica scored first. Not even the dogs dared bark. The town was silent, this was serious. In 1969 Honduras went to war with El Salvador in the famous “Football War”. At a game in El Salvador, visiting Honduran fans were attacked by home fans. In retaliation, the Honduran government evicted thousands of Salvadoran immigrants. El Salvador closed its borders and in the midst of the terribly mature political tirades that each country threw at the other, El Salvador invaded Honduras and bombed all its airports. Maybe Bill Shankly was right. Football isn't just a matter of life and death, it's much more important than that.

As well as soccer shirt sweatshops, Central America has coffee of course, and Honduras, like Guatemala, has loads of it, the beans drying by the side of the road and on flat roof tops. With the recession though, these countries are suffering dreadfully by default. The recent closing of so many Starbucks has been economically devastating for the region, as has the reduction in funds being sent here by those working abroad, especially the USA. It's the Hispanic community in the US that seems to be bearing the initial brunt of the recession and conservative estimates are that 1 million have come back to the region already since the downturn began. That's a whole lot more unemployment with no benefit system to help. That other huge earner, the tourist, is becoming an endangered species too. On this trip I have never been told a hotel is full, and I've rarely paid the initial asking price since crossing from the US, given the lack of tourists. The tourist markets and shops are usually completely empty too, which means great bargains if you are a callous bastard, and if you have some way of carrying your booty. A loaded bike isn't it. I'm already carrying a blown rear shock absorber with me and attempting to post it from every country I get to, but until I get a quote below £50, it is staying firmly strapped to the bike.

Camping high in the mountains outside the capital city Tegucigalpa was peaceful and the vast panorama of pine forest was a particularly wonderful view with which to savour a cup of tea and watch the sun go down. Of course after it got dark and the forest creatures came out to play, I remembered that it was Friday 13th. Given that I am no chicken, afraid of mad axe murders and other psychopaths, it only took me about 3 hours to fall asleep. Well, that breaking twig just might be a... no, that's stupid. And those repetitive thuds, that's bound to be pinecones falling. Isn't it?

Getting back on the road in the morning, it turned out we had turned off the road barely half a mile before a military camp. Talk about being surrounded by psychopaths in the forest!

Tegucigalpa, or 'Silver Hill' was an old Spanish mining centre and is beautifully nestled at 3000ft in a near perfect bowl valley, which is of course an absolutely essential criteria for containing and concentrating as much smog as possible. The descent into town really hurt the eyes and lungs and approaching from the west also meant that we got to see the worst the city had to offer. In Belize the houses were patched up. In Guatemala many of the houses were little more than palapas (a tall thatched roof on 4 legs) with rough walls of wood planks or branches. In Honduras the urban shanty home is just made of all the other bits. Just the patches if you like. Many of them teeter on their spindly legs, valiantly holding on to the hillside waiting for the next rainstorm to wash them away. It happens every year, though 1998 was the worst when 10,000 people died in Hurricane Mitch and many villages were lost in their entirety. The shanties continue to grow and the architectural integrity of the stick house continues to deteriorate.

With all the main bridges in the city destroyed that year, a mechano-style temporary replacement was installed. I crossed it gingerly. It has collapsed three times since installation, as people slowly nick all the bolts. Everything here is precious and the piles of waste that exist, over every slope or filling every gully, comprise primarily of plastic, the world's enemy. Everything that can be reused is. I was invited in for a night with a family and saw the cut open toothpaste tube that was to be wiped clean inside before another tube could be purchased. This was in their spotlessly clean, well appointed and tiled bathroom, that just didn't have any plumbing. Instead it had a 50 gallon oil drum in the shower cubicle that was filled daily and used as the water source.

This cleanliness was a constant in both Guatemala and Honduras. Everywhere I stayed was a fraction of the cost of staying in Belize, where everything was filthy. No doubt there is some free marketeer out there who'll tell me exactly how the hidden hand of market makes that little equation work.

In the village of San Antonio de Oriente high in the central Honduran mountains we played for hours with the village kids, who insisted on wearing our helmets and gloves and going through every pocket of my jacket trying to find out what everything was used for. They sat on the bikes and we talked for hours without any of the adult social embarrassment we learn to experience just because we don't use the same language. Piggyback rides and laughter amidst discussions of who lives in each house we walk past and who is related to who in the village.

San Antonio de Oriente, an old colonial mining town and beautifully preserved example of centuries old Honduran architecture, was made famous by the painter Jose Antonio Valesquez. His primitivist paintings of the terracotta tiled, whitewashed adobe buildings on the mountainside, huddled around the church and separated by cobbled streets populated by farmers and donkeys, have been reproduced thousands of times and have become as synonymous with Honduras as the vernacular thatched cottage has with the image of Ireland. Wilfredo, Luis, Nando and the other kids ran out of town after us, waving and screaming until we were finally out of sight and I was left with a wonderfully warm feeling that helped counteract the stresses that had been building between Jason and I.

Matt and I parted company with Jason before we left Honduras, which was good for all of us. It can be intense living with people on a 24hr basis, and Jason's travel plans involve no time frame at all, so when he discovered just how incredibly friendly the Hondurans all are, and how beautiful the women are, he was bound to stay. That old adage about the less material wealth the greater the generosity, really seems to hold true here. Everyone wanted to chat, even officers Maldonata and Espinoza who kept us for 10 minutes chatting at one of the many police checkpoints, about the bikes, David Beckham and the weather plus all the usual international male small talk.

In the centre of Tegucigalpa, Francisco the security guard from a shop near where we parked, switched his professional allegiance and stood guard over the bikes. I did give him a few Lempiras later, but he was overjoyed to just watch the bikes and explain to every passer by where each one of the bikes had come from and how many months we had each been on the road. Nobody asked us how much the bikes cost or where we got our money, but everyone wished us a good time and hoped we were enjoying our stay in Honduras.

Honduras stands alone in Central America as the only country not to have had a hideous war in the last 30 years, (the football war technically lasted only 100hours), so perhaps that is also why it is so friendly, but the only reason it didn't have a war was that the US used it as a base to train one of the parties in all the other wars, and even as a base to attack Cuba, so there was a constant supply of aid keeping things financially stable and politically controlled. Never enough aid to actually address any of the great questions of poverty, but aid nonetheless.

Now before you moan about me being anti

American again, note that this is the original Banana Republic, the one where the term originated because US fruit companies owned 75% of the productive land, controlled 66% of the country's economy and ran the two political parties, through the first half of the twentieth century. Economically it was much too important not to be 'protected' and prior to overt US military meddling in the Cold War, Honduras had managed to screw things up very well on its own, with rebellions, coups and irregular power grabs. They've rewritten the constitution 17 times since Independence from Spain in 1821.

It will be interesting to see how things pan out in the future, because Honduras has joined the long list of Latin American countries in the last decade that have voted for socialist or left wing governments. The current regime of President Zelayas is very popular with the poor and has been instigating change, but to the detriment of the wealthy, a policy which doesn't have a great track record for prolonging power in Central America. With a third of the population being under 16 years old I can't help but feel that the changing electoral dynamics combined with increasing poverty will bring more political upheaval.

And that is about that. More great scenery, lovely roads when they have a surface, friendly people, terrible poverty and just the odd shooting.

Honduras.

34 THE FAIRTRADE SANDINISTAS

I thought I could manage perfectly well on my own at the Honduras- Nicaragua border, becoming the savvy traveller. My Spanish is getting better by the day, and I've been getting the hang of learning to smile. True, it's taken me forty years, but it has never been quite as essential before. So when Frank approached me as I attempted to park the bike at the border building, I knew I could just palm him off with a smile and a polite, "no gracias". Official looking badge or not, I wasn't going to need any help thanks. Oh how naive!

Of course the window to the customs building doesn't open unless there is a helper on hand who knows how to knock! The woman in uniform was struck by a strange case of absolute deafness, until Frank's magic hand tapped the glass. The process had begun. Frank, to his credit, ran from building to building getting things going, occasionally calling me to come and sign something. I, in the meantime, tried to befriend some of the money changers by discussing El Comandante Che Guevara, given that they were wearing the T-shirts, I had a similar sticker on the bike, and because I really know very little about football. I thought that making human contact was infinitely preferable to kidnap and robbery which, it would appear, is a pastime favoured by many at the border.

I was doing really well I thought, until one guy was presented before me wearing a “kiss me I’m Irish” hat in the same colours as the flag on the front of my bike. This was clearly a conversational ‘in’ they all thought. Then the talk turned to football.

Damn. International revolutionary politics I can deal with, even in a foreign language, but football? Does that really mean I'm not a man? I fended off the football questions as best I could and took the decision that I probably wasn’t supposed to kiss the hat wearer, which was just as well when they tried another tack.

“Su espousa, she in Irlanda?” Ah, they want to know if I'm gay.

No, my wife is in England!

“Ah, she live Liverpool or Manchester United?”

Now I’ve got them. “No, she lives in Hereford United.”

Blank looks.

“Si. Hereford United. Reached the 4th round in the FA Cup last year. You don't know Hereford United? Soon to gain promotion to the Football League, where they shall take on Crewe Alexander and the famous Accrington Stanley. Much more important than the Premiership.” Ha. Now they're on the run. My authority re-established I even feel able to take on the bike watchers. The 5 to 10 year old kids that hope to gain money from watching my bike. “Why? What’s going to happen. My bike is perfectly safe thanks.” But they are the ones with the knives capable of slashing a tyre in seconds.

Matt and I are a team. By this stage we are able to speak volumes with our eyes, and deploy this communication skill to the max. One of us always watching the path that our passports are taking and the other guarding the bikes yet both watching each others backs and identifying the scammers and the gangs of hoodlums with a nod or a raised eyebrow. I'm so very glad

I'm not here on my own. After getting the bike out of Honduras, a process which involved reciting the chassis number quietly, by heart, in Spanish to the helper who couldn't read it off the frame, but who needed to relay it to the customs official, it was time to do battle with the immigration office. Emigration from Honduras shared the office with immigration for Nicaragua.

Frank was on hand, but we were starting to get pissed off in the heat. $3 was handed in for the exit stamp from Honduras and $7 was needed at the next window to get entrance to Nicaragua. I handed over ten.

"What do you mean you have no change? I have just given him $3 and you owe me $3. Give me that $3."

"We hab no dollares aqui"

"Yes you have. That guy at the next desk has!"

"No, you can hab Lempiras in change"

"Lempiras are Honduran and ever since that man stamped my passport I haven't been in Honduras, and standing that side of the desk, you aren't in Honduras either. Give me dollars or Nicaraguan Cordobas".

They were adamant. Matt was beginning to seethe. I was hot, sweating and feeling Celticly stubborn. The Nicaraguan officials were prepared to take me on. Stalemate.

In the end Frank gave way and ran back across the border to the money changers to get change for the immigration officials.

All up we paid $20 to get the bikes out of Honduras, $3 to get ourselves out, $12 for Nicaraguan "insurance" and $7 to get us in to Nicaragua. In total, we got a receipt for $4. Maths was never like that when I was at school. At least it was nice to see the shiny Lexus parked up at the customs office....

After another two checkpoints, we were cruising in Nicaragua. Sweeping through the flowing bends on perfect tarmac, admiring the scenery and the orange trees, and I don't mean of the Del Monte variety. Tall graceful and completely unidentifiable trees with the most exquisite orange blossom, helped paint the hillsides and provide a backdrop for all the red and black painted fence posts, tree trunks, flags and walls close to the road. This was hardcore Sandinista country, where the revolution began and where the fighting against the Somoza dictatorship was strongest. Even though that was the late 1970's, this mountain region still votes Sandinista and the rewards are obvious. There are schools everywhere. I mean, every two or three miles I was slowing for a "zona escular", be it primary or secondary. Education is one of those things that the Sandinistas are passionate about and they managed to lift literacy rates from their 1978 level of 30% of the population, to 80% by 1996, and to eradicate polio. No mean feat, given the continued war with the Contra rebels and then the imposed trade embargo after the Iran Contra scandal when the US could no longer fund the rebels directly.

What the Sandinistas could never provide however, was a shower of rain, and after riding out of the mountains it was sorely apparent that rain was what was needed most. It had been a very long time since we had seen so much yellow grass, and livestock of every breed so perfectly displaying their skeletal form.

During lunch beside a recently overturned 40 foot truck, we discussed what little traffic there was on the road. Rather like parts of Belize, there was a lot of bicycle traffic, but also a huge amount of horse or ox drawn traffic. We were to see a vast array of carts, built from various car and truck parts, some even fashioned in the style of a late nineteenth century covered buggy, suspended in a rudimentary way with cobbled together springs which nonetheless seemed capable of supporting a family of fifteen. Oxen, working in a team haul immense loads out of the sugar cane fields and at least appear a lot stronger and healthier than most of the working horses.

The Nicaraguans love their horses though and there are often fairs, parades and gatherings, it's just that the economic situation and the severe lack of rain means that everyone is short of a bite to eat.

Nicaragua has been hit hard by failed neo liberal economic policies introduced in the late 1990's when the Sandinistas were beaten in the polls, and more recently by changes in the West. Tobacco sales have fallen dramatically, coffee is down, even Fairtrade which the Sandinistas were very active in promoting, and the lack of rain means that this year is the first time they have been importing beans, a diet staple. So go on people, drink more coffee and smoke more tabs to support your friendly Sandinista revolutionaries!

Daniel Ortega and the Sandinistas are back in power now since November 2006 and attempting to redress the developments of the past ten years, but some of their socially structured, communal ideas are resurfacing in the strangest places. It is now possible to buy 'Contra Coffee'! Community cooperatives of coffee farmers who as US funded Contra rebels who spent their time during the war, fighting against cooperative farms, are now marketing their Fairtrade coffee in the US under the banner "Wake up to Freedom"!

The localised nature of the weather patterns in this part of the world means that while Costa Rica and Honduras are being flooded, Nicaragua hopes for another seismic shift that may tilt the land just enough to let some of the water flow their way. The Caribbean side of the country gets rain, and plenty of it, but it is generally a swamp and known as the Mosquito Coast. Very few people live there and as intrepid a traveller as you may think I am, I'm buggered if I'm going to go to a place called the Mosquito Coast just to see why it got its name. I can guess. Instead, my first port of call is the city of Leon, intellectual and artistic capital of the country, and mainstay of support during the Revolution.

The main road south to Leon caught us a little unawares. After swinging along, care free on the great surface of CA1, with no landslides to speak of, this other main thoroughfare, CA6, was ridiculous. I can't really describe it as a potholed road, more a collection of holes loosely connected by serrated pieces of tarmac. Although perfectly level and dead straight, after about 10 miles in 1st and occasionally 2nd gear, we decided to head off road and just drive through the fields, which were billiard table smooth in comparison. We even met a bus doing the same thing. The land became more and more arid as we lost altitude and neared the Pacific, and the dry desert heat became unrelenting. After pulling in under what was left of a tree, to use its remaining shade and grab a drink of water, Jacqueline appeared from a nearby house carrying two chairs.

We shared our crisps, water and very few words with her, partly because she kept hiding behind the multipurpose tree when any other vehicles approached. A lovely girl with a rather unfortunate face, she didn't smile once. As a window on the world, the face can be so expressive yet it's when it shows no expression, that you suddenly notice. She clearly had a kind and helpful demeanour, but remained impossible to read through that blank face. I made a note to self- try to smile even when someone isn't wearing a customs uniform. Maybe people won't think I'm quite so weird.

I used the brief roadside halt to dry my tent after the previous night's camping in the Honduran mountains and it actually took as long as it takes to eat a packet of Doritos. It was possible to watch the rain drops vanish between munches. That's proper hot sun.

Out of the shimmering haze rising from the barren plain, came a perfect line of volcanoes running north to south, some of which were smoking away while others bide their time waiting to surprise everyone, like Momotombo did when it did a Pompeii on the town of old Leon. Archaeologists are still busy uncovering the old town with all its gruesome reminders of the speed with which a volcano can turn a beautiful day at the market into something very shitty indeed.

But people never learn, and young westerners flock here, to a neighbouring smoker called Cerro Negro, or Black Hill, to sand surf. Yes folks, if you tire of snow boarding and the reflection hurts your eyes, come and get your kicks hiking up the side of an active perfect cone of explosive power, and then use your board on the black lava to escape from any potential danger. I'm sure there must be some god of fire somewhere getting mightily pissed off, and thinking "Right, just one more time and I swear I'll..."

Matt and I stayed three nights in a brilliant hostel right in the heart of the 'new' city of Leon, with a pool, wi-fi, and free tea, because it was run by an Englishman from Preston. Another couple of bikers turned up while we were there. Peter, riding from Australia and Reinhardt from Germany. Reinhardt travelled with his bike by sea to Argentina and said the five weeks of solitude in his cabin on the container ship was good for him. Umm...

Leon is a low rise, grid pattern Spanish colonial university town, with the largest Cathedral in Central America, though allegedly different building plans were submitted to Madrid for approval, because it was thought something grandiose wouldn't be allowed. I used this centre of (limited) commerce to finally buy another camera but had to settle for one with AA batteries, though I had vowed never again because they run out so quickly. I took twenty photos that night, all excited that I could again record stuff, so I got up the next day at 6am to use the great dawn light to capture some of the murals across town that still remain from after the '79 revolution. The camera wouldn't switch on.

I was seething by the time the shop finally opened. Apparently 20 pictures was quite good and what did I expect? No, there are no refunds. Why don't I just buy more batteries and leave a small trail of lead waste across Central America? At 20 photos per set of batteries I wished that I knew how to say ruder things in Spanish, and was then dumbfounded when he said that the batteries he had sold me with the camera were really crap and I should just buy better quality ones.

It's an odd sales technique, but one that at least meant I had a functioning camera to capture the intricate restoration of the canvases hanging in the largest cathedral in Central America by teams of young artists. It was still working when I got to the Museum of the Revolution and met Francisco, my guide, a veteran of the fighting who explained he was such a psychological mess after the war that he had to go to Cuba for rehabilitation. He brought the fantastically amateur museum display to life and showed me some of the homemade weapons that were used against the dictator Somoza's National Guard, like mortars made from scaffold tubing and grenades in baby food jars. The whole place is run by veterans of the fighting and operates entirely on donations, but it had an authenticity and helped fill in the background to the 40year Somoza family regime that I hadn't understood. All I knew was that famous Roosevelt quote about Somoza; "He may be an evil son of a bitch, but he's our son of a bitch."

Suitably enlightened we set off to explore more of the country and were stopped by some friendly cops who had been sitting under a tree waiting for some action.

"Buenos Dias señor! Bienvenue a Nicaragua. Passport por favor"

After a welcome handshake I gave the friendly

smiling police officer my passport. What a nice man.

" Now you give me 300 Cordobas for the offence or I keep your passport."

"What offence?"

"I'll think of one."

Using my phrasebook and after much discussion, I was able to ascertain that because he had my passport and a gun, he was bound to win. Ten pounds poorer I was back on the road to Managua the capital, and when we were right in the middle of all the city traffic Matt's bike completely died, forcing me to hotwire it after diagnosing a dodgy ignition switch. After neatly fitting a spare light switch we were carrying, to act as a key, Matt just looked at me and said "Should I ask how you knew how to do that?"

Having always been a bit of a fan of hypocrisy and after complaining about surfers on Cerro Negro, we then rode up the side of an active volcano, because we could. Right to the crater's edge where the noxious gases burst forth in intermittent plumes, and where a little sign said "Please reverse into your parking space", which is bound to help in case of an eruption, you wouldn't want to be fumbling with reverse would you!

The crater of the Masaya volcano is populated by a species of parrott that has adapted to life among the noxious gases, and no doubt enjoy the thermal updrafts that help it fly out in the morning to look for breakfast. The car park is littered with strange stones embedded in the tarmac, until we suddenly realised it was the result of falling red hot lava that melted itself in. In for a penny, in for a pound as they say, we set up our tents but opted for a bit of extra shelter in the old visitor centre/ restaurant complex that had been hit by a hurricane and partially destroyed. It still looked like it could fend off falling hot rocks better than a piece of nylon, and it gave me somewhere to examine the pool of oil that fell out of my new rear shock. Nearly a month. It lasted nearly a month and the thing is, I'm still carrying the old one.

Because the volcano was in a National Park and we had asked permission to camp, we were presented with Luis, our armed guard, who was to sit and watch us for the night. We never ascertained what it was that Luis was protecting us from, but it led to a sound nights sleep although I have my suspicions that all three of us enjoyed one. I watched the sun rise and before we left we brewed up for Luis and then Matt threw his bike to the ground in customary style as we rode away.

From there it was a couple of days on the beautiful island of Ometepe in the middle of Lake Nicaragua, a fresh water sea that has sharks who have adapted to the fresh water. Like the parrots in the volcano, maybe it's the mend and make do attitude the whole country adopted during the trade embargo that lasted for so long. Even the national fauna have decided to adapt themselves to cope with what they've got and just set up home regardless of where they were originally designed to live.

The island of Ometepe is made up of two volcanoes that rise from the lakebed and who are joined above the water's surface, by a spit of their conjoined lava flows. It is, not surprisingly, the home to an array of island specific wildlife, and also lots of plantain plantations. Getting there involves taking a tiny ferry on very rough water for an hour, and watching your precariously tied motorbike get soaked with water as it is slowly approached by a plantain truck that has broken free of its securing ropes.

The ferry sails from the little port of San Jorge, which has a big colourful statue of Saint George slaying his dragon. He really gets about doesn't he? Patron Saint of Ethiopia, Russia, Lithuania, Portugal, Greece and even England among others, he still has time to stand up for victims of disease and be one of the Saints that cross innumerable theological boundaries to be held in high regard by loads of Christian splitter groups. Not bad for a bloke from Turkey of Palestinian parentage, who didn't really travel all that much. I saw a snake on the island road that more than stretched across a whole carriageway, so a good nine feet long and proof that Saint Patrick never got here even if people like to think Saint George did.

The majority of the roads are dirt, or a combination of jagged lava and fine silt, so terribly entertaining and more punishment for Peggy and her failing suspension. She shed one of her rear subframe bolts in disgust and after getting a thorough soaking on the way back to the mainland, when the boat deck was practically underwater, she refused to start and three deck hands pushed us ashore. The deck hands are a multi talented lot. Given the height of the waves when it is rough, the ferry can't dock, so I watched one of them just dive over the bow of the ferry, resurfacing about 50 feet ahead, with the fine line of the docking rope in his teeth. When he reached the shore he pulled the attached heavy rope up to locate the boat so that it could spin round and reverse in. I'd enjoy seeing someone from P&O do that in the Irish Sea.

From Ometepe we headed to the Pacific again and San Juan del Sur, where all the rich Nicaraguans and it would appear, thousands of Canadians, have a second home. We met up with Lee again, remember Lee and his aromatic boots? And we met Baz, from London on a KLR with some great stories.

On day two of his journey he wrote off his bike by riding off a dead straight road in Utah while selecting a song on his ipod. Then he hit an old man in Mexico who walked out in front of him, breaking his leg. (The old man's). A crowd arrived, as did the local paper and the Federal Police (renowned manicurists and amateur electricians) who decided to take Baz away when the crowd started getting angry. They said it was for his own safety and first took him for a ride in their new Dodge Charger patrol car to show him how fast it could go. Then they showed him around town and took him out for dinner which was all terribly polite.

Then they put him in jail and said the judge would see him in the morning. The Federales must have had a soft spot for him, as they kept him in a holding cell with a handful of others just off the main prison cage. He was told if he needed the toilet he should take his clothes off before entering the cage, as all of his possessions would be forcibly removed by the inmates when he entered. There are times the smell of your own piss is bearable.

The judge didn't show up in the morning and although Baz contacted the British embassy they said it was nothing to do with them and he should just pay the 3000 pesos that a police appointed lawyer said he needed to act on his behalf and get him out. He seems to get in some very strange situations and while he was telling me this over a quiet beer, we were invited to Thelma's 19th birthday party, where we had pizza and cake on the beach with 10 people we had never seen before. How very normal.

San Juan may well be the second home for Nicaragua's rich and famous, but these things are relative, and for two days there was no power or water supply in the whole town and nobody thought that was strange.

All four of us set off for the border with Costa Rica. Rumour has it that Costa Rica has warm water in the showers, and I think it has been about three months since I've had one of those…

35 THE STEED BLEEDS

Costa Rica, or Rich Coast, is so called because of all the gold that seemed to adorn the locals when the Spanish first arrived in 1502. I expect the ruff wearing Spanish colonists would know better than to attack any bling wearing locals today, what with changing fashions, cultural identity, and the chance of being stabbed for looking like a poofta, but history brought us where we are today and Costa Rica is still a bit of a rich coast, in part I'm sure, because of one significant difference over all it's Central American neighbours: it doesn't have an army.

It tried it for a while at the start of the twentieth century but that just led to war, as you'd expect, so after 2000 people died in several weeks of fighting, the army was abolished in 1948. They haven't needed it since and the only time they were invaded, in 1856 by William Walker the American who wanted to set up slave plantations and build a Nicaraguan canal across the continent, it was the people of Costa Rica that got angry. Walker had already attacked Honduras and Nicaragua and soundly beaten the military of both. Having seized control he marched south into Costa Rica where he met a crowd of pissed off civilians who soundly beat him and his army and then chased those fleeing north to the Nicaraguan town of Rivas, where they attacked and burnt down the fort Walker was seeking refuge in, forcing him to flee back to the States. He returned to try again in 1860 but was shot by a Honduran.

The last ten years haven't witnessed any actual wars in Central America, yet military spending in the region has increased 21% in that time, to a staggering $4.5 billion, which must be some kind of madness given the poverty I've been travelling through. Not surprisingly, Costa Rica has been the most stable nation in the region for the last 60 years and is probably the most developed, preferring to spend all that military money on infrastructure and education. It now has the highest literacy rates in the region. This development is also why we were stopped five times in the 50 kms south of the border for passport checks. With development comes the fear of the illegal Nicaraguan immigrant. You can just hear the rich Costa Ricans

"Coming down here, cleaning our toilets, sweeping our streets and serving our burgers for next to nothing".

Costa Rica is also at the forefront of tourism, and especially eco tourism, since it has placed almost 30% of its land area under protection of some kind, be it local or National Park, or controlled area of agriculture. These tourist dollars, along with the bananas, coffee, melons and other produce, keep the country buoyant, but it was a manufacturing deal with Intel in 1997 that really boosted the economy.

With Intel inside, Costa Rica capitalised on the massive expansion in the electronics markets at the start of this century, and reinvested to further expand tourism. All this meant that I did indeed have a hot shower on my first night in Costa Rica. It had been so long I honestly can't remember how long I just stood there luxuriating in the cascade, or how many times I washed my remaining hair. We rented a small one room chalet in the mountains, which had that wonderfully musty aroma that part used holiday cottages across the British Isles have. It was so distinctive I was transported immediately to various family holidays in the 1970s and 80s.The experience was made even more familiar by the grey skies, wind and intermittent rain.

Although this is the dry season, we were up in the mountains for some respite from the Pacific coastal heat, and you just don't get all these tropical forests without water from somewhere. The rains also mean that this is productive land, and despite the hilly topography there are clusters of little green pasture fields. Combine that with my first view of the gorgeous Lake Arenal, under leaden skies with shafts of bright sunlight breaking through illuminating fresh wet vegetation all framed by a perfect rainbow, and I thought I was in Fermanagh looking at Lough Erne. Of course Fermanagh doesn't have quite as many palm trees, banana plants, hummingbirds or parrots, but just for a moment there...

The luxuriant greens were so rewarding and restorative after the dry Nicaraguan west, but trying to work out the money wasn’t relaxing. There are so many zeros that it is nearly as bad as Italy was before the Euro, when the price tag in a car windscreen would stretch round to the side windows.

It just doesn't seem right going to a cash machine to withdraw a hundred grand. There's always that moment of panic as you recount the zeros before hitting “accept” and worry that you'll go into overdraft, or worse, cause the collapse of a bank. As if that could happen. On the other hand, as poor Baz did, you can remain cautious and end up paying higher bank charges than you've just withdrawn!

The beauty and the photo opportunities meant that there were a few days that we rode barely 20 miles. I can't imagine the fit Russ Malkin would have if Ewan and Charlie let their schedule slip and stopped to look at stuff.

The area on the north side of Lake Arenal is covered in hot springs. The local volcano Arenal is still throwing out lava which steams on its cone sides as the near permanent surrounding cloud tries to cool it. What this means though is an abundance of thermal pools, but none of them smell sulphurous. It is just a water table that is geothermally heated and all the resorts in the area have hot fountains and other water features as decoration in the garden and to entice you in from the road. Cheapskate as ever, I stopped to ask a few locals where we should go for a thermal experience and followed directions down an unmarked dirt road opposite a huge resort hotel, to the loveliest complex of crystal clear pools of varying temperature and not a sinner was there but us.

One of the pools had a water slide but it appears that I have put on a little weight since I last experienced one in 1977, so I got stuck and rather than flow with the water, I simply created something of a dam and had to manually work my way to the bottom. The security guard didn't throw us out, but instead agreed to let us stay the night after we agreed to pay him four grand, and we had everything you could imagine. A clean toilet block, power for light and shelter in case of rain. I just set up my mozzie net and prepared for sleep on a table.

At about 8pm the locals began appearing, to create a huge social event, families all having prepared picnics or BBQs. Even though we were the only gringos, the striking thing about Costa Rica is that we weren't overly noticeable apart from the bikes, the tents and our clothing of course. Costa Rica is much whiter than anywhere else and has almost no indigenous population, so we could blend right in. Well the others could, I may still have been a little whiter than most...

While luxuriating in a pool, talking to a guy who sells stuff to tourist shops, I discovered that the owner of the land and the creator of the springs, refuses to pay a fee to the tour operators so none of them will bring their buses of tourists here and as such it doesn't appear in any of the guidebooks either. The good thing about that is that he won't be so badly hit by the current downturn in the industry, having instead a steady local clientèle.

After days in the beauty of the mountains, we rode for the coast and intercepted the Pan Americana. The heat and filth was unbelievable. Lines of trucks and buses all belching smoke, but it was only to be for 30 miles till we reached the turn off for Puntoareñas and the ferry that was to take us across to the Nicoya Peninsula. Two ferries leave from here to the peninsula. One goes straight across the bay and we were told takes an hour. The other, just about to leave, goes much further south, almost twice the distance and apparently takes an hour too! That seemed like more of a bargain and was scheduled to leave, but we were told it was full and so hurried to the ticket office for the other one, which, it turned out was also leaving. Literally.

Having finally sorted the tickets and with all the workers urging me on I raced up the gangway behind the lads and it was only at the last minute that I realised the boat had in fact already left. It was one of those moments when there was nothing to do but close my eyes. If Evil Knieval can get a Harley to fly, it was time to try out the "big air" training that Yamaha Canada had given me. The broken planks at the end of the gangway weren't the best launch pad, but the angle was OK and luckily the steel boat deck was dry which avoided the obvious embarrassment that heavy collision with the back of a cattle truck could have created.

The road on the peninsula was another rock, flint and sand bike-breaker with switchback climbs and blinding dust which meant I found the edge of the road through trial and a little too much error. After finally passing all the vehicles that had disembarked before me, I could see the road ahead, breathe, sweat profusely and concentrate on breaking the bike.

It was a front wheel puncture first. It had to be a front puncture, Murphy is never wrong. After carrying a heavy duty, 'unavailable anywhere' spare tube for the front tyre all the way from Europe, I had finally given it away in Nicaragua the week before. I rode on to the nearest village, which had the advantage of breaking the tyre bead and felt little different to riding the sand anyway, and found a hotel with swimming pool. Everyone was delighted with my choice of breakdown spot and Lee and Baz pulled up chairs to watch the repair while Matt set off to buy food and refreshments. They had both been carrying puncture repair kits for months but didn't know how to use them, so began arguing as to whose kit I should use, both of them wanting to know if their tyre levers were any use. All I had to do was appear convincing and knowledgeable before eager eyes. The truth is, it has been years since I've fixed a puncture, modern tyres being so incredibly robust, but I think I carried it off, with a few little gems of advice about possible scenarios just to add credibility.

To keep my feet firmly on the ground, the following day one of my front suspension fork seals burst. I don't mean began to leak, I mean burst. Oil sprayed all over the engine, the bodywork, my right leg, came out around the speedometer and coated my visor! As always, I ignored a potentially disastrous problem and pressed on to Montezuma and the famous beach, but left a pool of oil anywhere I stopped, and coated the front tyre in the stuff. An oil coated front tyre didn't really matter on the dirt tracks and I presumed the fork would be empty by the time I saw tarmac again.

As so often on this trip, we rode into a gringo zone. It's always weird, this crossing of paths with tourists. Our whole experience of a country is dramatically different from theirs, and although we can, undoubtedly communicate, (most of them being Canadian weather refugees) we find it hard to "hang out" the same way. It was here I met Jeremy Kroker's dad, like you do. Jeremy wrote a book a few years back about riding his KLR 650 down to Panama, which I read not long before I left home, and often recalled parts of, on this trip. Jeremy was riding with a friend who infuriated him by always leaving his indicator on and having innumerable near misses in traffic because of it. Everyday I watch Matt do similar and can't get him to change. It'll be terribly inconvenient if I have to watch him being brutally crushed by a truck, not least because I'll have to carry the air compressor.

We camped on a beach next to a hotel thing run by a Californian with a strange business model. His beer was 1500 Cordobas instead of the usual 1000 and rather than sell any he said, "if you've got a problem with that, go down to town and buy your own in the shop for 700" which we duly did.

Prior to setting up our tents, we tried to get a room from him, but at 50% more than anyone similar in town, his were all empty and he wouldn't take anything less.

Peggy wouldn't start in the morning. She'd returned to her old ways of complete electrical failure. I think she was sulking about her incontinent suspension components and my terrible puncture repair. Or should I say my second front puncture in as many days? Given that the front and rear suspension were suffering, I elected to head back for the ferry and find some tarmac, rather than continue with the peninsula and all the promised river crossings. To be honest I also wanted to get away from the heat and the dust and return to a little greenery, as did Matt, so we left Lee and Baz (who fortunately didn't witness my early morning air free front tyre) and headed back to the boat. On terra firma an indicator fell out and hung limply by its wires, the plastic body having fractured and I noticed that the rear subframe had shed a main supporting bolt. The fork oil was now also getting on the brake caliper rendering the brakes next to useless and I really started getting concerned about where it was all coming from. Surely Peggy isn't the only bike in the world that has fork legs connected to the engine oil tank. Or is she? That speedometer is still rolling backwards....

Oh Peggy, tell me this isn't the end!

We turned south towards Panama, where everything is apparently cheaper, and to the Costa Rican town of Quepos where a work colleague of Matt's was going to be. All perfectly smooth tarmac, but it was lined by white tower blocks of apartments, small airports, KFCs, Burger Kings and of course the Golden Arches. A consequence of development it may be, but Costa Rica is also the first place where I have seen joggers and flab. Where the rich food trappings of wealth lead to an industry of weight loss and fitness and tracksuits. Where it is impossible to get fresh orange juice and where bicycles are for children or recreation use only. Gone are the lithe bodies of further north, eating cheap fresh fruit and vegetables and living active lifestyles, replaced instead by air-conditioned cars, processed food and obesity.

Unfortunately the girls here still adhere to the Latin American fashion of wearing spray on tight jeans regardless of aesthetic outcome.

We crossed Rio Tarcoles and stopped to see Central America's largest collection of wild crocodiles, all just hanging out, as they do, semi submerged in prehistoric fashion, while the surrounding cattle stand around until heat and thirst gets the better of them and they head to the water to drink and risk dying horribly from a rather severe case of decapitation. We turned off the thin coastal plain and headed inland on the first road that looked like it climbed into the cool of the mountains. Riding past empty expensive resort after empty expensive resort, we found a village and stopped for a rest. It was definitely cool(er) and all the cycling kids gathered around to chat and pop wheelies on their bikes. One little lad, Fernando, made me jealous with his mono wheel antics the length of the village, on any size and shape of bike. Later in the evening he did the same with a DT175 even though he looked about nine. Upon return to the UK I will be enrolling at a wheelie school so that in future I can hold my head (and front wheel) high in the company of school kids.

After bargaining with the local shopkeeper, we rented his sister's house for the night, for the same price as an official campground. A mere ten grand for a four bed house with secure parking and a tiled area to work on the bikes. I fixed Peggy's second proper puncture and planned to clean the oil off the brake pads as best I could, but realised part of the caliper may have broken and the pads just fell out. This was to become a regular occurrence and seems to just be a result of metal fatigue on the rough roads, like the plastic fatigue that is making the bodywork slowly disintegrate. The love and attention she got that night was enough to convince her to fully cooperate again in the morning and we rode on towards Quepos.

There was much concern over the state Peggy was in when we luncheoned with a large group of Costa Rican bikers out for a leisurely weekend ride. She was still leaking oil at a rate that meant creating puddles the size of a £20 note in just a few minutes and was flowing down the fairing from behind the indicators. The rear shock had come out in sympathy too, which surprised me as I was sure it was already empty. My new friends said there was an Aprilia dealer in the capital city San Jose, but then said it was doubtful that they would have any fork seals in stock....

In Quepos we managed to meet Matt's friend Laura who had actually come down here to do a TEFL course so that she could continue travelling south through the

Americas by teaching English en route. The town was in the middle of a cowboy festival and it would have been rude not to join in the revelry, so as the sun went down the brass bands and Spanish guitarists played country tunes from the backs of trucks, while horses were paraded and the Queens of the event waved excitedly to everyone from their lofty positions atop quad bikes. A constant throughout the region so far, regardless of a nation's wealth, is the love of horses, bad hats and terrible music.

I embraced the whole tourism thing briefly and went zip lining through the jungle canopy, which was stunning even if the humidity and my perspiration meant that my funky trousers stained my legs orange. I was surrounded by some of the 800 species of birds, the poisonous and venomous frogs and snakes, various monkeys and butterflies that Costa Rica is famous for. But as much wildlife as I watched, I was never quick enough to catch sight of a sloth. They're flighty you know.

A few days later it was off towards Panama, but first I really wanted to ride to the highest point in Costa Rica, (3135m) along a fantastically twisty section of the Pan Americana highway. As we rode up above the clouds I really felt like this is what the Pan Americana is all about. I could sense all those racers in the 1950s, Fangio, Ascari and Hill who took part in what was to become the most dangerous motorsport event of all time. I know it was only held in Mexico and never came this far south, but that's not the point, I can dream.

Our arrival at the summit was greeted by a sign that said 3050m so, feeling a little short changed, Matt found a tiny track going up further which we followed over rock, leaves, moss and mud until we made the very top and an old observatory station that was overgrown. Then the weather changed and we got soaked and frozen trying to make the descent to San Isidoro and a real live, Central American first division football game, with fire crackers and hooters and mayhem. Thankfully San Isidoro won so it was a very happy place to stay the night and prepare for the assault on the border. Again.

I just quietly prayed that Peggy would make it. She should- I've explained she needs to get to Panama and then she'll get a rest, 'cos that is the end of the road. You can go no further south without using a boat or a plane, so I have already described all the shiny parts I'm going to buy her and the warm soapy water I'm going to wash her in.

Well a girl needs some pampering...

36 THE DARIEN GAP: LITERALLY THE END OF THE ROAD

No no no, not now!!

Panama City, traffic chaos, eye stinging smog, 11am, sun high in the sky and Peggy cries enough.

She grinds to a halt at the side of the road with complete electrical failure again. With not even enough power to make the horn go 'ting', the fuel pump can lift no more fuel and the plug no longer sparks.

Shit.

I can see her point, I've asked for the last couple of weeks that she get me to Panama and this she duly has, but I didn't mean it literally. I mean I still need to get to the Darien Gap, the very end of the road, the point where there is no more, but jungle, swamp and eventually Columbia. And so it begins again. I push her across the street to where I can see a little shade outside a cafe that has closed and proceed to strip her down. The battery has a full 12.8 volts which is respectable enough and as such gives me no pointers to the same damned problem that has plagued me since Mexico.

With all the bodywork off and the loom apart, Matt and I proceed to clean the fork oil off every connection and open the main harness to check again for any damaged wires. Vivian then appears from the Dental laboratory opposite with spaghetti, salad and chicken on two plates for lunch and asks if we would like to use the loo. You see great things happen when you break down. There is never really any need to panic. By the time the bike is back together with no obvious problem found, it is 4-30 and getting too late to try and get out of the city and head south. She starts on a push and is running perfectly when the police arrive and wonder why I'm not wearing a helmet, but sensibly back off after just pointing to their head. Vivian appears so that we can follow her to a hostel she has found for us, one complete with free tea and coffee. The kind of place that will provide ample opportunity for me to muse about the fact that I can take Peggy apart, find nothing at all wrong and put her back together again completely fixed and functioning perfectly. Infuriating!

The following morning we set off for the Darien Gap. It starts 285kms away on unknown road conditions. The information we can glean is limited, from "most of it is dirt and mud" and "well I suppose you are on bikes so you have a chance", to "no problem, most of it is paved". Everyone said it was dangerous though, and that we shouldn't go. The guide book says of El Real and Yavazi, the towns at the bottom of Panama, that they are full of security services, bandits, drug cartels and Maoist rebels from Columbia. But it is a point on a map and I didn't make it to the top of Alaska so was determined to make it there.

Within 50kms of the cosmopolitan, vibrant Panama City limits there is a whole new country. The mighty Pan Americana, the transportation artery that connects all of the rest of the Americas, is reduced to a potholed twisting country road with single carriageway wooden or steel bridges. The villages revert to collections of thatched single roomed huts on stilts and the children scream in delight and rush out to wave at us. The jungle gives way on occasion to cleared farmland and cattle grazing and there are military checkpoints. Lots of them.

At each one our passports are taken and their details entered in a ledger that no one will ever look at. The time taken to do this varied, especially if the guy with the pen decided it was thirsty work and first needed to go and get a bottle of pop. I don't know why he couldn't have anticipated some traffic, he had all morning from what I could gather. There isn't a whole lot happening around here. The odd small town appeared and if my map was even mildly accurate (most of the ones I'd been using turned out to be purely schematic) it was going to be important to stock up on potable water and fuel. The shops in these parts reminded me of Belize; run by Chinese, badly lit, terribly arranged and smelling of damp. I checked the sell by dates carefully but couldn't find anything as old as a five year old Snickers.

We'd made an early start and kept waiting for the expected deterioration of the road, but the tarmac continued. True, it wasn't all great, but there was a lot of fresh stuff, for which Peggy and her ailing suspension was eternally grateful. Stopping at Agua Frias checkpoint, I once again checked with the military commander as to the state of the road. He assured me the road was 'bueno' the whole way. No problem. Perfecto pavmento. And it really was perfect pavement, for almost a mile before deteriorating into dusty jarring potholed gravel. Damn. And still 300km round trip just to get back to this point. Then as if by magic 5kms later it was fixed. For a while. I po-goed over one rough patch and then the next, all the time hoping that the remaining fork leg would take the strain, that nothing else would break or fall off and that the electrics had decided today was a good day to pass current. The jungle got thicker and steamier.

Then one of the last checkpoints, only 50kms from the end, took me by surprise. We were asked to go inside the military barracks and answer some questions. I duly followed and then took a double take of the troops, all milling around, chatting Spanish. Some of them, in their identical camouflaged uniforms, had little "US Army" badges sewn on. I was confused, given that the US military left in 1999. No doubt the Panamanian military use whatever clothing they can get. Then I was approached by Stanley SomethingEasternEuropean andcompletelyunpronouncable, from Louisiana, who offered to translate if our Spanish wasn't great. He said, before I asked, that the US had provided some troops to the Panamanians for 'training purposes' and that he was a health and safety officer. A health and safety officer! It's important that the employee doesn't hurt his finger or perhaps shoulder in any way, whilst filling someone full of lead. Safety First!

We promised the commander we were going to the end and then would come straight back. Stan could provide no first hand details of the road ahead because he said they weren't allow go there as it was too dangerous. Matt freaked out.

"It's too dangerous for the US military and you want me to go! Listen, I was only going to Vermont to see my mum!"

I talked him into it on the proviso we got there and turned around and left. I omitted to mention the 51 US citizens taken hostage in the recent past in case it weakened my argument.

As we got closer, the whole road now dirt, there being no more little tarmac islands of respite, I contemplated the military warnings, and wondered how it was that I should identify the Maoist rebels I had to watch out for. Mao himself, I could do. I've seen the T-shirts, but all the others might just be able to sneak up on me. Maybe they are all working in the shops we'd just passed...

Yavazi is the end of the road. Across the river from

the potholed expanse of earth the trucks use to turn around, I could see some houses through the jungle. Boats are used from here on. Another 100kms as the crow flies and it is Columbia, but not the end of the famous Darien Gap, so there probably aren't any customs officials. The end of the Darien is a further 100kms. A handful of people have made it across the 201 kms using automotive power. Chevrolet set out on a big expedition in the late 1960s to demonstrate the power of Detroit and the auto industry. All the cars are still in there, claimed by the vines and the ferns and probably making leather clad homes for monkeys or toucans. The British Military made it in Range Rovers in 100 days in 1972, but they cheated a bit, using boats for the vehicles and helicopters to keep bringing in supplies. The first non boat supported journey took 741 days and was achieved from 1985-87 by Messers Upton and Mercier in a Jeep. 741 days for 201kms. Think about it.

Helge Pedersen rode it with his R80 GS in the early nineties. On his own, which is hardcore. I can't remember how long it took him, exactly how much weight he lost and don't know whether or not he required psychological help afterwards, but you may have seen his classic timer taken photo, as he dragged the bike using block and tackle, the whole length of the gap, with a machete to cut a route.

That is adventure biking. I am just out for a Sunday spin by comparison, but I have had a lot of time to think and reflect. I have asked a lot of Peggy the Pegaso with very little real preparation. She is after all a road bike, with some posey off road, Chelsea style pretensions, and she has coped tremendously well under terrible conditions. The suspension may have collapsed twice, but it was aftermarket and not Aprilia's own. The lights and brakes may no longer work, along with the speedo, but the engine is a gem and she only stops when the phantom in the wiring loom is awake. But I have taken her for granted, in exactly the same way as I have taken the other woman in my life for granted, Siobhan.

I hope that I haven't broken her in the same way, and for that reason this really is the end of the road in more ways than one.

I'm heading back to the UK, and now that I can answer the shipping agent's rather large, "What is your destiny?" question, we have only to make it to the boat in the city of Colon and begin the nightmare bureaucracy that is international shipping.

There just remained the return journey from the Darien to Panama City, and for some crazy reason we decided to do the whole thing in the same day, opening the throttles wider than we probably had since Texas, in the race against the sun. Panama City has truly dreadful drivers. They are the most aggressive I have ever encountered and as the Lonely Planet advises, things like traffic lights are purely for decorative purposes. The blowing of horns surpasses even the Latino love of terribly loud music and the whole resultant cacophony never subsides. The city streets occasionally have names, but as it is customary to change them every year or two in honour of someone recently deceased, maps, road signs and local knowledge never tally. Given this back drop we headed for the hostel and the last 2 hours of the journey were undertaken in the dark, through the city.

Without any lights.

Did anyone mention adrenalin junkies? Matt and I figured it was our swansong, the end of a journey of adventure, and since the rebels didn't take us hostage and the boat was booked, maybe we were seeking the last great buzz. It certainly was that alright, but it was also incredibly stupid. Like scything through London traffic on an emergency delivery, but doing it wearing an invisible cloak. I was expecting everyone to fill the gap we were in and turn across our path and I don't think a single vehicle disappointed. We stuck together, reading each other and everyone else, riding like locals and yet with an understanding of each other that is truly rare and I thought of Matt four months earlier, encountering the traffic of Chihuhua in northern Mexico and freaking out. My oh my how things can change.

And as it happens, it fell way short of the unforeseen buzzes still to come.

37 INTERNATIONAL SHIPPING- A SEAMLESS PROCESS.

I'd entered Panama a few days before the trip down to the Darien Gap. This shouldn't surprise you. Peggy may well be the 'The Flying Mythos', but alas she rigidly adheres to your common or garden space time continuum, so to get into Panama I had first crossed by what is probably the busiest of the Central American border crossings. Constrained by oceans, jungles and mountains, there are only two vehicular crossings into Panama. Both are from Costa Rica. I had long hoped to make the northern one, on the Caribbean coast because the international divide is symbolised by a single river bridge a few hundred yards long but only one carriageway wide. This single track takes trains, trucks and pedestrians and only the bravest of motorcyclists, because a large proportion of the cross planks are somewhat absent and the iron rails can be tricky in the wet, especially with a few thousand tons of locomotive bearing down on you.

All right, if I'm honest it wasn't the extreme riding I was after, more the infamy of the crossing which means that next to no one uses it and therefore there is peace, tranquillity and hopefully a little more bonhomie amongst the officials. Alas, the state of Peggy's running gear had dictated the shorter, smoother, more tarmac route on the Pacific side. The route that almost everyone in a truck going north or south uses. In for a penny as they say, my last Central American border was to be the biggest.

Our border helper had no name, but did possess a huge pair of Raybans of the sort last seen on Starsky and Hutch, plenty of gold teeth and the unfortunate after effects of bad teenage acne. He also undertook a continuous textual conversation on his phone during the 2 hours we spent getting through the border. There was a part of me that desperately wanted to shout "for god's sake just call her". I didn't. Instead I stood, quietly perspiring and marvelled at the permanent nature of the market that has developed in what is effectively no mans land, and the accompanying human and vehicular traffic that seems to completely ignore officialdom and goes on its merry way over and back across the political divide. One chap was producing sugar water refreshment in the back of his pickup truck with a sugar cane crusher powered by a little diesel engine. A bucket on the lowered tailgate caught the resultant fluid and added to the overall complete lack of appeal.

My fear with this crossing had been attaining the "tourist visa" that is the source of many a thread in online travel forums. The requirements for Panamanian entry seem to change on an almost daily basis, with the visas available at the border one day, and back at the embassy in San Jose, Costa Rica the next. There are stories of the border service "running out" of visas by 8 am, an hour after opening, but being able to find some more when your wallet has fallen open. It is also necessary to prove how and when you are leaving Panama again. It was my lucky day, and not for the first time was I delighted to have been born in the internationally disputed territory of Northern Ireland.

"Irlanda eess no beeza"

Yippee! I start the importation of the bike in triplicate as Matt joins the queue for citizens of less desirable nations who need a visa. Other than my helper insisting that Aprilia was an Italian bike (he knew!), and therefore couldn't be Irish, if you know what I mean, the process went quite smoothly.

Finally it was on to the Dept of Agriculture for the formality of fumigation. After getting our paperwork I tried to find out where actual fumigation took place, but was simply told "you hab documentos si?"

"Si, but where is the wee man with the chemicals?"

It turns out fumigation really is a formality. There is no wee man with a load of weedkiller, just a form to show that there might have been! As it happens 20 miles down the road a police checkpoint pointed out that my fumigation form hadn't been signed, so asked me for a pen so that he could P.P. it!

From there it was dual carriageway for 550 kms to Panama City. Dual carriageway! How mad is that? Ok, it didn't last, but we revelled in the expanse of broken concrete right up until we got nicked for speeding, by a policeman who swore that he didn't need radar because his spatial awareness was second to none. We begged to differ, I with my phrasebook and Matt with his mad staring eyes and one of the digits on his right hand. The fine was reduced from $50 to $20, so I asked for proof of the offence and Matt stood, legs apart, his arms crossed, with chest out and all 6'2" of him scowled at the little chap. A small part of me felt pity until I let my prejudices remind me that he had probably been a bully at school before joining the police, so deserved all the intimidation he got. We ended up walking out without spending a penny and carried on up the road to a hotel in the town of Santiago (every country's got one!).

Everything is so cheap! After Costa Rica, it was just so refreshing to pay $7 for a good clean hotel and next to nothing for food and drink. Granted, the cold shower smelt just like an over chlorinated swimming pool, not dissimilar to the one in the centre of the courtyard as a matter of fact and we ruminated on just how they must have the pumping system rigged up so that the pool and showers could interconnect so efficiently.

The following morning we began filtering past miles of stationary traffic on the Pan American Highway, expecting to come upon some hideously mutilated bodies as a result of the all too common traffic accident, but instead witnessed people power in action. In common with South America, one of the ways that local people try to draw attention to a political issue is to block main traffic arteries.

We got to the front of the queue to see TV cameras and lots of police and military milling around behind the makeshift barriers of rocks and branches that the locals had placed across the road. It turns out that as is so often the case, local Panamanians were losing out to big finance in the name of development. A property developer had enclosed a huge area of public beach to service a new resort for tourists that was being built, with the result that fishermen and all those who had always used the area and its access to the ocean, were banned and denied livelihood. The age old practise of public land appropriated and enclosed by private wealth is alive and well in Panama. To their credit, the police and military were just hanging out, not attempting to move the road block or hassle anyone and we had plenty of opportunity for conversation until the Speciale Police arrived.

Calmly, and without a word spoken on either side, this mutant breed of Panamanian giants in their tan uniforms with brown leather belts, began removing the obstruction and we were off. It's clear that some reputations may have a solid grounding in truth as no one attempted to interfere. And so we headed on towards the Canal, that great slice through the middle of the country that divides the American Continent whilst unifying the world, or so the catchy slogans go. Is there anything else that you know about Panama? Well, before I begin to blow you away with very male statistics about engineering masterpieces, you should also know that 'Panama' in Guarani Indian, means 'abundance of butterflies'. There are over 600 species of butterfly in this skinny country, but as far as total flora and fauna, that is but a drop in the ocean. There is a thing here called the Tarantula Wasp, which you have got to admit, is one hard creature. This wasp attacks tarantula spiders and then manages to drag or carry them back to the den. I don't know if they are restricted to any particular type of tarantula, but remember some of those even eat birds! Next time that evil black and yellow resident of the English country garden lands on your jam sandwich, count yourself lucky that you aren't sitting in Panama and stop being such a pansy.

I went to the Miraflores Locks which are one of three sets of locks on the canal and are those closest to the Pacific, which incidentally, is several inches higher than the Atlantic. I suppose that's why no one likes going down round Argentina. It's that slope they have to deal with at the bottom and thinking about it, what exactly is sea level then? After a distance of 82kms, boats coming along the canal from the Atlantic are lowered into the Pacific here and it is an amazing sight. These huge vessels, built around the world with the dimensions of the locks in mind, have anywhere between 24" and 11" of clearance as they make their way through, and I could see from the sides of the boats that I watched, that they didn't always manage to maintain a steady gap.

Vessels pay a fee to go through depending on weight, size and cargo, with some paying more to jump the queue. Cruise ship Disney Magic allegedly paid $331,200 for the privilege rather than bob about for a few days in the Pacific and Richard Haliburton famously paid 36 cents, the lowest ever toll in 1936 when he swam through. I can't imagine how he dealt with the currents when they open all the gates that let the water in and out, but the mechanisms controlling those gates were on show in the museum in model form, which really helped to put the system in a manageable scale. Thing is, they had the old mechanical system on show and the new, upgraded, low maintenance hydraulic one. You could operate the models, but the new, low maintenance, hydraulic ones had broken. Oh progress.

The whole system uses fresh water believe it or not, 52 million gallons per vessel being dumped in the sea. It does rain a lot in the region, but with the constant increase in traffic, the water table is starting to suffer badly, with the 40 passages a day. Because of this, work has begun on new locks which are being designed with a 60% water saving, and the museum display was full of water information exhibits; about its importance for life, agriculture and the global ecosystem. Shame then, that the new state of the art museum building didn't have urinals in the male loos, only flushing toilets!

The hope is that the new locks will be open in 2014, the canal's centenary, though the earliest plans to start digging were actually 1524, when Charles V of Spain reckoned it would be a good idea after the Conquistador Balboa had mentioned it over dinner on his return from the area. I'm sure the new opening will be celebrated with much gusto but I wonder how many of the original dead will be honoured. It's not known exactly how many thousands did die during construction, but the greatest cause of death was yellow fever, dengue fever and everybody's favourite, malaria.

Of course the canal has inadvertently killed many thousands since, what with the various invasions by Panama's larger north American neighbour, the most recent being in 1989, as the struggle continued for economic and political control of this most lucrative area.

Panama has actually fully owned and operated the Canal since Jan 2000 and when you realise that the canal netted $1,317,474,779 in 2008, you can see why people feel it is important. Important too, it seems, is the Canal Authority's ISO9001 certification standard, which ensures the provision of a quality service and commitment to provide fast, efficient and reliable service to it's customers.

"The Canal works day and night to become world leader of services to the maritime industry, cornerstone of the global transportation system and model of excellence, integrity and transparency."

What a load of bollocks. I mean really, if it loses its ISO9001 Quality standard are all those shipping companies going to use the opposition? The other trans American canal? And who designs these international trans-continental canal standards anyway, the Association of Panama Canal Operators?

But Panama is so much more than just a navigable waterway through a continent. It is also proud of its banking sector, which has more secrecy and privacy laws protecting bankers than anywhere else, and we all know how much they can be relied upon to manage money well when nobody is watching!

Panama also of course is home to almost a third of the registrations of the world's shipping fleet because of its policy of not interfering in industry with such things as rules, regulations and safety legislation. They're not called flags of convenience for nothing.

Because this is rapidly becoming a tirade on behalf of Concerned Global Citizens I shall move along swiftly to the section entitled 'personal experiences as a foreign motorcyclist engulfed in a sea of unbelievable bureaucratic nonsense'. You may however, have some idea what lies ahead.

After the night of madness returning from the Darien in the dark, we had little to do on the Thursday other than contact the shipping company to ensure everything was still on for Friday and to check there wasn't anything else we needed to do before presenting the bikes at the docks for shipping. The ship was due to sail Sunday, but the cargo needed to be in the bonded warehouse 2 days before.

We spent the day cleaning the bikes and hiding about the frame, all the bits and bobs that we wanted to get home but didn't want to carry on the plane. I gathered together a pile of stuff that I was going to sell; cooker and pots etc, some tools, waterproofs, first aid kit, anything that would help off set the cost of the flight. Then we sat back, had a cool beer at the hostel where we had camped in the yard because it was half the price of a dorm bed, and watched the parrots and hummingbirds that frequented the foliage. I got on well with one parrot in particular who lived at the hostel and climbed onto my arm so that I could carry him around. All was done to a backdrop of blaring horns that never ceased, day or night, and a hot, humid, smog filled atmosphere. The perfect tropical city.

The road to the City of Colon on the Caribbean was 90kms and started with brand new tolled dual carriageway, cutting its way right through the centre of the national protected park land north of the city. It rapidly deteriorated to the sort of thing that I hadn't seen since Nicaragua. This main artery between the two most important cities in the country, and parallel to the Canal, was a pot holed, dusty/muddy disaster that saw most vehicles swerve around in first gear hoping for a smoother ride. It was also missing a large percentage of its man-hole covers, leaving gaping holes that were larger than a motorcycle wheel.

With no directions and an address that nobody understood, we didn't get to the shipping office until 1.30pm, but figured that was still OK given we were just to pay and leave the bikes. Addresses in Panama are really superfluous, because as I mentioned before no two people will ever know a street by the same name and anyway the names aren't written on the roads. We were sent to 6 different port entrances by security guards and held for ages at each one as they tried to find the office we needed.

"So ave you bin to de Aduana yit?" said Joel in the shipping agents office, referring to Customs.

"No, should we have? You assured us there was nothing else we needed to do."

"You muss go Aduana to get the stamp for exit the motos. It is back in Colon City near the big sign on the road say 'Colon Free Zone', or Zona Libre. But you muss be fass or day close. Then everything is finished."

Bugger, we rode like couriers for nearly 20 mins to get to the free zone through stationary traffic and fumes. We were greeted by a row of armed guards.

"No, the only Aduana office is at the Manzanillo Port, in gate number 1" near where we had just been.

Breaking even more laws we made it back there, though there was definitely beginning to be an air of desperation in our actions. We sat and were ignored for 15 minutes by all the customs staff, who needed to read books and play computer games, as well as do their nails and chat. It was Friday afternoon and only Romero seemed to be working. He also seemed to be the office skivvy and he left his post continually to take phone calls at other peoples desks, and to do any piece of paperwork the boss shouted for, in his adjoining office. Queen bitch of the nail file finally acknowledged us and sent us to sit in front of Romero. I explained what we needed and he started the laborious process of exiting our bikes out of Panama. Nearly there. Breathe deeply and try not to look at the clock. He went to take another phone call.

Ten more minutes and it is now 3.05pm.

"What? What do you mean the computers have

crashed?"

15 minutes later an eight year old kid arrives to sort out the computer system and Romero starts at the beginning again.

"When is you moto to leaving de Panama?"

"NOW, TODAY, at 5 o'clock for fucks sake!!"

We leave the office at 4.10 relieved that at last all the paperwork was all out of the way, even if it was a bit close, and laugh with the guys immediately outside the customs office who are selling knocked off cologne from the back of a lorry.

In Joel's office we discover two more things that seem to have cropped up completely out of the blue. First, that they cannot take visa or cash even though they could earlier, and only a Bankers Draft will do. And second, that we need a Paz y Salvo form from the police to show that the bike hasn't been stolen. I try to convince him that of course it hasn't been stolen. I only arrived in the country a week ago and it's parked outside now! I have the proof of ownership and the entitlement to enter the country and now even to exit the damned country. I even have the spare keys!

"Ba de police don't know ees naw stolen"

"The police don't even know it's in the country, so of course they don't know if it's been stolen. I've never reported it. It's got nothing to do with them!"

"But you muss have dis form from de police"

"And you never thought of telling me this before?" He smiles and shrugs.

"Right. Can I get to the police station and back here by 5pm, with you on the back showing me the way?"

"Eess naw possible. De only police station wit de form ees in de Panama City".

"You are shitting me. A document necessary to exit the country by sea is kept 90kms away? Well how do I get there and back? My bike is not officially in the country anymore!"

"De good news I forgot to say is dat de boat, he is delay until Monday night, so you can come back Monday and we special get you into the port"

"But I can't ride the bike you fuck wit, because you got me to sign it out of the country"! I remember to smile.

We headed back to poor overworked Romero in the customs office and begged him to give us an extension till Monday. With everyone else leaving the office for the weekend he set to and fired up his steam powered computer to create new exit forms with later dates. I could have hugged him. 4.55pm and we have a reprieve. A weekend to get one form from the police station in Panama City and some money in the form of a bankers draft. Then the face behind the previously barked orders from the boss's office appeared and swaggered over to see what was going on with the gringos.

Panic ensues, but it's mostly mine. Romero has in effect now exited the bikes twice, but they only entered the country once. A call is placed at 4.58pm to the border with Costa Rica to get the staff, if they haven't gone home, to do the paperwork to enter two motorcycles that they can't see, because they are 500kms away. Presumably that means another truly effective fumigation process too! The previous two hour entry process takes barely 2 minutes and the job is done. We are free to go, nearly 100kms from the hostel, on the worst, yet busiest road Panama has to offer, have no fuel, no lights and it's getting dark.

Deja vu? We set off and tried to remember where the manhole covers weren't.

Right- NEVER again. I swear that is it. NO MORE NIGHT RIDING in this country. With that and the bonkers bureaucracy, my heart won't take it. I get the receptionist at the hostel to call the cops in the morning so that we can go and get the form but it transpires that they aren't open until Monday, 8am -2pm, and no, they don't know the address.

"None of the policemen in the station know the address of the station? Really?"

"Yes, they say it is opposite the market in Ancon district, everyone knows."

Everyone except people who need to go there, like foreigners trying to leave....

How exactly the emergency system works in this country is still a mystery to me:

"Hello, you say there is an emergency?"

"Yes, yes, Paulo Hernandez Street. Please come quickly".

"Is that Juan Carlos Avenue?"

"I don't know, maybe".

"Do we turn right where Alberto used to have a shop?"

"Alberto who? Just go left by the post office after you have crossed the big street".

"The big street near Burger King, or the big street with the banks on it?"

"The one with the traffic lights!"

"The what?"

Baz had arrived at the hostel after paying to follow a taxi driver who didn't know any of the current names for the streets in the area so had driven around in circles as blindly as Baz could have done on his own. He was hot and tired and his bike was sick, so I spent the weekend showing him how to take the engine out of his ailing Kawasaki under the watchful gaze of the parrot that had begun to imitate the sound of the zip on my tent and attempting to impress on him the necessity of carrying more tools than just a socket set that went from 4mm to 10mm even if it would take up more room than a pack of cards. We went shopping for spanners, which is pure male retail therapy and must surely be as rewarding as when women buy shoes.

And so it was, 8am on Monday morning Matt and I had found the correct Police building and were sitting in the cool of an air-conditioned office. Then god walked in. Stocky with a thick neck and unfeasibly short legs, baggy suit trousers and unbuttoned shirt. He surveyed his quarry and began establishing power structures. This was his office, he had a gun, a badge and bad memories from school. We were going to wait. He could deal with us between 12 and 1.

"It's OK, we'll wait. It's cool in here".

Turns out we wouldn't wait. At least not in his office, so we headed for the bank to get a bankers draft made up.

"You will need to open a Panamanian bank account" (which, I hasten to add, gets you a passport as introductory gift!) Let me guess, with the signatures of all four of my grandparents? Of all the banks we tried, The National Bank of Panama was the only one that could write a cheque without my having a bank account. On the plus side, that had used up the morning and meant it was time to go back to the police.

Back at god's office we were greeted by the unnerving sight of people already asleep in the queue. Not a good sign, but an ignorance of social etiquette can occasionally reap rewards and so we stood and smiled at the hatchway.

"Where are your copies?" (of the four bits of paper we weren't sure that we'd even need).

Of course there was nowhere in the police station where it was possible to get copies, or in the Dept of Justice building next door, or the other government buildings in the area. I ran blindly down the street through the slums looking for anything plausible. Courier work had taught me that anywhere near Justice buildings there were lawyers and thankfully I found one. Lawyers always have copiers. And air-con. I returned triumphant, if a little flushed and didn't take kindly to being told to come back for my paperwork at 3pm. I may have shouted and Matt may have delivered a crushing stare, but the power balance in that room was shifting. In only an hour and a half we had our new bit of paper to prove the bikes weren't on the stolen list and he'd looked at them to see they existed. A victory! We'd scored a victory!

But oh how hollow it turned out to be. We followed a minion in uniform as he darted across 6 lanes of uncontrolled traffic with our form, to another Justice Dept building. He disappeared inside and was gone while we secured visitors passes. Damn. The receptionist and the two hundred members of the public waiting, looked at us. I explained my plight as best I could, and was directed down some corridors to the general secretary's office. This seemed odd. Would my policeman be in here?

No of course not. The process was to begin again. There were two girls in the office. The one who did and the one who didn't. "Where were my copies please?"

There was time to go and get some more copies made because first she had to go up to the 9th floor and see if she could find the page that had the stamp to show that the bike had been inspected at the building across the street ten minutes before. The stony faced cow who did nothing sat and did nothing.

I legged it to the lawyers office and got five more copies of everything, just to be sure. Was this really the last thing that we had to do to get this Paz y Salvo? She said it almost was. Almost? Just one more stamp on the page and we were done. Great!

"Oh, no, that isn't in this building. Only a five minute drive...."

I do believe I actually screamed. It was 3 o'clock so she found the stamp and did it herself.

Once more into the valley rode the two. Like demons. Footpaths, grass verges, under and overtaking we made it to the port of Colon in 50 minutes and Joel seemed surprised we had taken so long.

"Now just Aduana"

"No bloody way. We've done that already, remember? You said there was nothing else".

"This is different Aduana, just around the corner. Please, be quickly".

We stood in a queue with Joel telling us to hurry up and the woman at the front busy arranging a date with the guy in the office. Only three more windows to go. Window number one takes a look at all our stuff and hands it back, untouched. Really? No stamp, no entering details in a ledger. Nothing?

Window number 2 is a longer queue and needs copies of the one new form we've just got and haven't managed to copy. Believe it or not she has a copier!!

That leaves window Number 3. It's 4.28pm. She takes Matt's papers but not mine because it is now 4.30 and closing time. We plead. She opens the hatch and takes the papers. We stand in the heat for 20mins and then she hands the papers back, untouched. "I said I was closed".

Joel seems surprised to see us, as though we must have headed on without him. He gets on the phone so that we can still enter the port area.

"There is a $100 charge for a late processing fee". Unprintable response. He gets on the phone again and they agree to waive the fee if we go to the office immediately.

The woman at Number 3 who was closed is now open but wants $10. We get the stamp.

"Joel, is there anything else we need to do? Any more surprises?"

He assures us we have only to ride to the security gate Number 5 where they are waiting to take our bikes, and oh yes, that he has just remembered, the boat is delayed for another day, so there is no need to rush. Not surprisingly security have no idea about after hours access and assure us that the gate is closed after 4.30pm and we must come back tomorrow. No more arguing. We look at each other and race against the sun back to Panama. We lose. Again.

I shan't bore you with the following morning, but Baz came on the back so that after we left the bikes we could all get the scenic train back across the country and be tourists. Even though it was "just drop them off at the gate" we weren't surprised that three hours later we were still getting new forms completed and standing in queues. I think it was a good experience for Baz. He needs to get the hang of how all the shipping bureaucracy works so seamlessly in Panama, the country that unites the world through logistics expertise.

We grabbed a cab and headed into Colon. All the schoolboy humour and play on words you can imagine isn't apt enough. With 50% unemployment and social and economic poverty on a par with anything in Latin America, Colon has a deserved reputation as the most violently criminal, filthy centre of human misery and decay in the region. One guide book advises the tourist to never leave their taxi, another says that if you need to use an ATM you should use one in another town and I think this report from 1886 is telling: "In all the world there is not, perhaps, now concentrated in a single spot so much swindling and villainy, so much foul disease, such a hideous dung-heap of moral and physical abomination as in the scene of this far fetched undertaking of nineteenth century engineering." James Froude may have been disgusted at the city built as a rail terminus and expanded during the building of the canal, but decades of decline since really haven't helped the city and many of the same actual slums remain, which quite a testament to the quality of the original buildings.

The walled off part of the city known as the 'Free Zone' where tax free goods and services are available and international trade is undertaken with such fervour, serves only to highlight the desperate plight of those trapped in the tenements who are denied access to basic services. Plans are underway to regenerate the old buildings in the centre of the city and transform the place into a Caribbean haven where cruise ships can dock, but I think there is quite a task ahead. Work has begun to refurbish the area though and one symbol of tremendous change that I decided not to visit is Hotel Sol Melia.

Perched next the canal and prior to its current recreational status, the building was known as the School of the Americas. A military complex run by the US that taught such fine arts as extortion, torture and execution, it includes in its list of graduates and honorees such upstanding statesmen, generals and all round dictators as Noriega, Galtieri, Callejas and Suarez. Known in Panama as the School of the Assassins, not a single troubled country in the Americas was untouched by the training methods employed by its 60,000 graduates.

The ride through Central America had been a journey of historical and social awakening for both of us, but something that must have been a real onslaught on Matt's national identity. I know that I am perhaps excessively interested in the social politics of the region and the involvement the USA has had in the shaping of it, but I hope there is at last real change in the White House and that that change will be tangible and beneficial to all.

With the exertions of the last few days and the overload and processing of recent information I decided to give it a miss. What did it matter? The bricks and mortar weren't responsible for their history and I doubted I'd be able to engage any of the staff in conversation about the old days. The School of the Americas still exists and currently trains people who are yet to become famous on the world's genocidal stage, it just resides in Georgia now where the rent is cheaper and the locals don't campaign outside quite as often. It has also had a makeover and now calls itself the Western Hemisphere Institute for Security Cooperation, but I'm not sure if that means it has stopped concentrating on ways to kill church folk, labour activists and the poor.

The train back from Colon was a delight. Built in 1855 it was the first Trans-Continental railway in the Americas and carried all the gold diggers from Europe and the east coast of the US across the land to their waiting ships on the other side that would whisk them up to California. Trans-Continental seems a little grandiose for a 50 odd mile stretch of track, but it is geographically correct and a PR department is never going to miss a trick like that. We half expected to be sent to Costa Rica to buy the tickets though. We drank Nicaraguan rum and coke in our up stairs glass domed carriage and watched the jungle go by, with occasional glimpses of the canal. Tourists at last and with a moment to ruminate on how different things in Colon might be if the Scots had got their way.

Panama is the only country the Scottish ever attempted to colonise and I don't think a lot of people know that. They invaded England a few times but always seemed to lose interest by Derbyshire or wherever they encountered bright sunshine and it's true they settled rather extensively in Northern Ireland where at least the crap weather suited them fine, but the organisation of that event was pretty much orchestrated in London. So what on earth brought them to Panama under their own steam?

Well, it was something more closely related to the Colon Free Trade Zone than I could have imagined. The dream of one man became reality in 1698 when 1200 men in five ships left Leith for the Darien, though not quite how he had ever envisioned it. William Paterson, a Scottish economist and founder of the Bank of England, dreamed of a colony founded on peace and freedom, hard work, free trade, honesty and Presbyterianism. It would help the development of the world through the transportation of goods across the Central American isthmus, initially by land but eventually by a canal and which would enrich Scotland as an independent nation the way trade had enriched England. The difference of course was that England found war and the use of force a much more efficient method of getting native peoples to see things their way. And the English didn't expect to do a roaring trade in the finest tweed suits and woollen stockings with people who lived in the tropics.

That bit wasn't Paterson's fault. He was much better at target marketing than that, the problem was that his vision, through which he had secured the necessary legislation at the Scottish Parliament and raised the requisite funds, went horribly wrong when he went to Germany to order some ships. "The Company of Scotland Trading to Africa and the Indies" was founded in 1695 before corporate branding had really got in its stride and it sent Paterson off to Germany to order some ships with £25,000 in his pocket. The fact that they didn't order them from a shipyard on the Clyde may have been a bad omen, but getting his mate James Smyth and the only Englishman involved with the project, to hold onto £17,000 of the £25,000 they had, was a very bad idea indeed. Smyth was not to be seen again and Paterson's reputation for financial integrity was destroyed. He did go on the expedition but only as a lowly planter, having lost all of his governing and organisational powers. He was not therefore permitted to ask why they didn't have enough rations for the journey, or why they had packed 1,440 Scotch bonnets, 23,000 clay pipes (when it was the

Americas that had been using tobacco for years), hunting horns, gudges, fish-giggs, periwigs or even 100 Wombles in three different sizes. And no, I don't know what any of those are either, but I managed alright in the tropics without them and I suspect most people did back then too.

The colonists got on well with the Indians (indeed many Cuna Indians still use Christian names such as Andrew and Alexander), but no one had reckoned on the rain, the mosquitos or the fact that nobody wanted to buy their tweeds and periwigs. Their German ships couldn't sail against the wind so they couldn't leave the bay once they'd arrived and they didn't organise a proper system of government so couldn't agree on anything. When Paterson finally took charge and organised some form of council and judiciary six months after arriving, a quarter of the colonists were already dead. New punishments were to be meted out for the worst offences, like blasphemy and disrespect, which were listed way above such minor misdemeanours as duelling, murder or the abuse of a woman even if she did belong to an enemy.

In the end the remaining colonists simply fled amid disease, rumour and fear, though none landed back in Scotland soon enough to stop a larger expedition of reinforcements from setting sail, who, under the appalling command of the unscrupulous, autocratic and very stupid James Byers made all the same mistakes and more, failing to acknowledge any of the advice from 20 men who later returned from the first attempt.

Barely 18 months later, in April 1700 the Spanish arrived on the scene and finished the job. Most of the colonists perished, but a few hundred escaped, including the Presbyterian minister who made it to Carolina and found a new flock to minister to. Six generations later it was one of his direct descendents, Teddy Roosevelt who made something of a canal shaped mark on the Panamanian isthmus. By using warships to defeat the

Columbians in 1903, he thereby granted Panamanian Independence, assured American control of the Canal Zone and then funded the building of the canal we have today. In a way the Scots got there in the end and Paterson's dream of a passage to ensure the free movement of goods around the world was realised, it's just that Colon City doesn't live by quite the high moral Presbyterian standards he had envisaged.

At the railway station in Panama we reverted to type, shunning the tourist moniker and laughing off the taxi drivers with their 12 and 15 dollar fares. Instead we walked straight into the four lanes of traffic outside, flagged down a cab and offered him $5. We cruised through the city, shouting above the stereo that was so loud everything in the car reverberated and back at the hostel a Canadian asked me to sleep with her. You see, I can't emphasise enough how accommodating Canadians are, but it was of course out of the question. I had a plane to catch in the morning.

In the airport after check in to my flight to New York I had a quick browse of the gift shop for last minute mementos.

"Would you like a bag, sir?" She held up a Davidoff bag emblazoned with Ewan's smiley face and jauntily angled scarf oozing a 'spirit of adventure'.

"Ah. No thanks. I think I've got an old plastic bag somewhere that'll maybe do the same job."

Settling into my Continental Airlines flight I read the adverts in the magazine that said "What's an old plane called? Theirs, ha ha!" and then wondered why there were still ash trays in the arm of my seat and in the toilet....

I checked into my New Jersey hotel, said I would certainly try to have a nice day, thank you very much, and headed to the restaurant, where I inadvertently seemed to order a meal for a family of four.

After a full day sightseeing in New York, I can vouch for the fact that it really is no place for the old, cos the wind does go right through you. From there it was a flight back to the UK with Air India where beer was served in multiples as the air hostesses said it saved them time and I attempted to while away the hours with a little sleep.

Nearing arrival in London one of my fellow passengers commented, “I find that the space provided is most inexacting for the successful execution of sleep”. Quite.

I couldn’t have put it better myself. Perhaps I should take Peggy to India next, if only for the quaint turn of phrase. Oh, but then there’d be the curry…

EPILOGUE: IN DEFENCE OF LAW SUITS

I expect you are wondering how I got on with the suppliers of my moisture absorbent riding jacket. It would not after all, be fair to go to print without giving the manufacturer some redress. I contacted my Rev'itt supplier on my return to the UK and told them that much as I liked the colour and the fit of their jacket, it let the water in just about everywhere. I was told that it didn't and that I was mistaken. After some protracted discussion it was agreed that a new liner should be ordered as a good will gesture, but that really the problem was just my imagination. As for the failed stitching, broken zips and collar retainer, I must have maliciously mistreated them. I thought you might like to know.

Hagon Suspension built me a new shock absorber to the specification I'd originally requested and they gave me a cup of tea, which was nice, while I fitted it myself outside in the rain. This one, the third, seems to work.

And then there's Aprilia of course, who created my little steed in the first place. Peggy disembarked in Southampton three weeks after leaving Panama, but alas, not under her own steam. The dockhands pushed her off the boat and left her on the quayside, her battery lifeless. When I arrived I was under strict instructions to get her out of the area as quickly as possible because as a civilian in a forbidden zone it was feasible that I might cause the world to end.

I was equipped with booster cables and in a frenzy of efficiency, born of familiarity, I had Peggy running and on the road north in no time. The weather was fine and clear and with Siobhan following in the campervan, we headed off to explore the New Forest and slowly meander home.

That first campsite evening was spent fitting some of the bits necessary to make it back through the UK without incurring too many points on my licence. Parts like the wiring to the lights, some new indicators and a speedometer, but the end of the road trip story isn't a rosy one. In deepest Dorset, near the village of Cerne Abbas, there is a man with a 26 foot long cock and the following morning the shock of it was just too much for Peggy. She coughed her last at the side of the road almost beneath the huge chalk figure carved in the hillside and suffered the terrible embarrassment of arriving home late that night on the back of a rescue truck instead of under her own power.

I know she's been the butt of a few cheap jokes and insults but other than the recurring electrical gremlins there really has been very little that has gone wrong. Remarkable really given the abuse and the appalling roads with which I forced her to contend. The failed suspension was an aftermarket upgrade that I had thought would help and the fractured plastics were born of the vibration from the road surface, which, I hasten to add, led to the loss of only one structural bolt the entire 50,000 km trip.

The litmus test is always would I buy another Aprilia for a similar trip? Well the answer is no. I don't need to. I'm just going to repair a few of the broken bits and get Peggy ready to set out again. Somewhere out there is a village called Puerto del Faglioli and Peggy and I are going to find it. In the meantime, I'm just waiting for the delivery of a few new Aprilia parts. Apparently they'll be here any day soon…

THE UNASHAMEDLY BIKEY BIT.

Right, here goes. If you don't ride, look away now, these are the bits that worked and the bits that didn't and remember nobody gave me a penny in sponsorship, though if they want to do so now, I'm open to offers...

I used a 2002 Aprilia Pegaso 650ie, which was completely standard apart from:
Upgraded replacement rear shock from Hagon in London, two of which failed completely.
Upgraded front fork springs, spacers and oil from Hagon, which worked well even though the oil seals failed.
Hepco & Becker crashbars, cut, reshaped and extended by Tom to encompass two 5 litre jerry cans, for fuel and water and to locate 2 spotlights from Halfords at £20. Tom also reshaped the Hepco & Becker side luggage frames to hold my very second-hand 'Gobi' plastic panniers, one of which is still waterproof after all the incidents, although 3 locks broke on the trip.
A larger 'foot' was welded to the side stand and a headlight protector was made using a radiator guard off an RD125. I fitted a centre stand and a spare clutch cable from a BMW f650.
My friend Mark wired in the spotlights, (second hand) Oxford heated grips and the charging system for my computer, camera and phone.
A Baglux tank cover and small tank bag with map pocket were used to hold all important electrical equipment, valuables and paperwork.
I got through two sets of both front and rear brake pads, two sets of chain and sprockets, three spark plugs and air filters, seven oil filters, one set of front wheel bearings,

two rectifiers and a wiring loom. No partridges were harmed in the making of this journey.
Front tyres: Bridgestone BT45, Bridgestone Trailwing both used way beyond legal limit, but the Trailwing was crap and suffered two punctures.
Rear tyres: BT45 (worn to canvas quickly), Metzler Tourance (great mileage, vague feel, huge price) Trailwing (good stability but no grip), Pirelli MT60 (I love it and great mileage given the blown rear shocks). I desperately want a new pair if Pirelli are listening.
Two new tubes given and fitted free in San Francisco.
I used a crap bicycle pump which I threw away after Matt bought a $15 compressor in El Paso that said it was good for 250psi. That is about all it managed.

Clothing and equipment:
Shoei Multitec (£300) flip front helmet with duck tape all around the visor edge to keep the interminable whistle at bay.
Rev'itt Cayenne Pro (£250) jacket- you've read the book...
Hein Gericke 'Air' (£29) summer gloves (wonderful, have had them for years) and Gericke (£39) thick winter ones I bought 4 years ago and they are still great.
Held Kevlar lined (£79) jeans, worn everyday, scrubbed clean and crashed in with no (major) ill effects. Fantastic.
German Para boots (£25) good for walking and riding, with Hein Gericke waterproof over boots (gift). Great.
Old waterproof trousers that failed in Quebec.
Plastic over jacket and trousers ($69) purchased in Ontario and given away in Panama.

Very Nice People who deserve a mention include:
Motorcycle Mojo Magazine and Yamaha in Canada; SF Moto, San Francisco; Motos y Mas, San Miguel, Mexico and Motor Solutions, Belmopan, Belize.

ABOUT THE AUTHOR

Born in 1969 amid the incessant rain of County Fermanagh in the north west of Ireland, he has been travelling in search of anywhere with sunshine ever since, which is odd, given his complexion.

His first road trip took place, ironically enough, during the hot dry summer of 1976, and was a coast to coast road-trip across North America as a 6 year old, with his mum and big sister. Predominantly using public transport he was able to discover the beauty of a nation and the diversity of its people while simultaneously providing his mother with the makings of a nervous breakdown after wandering off at 2am in a Chicago bus station to engage some nice old men in conversation and look for change in the phone booths.

He was taught to play chess that summer, by a hairy hippy in the back of a bus somewhere in British Columbia and is forever grateful for being woken up to watch the sun rise over the endless prairies of the US mid west, the vastness and beauty of which he shall never forget.

Winter evenings as a child were spent leafing through the endless possibilities of the 'Global Coach Tours' brochure, and there was nothing as exciting as hearing 'Here comes the sun' when the BBC Travel Programme was about to start on a Sunday evening.

He first combined motorcycles with travel while at university in England and set off on a woefully unprepared 125cc Honda to try and see as much of Europe as he could in 4 weeks. Being arrested once or twice just seemed to add to the adventure, and the whole thing sowed the seeds of a plan for a two wheeled global assault, which has been undertaken in sections ever since.

He has been a motorcycle courier and instructor, a University lecturer, a writer, a builder and even collected litter at a landfill site to fund his travels. Indeed he may be the only person to have never successfully got a job in a fast food restaurant.

(His solicitor says he should mention that he is now and always has been, a really big fan of all Ewan McGregor and Charlie Boorman's work and if either of them wish to endorse this book he won't mind.)